Dawlish Remembers

The First World War

How the War was brought home to a Small Devon Town

Part Two   1916-1917

Robert Vickery

The Dawlish WW1 Project started in response to invitations by the Heritage Lottery Fund (HLF) for funding to commemorate the people and events of the First World War during the Centenary years of 2014-2018.

An application under the heading " How the War was brought home to a Small Devon Town " was made to the Heritage Lottery Fund, and to Dawlish Town Council, and was successful. Funding offered by HLF for two years was matched by Dawlish Town Council. The Town Council gave further support when the HLF funding was brought to an early close and the project group has been very grateful for the continued support by Dawlish Town Council.

The material that follows was first compiled for the individual commemorations on the anniversary of each death, contributing to the website www.dawlishww1.org.uk

This book form links individual mini biographies with other text that follows the course of the war and the impact on life in the town itself.

Part 1 1914-1915 was published in 2021.

Part 3 1918-1919 will be published in the same format in 2022.

All photographs by the author unless otherwise credited.

Cover photographs:

Upper, the display of shrouds in Northernhay Gardens, Exeter on 30th July 2016. Rob Heard wrapped 72,396 small figures in shrouds to represent all those British Commonwealth dead who died in the five month Battle of the Somme campaign and have no known grave.

Lower, Dud Corner Cemetery overlooking the plain surrounding Loos where eight men from Dawlish lost their lives in a single day on 25th September 1915.

Dawlish World War One Group

Campbell Brown

Michael Clayson

Tom Elliott

Keith Gibson

Ann Leigh

Sheila Ralls

Robert Vickery

Rev Roger Whitehead

with the active support of

Dawlish Town Council

Dawlish Museum

Churches Together in Dawlish

Dawlish Local History Group

National Lottery Heritage Lottery Fund

Related material from the website of the group

www.dawlishww1.org.uk

ISBN   97987 13064648

INDEX

Dawlish World War One Project

'How the War impacted on a Small Devon Town'

The project told the story of the impact of the First World War on Dawlish and its men and women, and the families who waited for them, of those who left, and of the 114 who did not return. Others died from the effect of the war on their minds or bodies.

The list of names recorded on the War Memorials of Dawlish, Cofton and Holcombe, provided the starting point for research. There are also individual graves or private memorials, and the project researched any sources that add further information about service careers and of the families at home. It has resulted in a further 13 names being added to the town War Memorial on a supplementary plate which was dedicated by the Deputy Lord Lieutenant of Devon at a ceremony on 28th June 2019. Contemporary sources of information have been the collection of issues of *The Dawlish Gazette* held by Dawlish Museum and the National Newspaper Archive. The War Memorials in Dawlish, Cofton and Holcombe are illustrated in Part One, 1914-1915.

We have not attempted to rewrite a history of WW1, as material exists in so many sources and has been explored in many film and television presentations over the centenary period. This account is mainly chronological but occasionally the names will be grouped according to a military event (e.g. The Battle of Jutland) so that a limited narrative of the war can be followed.

On the centenary of each death a Service of Commemoration was held in one of the area's contributing churches. The individual Services provided the opportunity for family members to speak about their relative and to light a candle of remembrance. Members of the organising group have spoken about each casualty adding their own appreciation of the context of each death. 93 such services have been held, sometimes commemorating a number of men killed on the same day, e.g. eight at the Battle of Loos, six in the Battle of Jutland. Each Service has been advertised by a detailed article in the *Dawlish Gazette*, giving a continuing narrative of the war.

Exhibitions have been shown in Manor House, Dawlish; on Wilfred George Jackson whose family lived at Manor House at the time of the Great War; on Richard Rooth who led his regiment ashore at Gallipoli; on the casualties from the Battle of Jutland; and on Nurse Margaret Jane Fortescue. These have been linked to the Services of Commemoration. The exhibition panels are available for group or educational purpose on request.

Dawlish Town Council has supported this project throughout. Heritage Lottery Fund also awarded funding which has been a partnership between individuals and drawing on Dawlish Museum, Dawlish Local History Group, Dawlish Branch of the Royal British Legion, Dawlish Repertory Company and Churches Together in Dawlish and District.

We have been grateful to those who have offered material from their family histories and photographic records. The website www.dawlishww1.org.uk has allowed our material to be seen across the world and some families have reconnected in this way. We are still keen to hear from anyone connected with the local casualties of the War. All material is shared with the partners in the project.

This is the second part of a three volume account of the known Dawlish casualties.

Dawlish War Memorial, Memorial Garden by the Parish Church of St Gregory

Cofton St Mary's Memorial 1916-1917 face

Dawlish War Memorial - original plaque 1914-1918

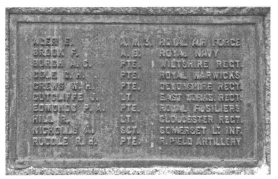

First supplementary plaque 1914-19

The "Missing Names" tablet added 28th June 2019

The Missing Names plate was provided by the project and fixed to the War Memorial with the approval of the planning authority, Teignbridge District Council. It was cast in a form similar to that of the original tablets and has been funded by the project account held by Dawlish Town Council.

This project has looked back just 100 years to a time before the widespread ownership of cars, of electricity and telephones in most homes, and a time when most family needs could be found in shops at a short walk from the front door.

Known as Manor Row in 1914, we are familiar with it as Brook Street.

The Manor Inn on the right is bracketed by two of the only visible street lamps, most probably lit by gas from the local gas works across the brook. The Inn Keeper was Robert John Sampson, a familiar surname today.

There is no date on this photograph and the childrens' straw hats may suggest it is summertime.

Compare this with Brook Street as it is now known, in midwinter and subject to 'lockdown' due to Covid. Not a soul in sight and the Manor Inn has been lost to redevelopment as housing. The evidence of double-yellow lines hints at the difficulty of car ownership here, where there is little prospect of finding a private parking space, but satellite TV is popular.

In 1914 a number of households here had surnames which are still familiar in Dawlish. A scan of the census of 1911 shows that in Manor Row were Combstock, Dart, Mudge, Pike, and further along, the section then called Brook Street, Shelston, Ford, Lambshead, Melhuish, Pike, Morrish.

Linking Manor Row to Town Tree Hill is Golden Terrace where Crook, Gilpin, Combstock, were found.

On Town Tree Hill were Dunn and Stoyles families.
Leading off Town Tree Hill towards Strand is now Albert Street but it was known as Chapel Street where Cotton, Dart, Dew, Monk, Way and Edmonds families were living.

In such a concentrated area it is inconceivable that partners might not be found and marriages develop. Reference to individual mini biographies will bring some of these to light, and for the remainder it can be a project for a family historian to explore. What is evident is that parts of this neighbourhood must have mourned the loss of family members many times between 1914 and the 1920s.

Old Town Street, ca 1908

Old Town Street 2021, *below*. In this picture the most glaring intrusion is made by the overhead distribution of electricity and telephone service. It replaces a single gas lantern that would have been adequate for slow moving horse-drawn carts or cabs.

January

Febuary

Gerald Easterbrook RUNDELL

Born: Q2 1894, Tiverton

Private, 20657

Died: 23 March 1916, Wareham, Dorset, aged 21

9th Battalion, Somerset Light Infantry

James Rundell (1853-1926) was born in Walsall and moved with his mother to 52 Fore Street, Tiverton by 1871 (census date). In 1892 he married Winifred Mary J Randell [1](1861-1926) of Portsmouth, Hants, and was in business as an ironmonger.

They were still at Tiverton when Gerald Easterbrook Rundell was born, and for the 1901 census.

By 1911, James had retired and the family were living at 3 Sea Lawn Terrace, Exeter Road, Dawlish and Gerald is described as a Student. He was then 17 and is not shown on Dawlish Boys' School Roll of Honour and so is likely to have finished his school days in Tiverton.

The account of his death in the *Western Times of 28 March 1916* shows that **Gerald Rundell** had been working as a bank clerk in Warminster before he enlisted. The *UK Register of Soldiers' Effects* reveals that his father was not paid a War Gratuity because it was "not admissible under six months service". He appears to have enlisted at Yeovil, Somerset, some time in January 1916 and was attached to the 9th Battalion of the Somerset Light Infantry. This was one of the battalions of Kitchener's New Army of volunteers and was in training before being sent to one of the theatres of war.

The *Western Times* account shows also that G.E.Rundell had been in the army about eight weeks, and had been ill for some days. On March 16th he reported sick and the Medical Officer attended him at his hut. However, he "did not keep his bed, and after three or four days looked brighter.

R.A.M.C. evidence [to the inquest] showed that deceased was in a state of collapse on Thursday last. He was treated and placed in an ambulance for [the military hospital at] Wareham." He died in the ambulance on the way to hospital.

Lieut Chas Salkfield, M.B.,B.S, R.A.M.C., describing the result of a post mortem examination that he had made, said that the body was emaciated, and he attributed death to tuberculosis of the lungs, with an attack of acute tubercular brocho-pneumonia. A verdict of "natural causes" was returned.

---

1   Winifred Mary Jane Randell was baptised in St Mary's Church, Portsea on 28 September 1862 but her surname appears in other records as Rundell.

Dawlish War memorial inscription: RUNDELL G.E.   PTE.   SOM. L. I.

Commonwealth War Graves entry: RUNDELL, Gerald Easterbrook, Private, 20657, 23/3/1916
Somerset Light Infantry,
He was buried in Dawlish Cemetery on Thursday 30th March, 1916.
Grave 612, Dawlish Cemetery – photograph by Robert Vickery

April

Thomas Pounder DAVIS

Born Dawlish, 8 April 1876   Died Edinburgh, 19 April 1916, aged 40
Able Seaman, Royal Navy, Service No: 162870   H.M.S. VIVID

Thomas Pounder Davis was the third of six children of the first marriage of John George Davis (1853-) to Frances Ann Cox Pearce (1851 – 1881) in June 1871.
In 1881 the family lived at 6 Church Street, Dawlish and John G Davis was a joiner.
Their children were William J G, (1873-), John P, (1876-), Thomas Pounder (1876-1916), Charles George, (1878-) Frances William Pearce, (1881-1961) and Henry P, (1881-1964).
Their mother, Frances A C Davis died in 1881, possibly after giving birth to twins.

The second marriage of John George Davis was to Mary Ann Evans (1858 – 1900) in June 1882 and there were four more children, the eldest of which was Frederick Albert Davis (1883-1914)[2], Beatrice Mary (1885-), George John (1888-) and Ethel Frances (1888-1954).

In the 1891 census John George Davis is shown with his second wife, living with seven of the children, including **Thomas,** 14, at 2 Manor Cottages, Dawlish. Unhappily, Mary Ann Davis died in 1900, leaving John Davis a widower once more.

Thomas joined the Royal Navy as a Boy Seaman, 2nd class, on 17 September 1891 at the age of 15, when he was sent to the Boy Seaman's training ship H.M.S.IMPREGNABLE. His record gives a previous occupation of 'errand boy'.
At the age of 18 he signed on for 12 years and served on various ships, being rated Able Seaman after three years. On 30 March 1905 he was discharged to the Royal Fleet Reserve, following a six month spell in the Naval Barracks at Devonport (H.M.S.VIVID). At this point he was given the service number R.F.R. Dev.B.929.

The Royal Fleet Reserve was established under the authority of "The Naval Reserve Act, 1900," and of "The Naval Forces Act, 1903," to provide a reserve of trained men for service in His Majesty's Fleet in time of emergency.
  • Class B, received a retainer of 6d. a day, and a gratuity of £50 when they are 40 years of age and have completed 20 years' service in the Fleet and Royal Fleet Reserve combined.

Thomas Pounder Davis married Frances Lily Steer Leaman (1885-1937) in September 1906 in St Thomas district, Exeter. The registration district circles Exeter and includes the Teign valley village of Dunsford where the Leaman family lived for some years. Frances' father was a 'rabbit trapper'.

_____

2   another Dawlish War Casualty, died on 1 November 1914, described in Part 1 1914-15

By the 1911 census, Thomas and Frances were living at 1 Church Cottages, Dawlish with four children, Beatrice, 4, Edith Mary, 3, Thomas William G, 1 and Frederick J L, 2 months. Thomas is shown as a gardener.

Thomas re-enlisted with the R.F.R. on 14th August 1910 for another five years w.e.f. 30.3.10.
He was called up for service in the Royal Navy once more on the 2nd August 1914, with his original service number 162870, and joined H.M.S.ENDYMION in Plymouth. Two days later War was declared and this elderly cruiser was heading on patrol between the North of Scotland and the Faroe islands to enforce a blockade of any cargoes that would help the German war effort.
Thomas Davis left H.M.S.ENDYMION on the 28th November 1914 to return to R.N.Barracks and on 6th December he joined H.M.S.HILARY in Liverpool where she was first commissioned by the Admiralty as an Armed Merchant Cruiser. Much of her ship's company was drawn from Devonport.

A captioned photograph appeared in *The Devon & Exeter Gazette of Friday August 6, 1915* in which "six sons of the late John Davis of Church Street, Dawlish and a grandson" are shown. Thomas Davis is referred to as an Able Seaman, R.F.R., H.M.S.HILLERY (*sic*).

> H.M.S.HILARY, originally named SS "Hilary", was a cargo and passenger liner built in 1908 by Caledon Shipbuilding & Engineering Company, Dundee, for the Booth Steamship Company to operate on the Europe/South America route. She could accommodate 210 first-class and 372 third-class passengers. On the outbreak of the First World War she was requisitioned by the Admiralty and converted into an Armed Merchant Cruiser. Fitted out in Liverpool and commissioned 7/12/1914 as the Armed Merchant Cruiser H.M.S. "Hilary" with the 10th Cruiser Squadron.

She formed part of the Northern Patrol blockading trade to Germany and was employed patrolling the area South of Faroe Islands.
HMS "Hilary" was sunk, after being torpedoed by German submarine U-88, on May 25th, 1917, whilst en route for Swarbacks Minn to coal.

Image from naval-history.net

Thomas Davis' service on H.M.S.HILARY ended on 31 March 1916 when he was transferred to the strength of H.M.S.VIVID.
*From the ship's log for **1 April 1916***
At Busta Voe, Lat 60.38, Long -1.35
5.30am: Commenced coaling
7.55am: Sub Lt Cleary left ship
8.10am: Ceased coaling,   9.15am: Resumed coaling
        *10.0am: **1 AB sent to hospital***

It seems very likely that this was A/B Davis, as the ship proceeded on patrol and was at sea until after the date of Davis' death. During this period the sick list averaged three persons per day.

Tom Davis would have been transferred from Busta Voe in the Shetlands to Glasgow and then to hospital in Edinburgh where he died 'of disease'. At the time of his death the naval-history.net website shows him attached to H.M.S.VIVID/R.N.Barracks, Devonport, and this may be a pay record for him while in hospital ashore.

Thomas Pounder Davis died at the Royal Infirmary, Edinburgh, on 19 April 1916 "from disease." He was buried in Dawlish Cemetery, plot 2459.

Headstone to Tom Davis in Dawlish Cemetery

He left £128.7s.10d to Frances Lily Steer Davis.
His widow married again in June quarter 1925 to Ernest Aggett and she died in December 1937.

Commonwealth War Graves entry: Wed 19 April 1916, illness, H.M.S.VIVID, R.N.Barracks, Devonport. Davis, Thomas   Able Seaman   162870. Grave ref 2459, Dawlish Cemetery. Husband of FLS Davis of 5 Swan Court, Dawlish

Dawlish War memorial inscription: DAVIS THOS.   Smn   R.N.RESERVE
He is recorded on the Devon Roll of Honour

Last known address: 1911 census - 1 Church Cottages, Dawlish
                         CWGC site - 5 Swan Court
                         Probate entry (1924) – Town Tree Hill
Next of kin: Frances Lily Steer Davis, wife.

References:
Naval-History.net (Royal Navy Log Books of the World War 1 Era, HMS HILARY – December 1914 to March 1917, Northern Patrol (10th Cruiser Squadron))
Naval service record (National Archives, Kew)
Wikipedia – refs to H.M.S.HILARY

14

MAY 1916

THE BATTLE OF JUTLAND

Although the warring armies in France and Belgium were engaged in furious trench warfare, there were no casualties reported back to Dawlish. It was not a 'quiet time' as planning was going forward for a major assault on the Somme.

In the meantime, the German navy was preparing to test the strength of the Royal Navy in the hope of demonstrating superiority that would allow capital ships to break out of the North Sea and raid shipping that brought supplies to Britain. The Battle of Jutland was the occasion on which the two fleets met in the North Sea and engaged in brutal confrontation with severe losses on both sides. Dawlish was to hear of the deaths of six naval personnel in this battle.

The Battle of Jutland was the largest naval battle of World War I, fought between 31st May and 1st June 1916, in the North Sea near Jutland, Denmark. The German plan was to use five modern battlecruisers to lure the British through a submarine picket line and into the path of the main German fleet. The plan didn't succeed, but the battle is considered to be won by the Germans, dealing the Royal Navy a heavy blow[3].

The Royal Navy's Grand Fleet of battleships were under the command of Admiral Sir John Jellicoe at Scapa Flow while the battlecruiser squadron led by Vice Admiral Sir David Beatty was in the Firth of Forth and closer to the German Navy base at Wilhelmshavn.

Revd Guy Arrott BROWNING

Born Wimbledon, 15 Dec 1876   Died 31 May 1916, aged 39
Chaplain & Naval Instructor,   Royal Navy   H.M.S. INDEFATIGABLE

Guy Arrott Browning was the second son of George Alexander (1838-1913) and Mary Elizabeth Browning, nee Kendall (1849-). He had joined the Navy on 12 January 1854 at the age of 16 and became a Lieutenant with a specialism in navigation.
They were married in King's Lynn on 22nd February 1872 and had lived in Wimbledon (1881) with four sons, Kendall Colin (1875-1936), **Guy Arrott (1876-1916),** Hamilton Arthur (1879-1891), and Herbert Acland (1880-1955). George Alexander Browning was a retired naval Captain. In 1891 they had moved to 20 Macaulay Road, Clapham.

By 1901 they were living at 2 Longlands, Dawlish where the household consisted of George A Browning, 61, Mary E – his wife 52,   Kendall C, son 25 (M.A. Cambridge Univ), **Guy A, 24 (Clergyman, Church of England),** Herbert A, 21, (Univ graduate, Medical student), Helen M Browning, 42, sister-in-law.
By 1911 the parents had moved again to 11 Barton Terrace with Helen M Kendall, the wife's sister.

Captain G A Browning died on 25 March 1913 at the age of 74 and his widow still resided at 11 Barton Terrace at the time of her son's death.

---

3   Ref 'JUTLAND 1916' by Nigel Steel and Peter Hart

The Cambridge University Alumni record summarises **Guy Browning's** life as:

"Adm. S. of George Alexander, Capt., R.N., of West Dulwich. B. Dec. 15, 1876, at Wimbledon, Surrey. Schools, Clapham (Dr F. C. Maxwell) and Dulwich College. sizar at ST JOHN'S, Apr. 27, 1896.

Matric. Michs. 1896; Scholar, 1898; B.A. (30*th Wrangler*) 1899; M.A. 1903. Ord. deacon, 1900; priest (Exeter) 1901; C. of Dawlish, 1900-3. Chaplain and Instructor in the Navy, 1903-16. Served in the Great War. Went down in H.M.S. INDEFATIGABLE, at the Battle of Jutland, May 31, 1916. Brother of Herbert A. (1898), etc. (*Dulwich Coll. Reg.*)"

right, The Memorial plaque in St Gregory's Church, Dawlish

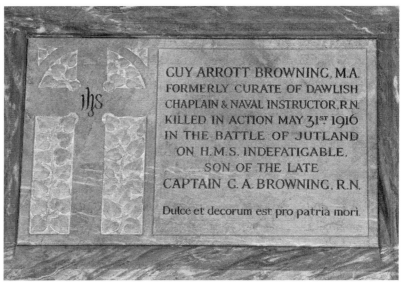

The battlecruiser HMS INDEFATIGABLE (Captain Charles Sowerby) was locked in a gunnery duel with the German battlecruiser *SMS VON DER TANN* when a German salvo was observed to strike HMS INDEFATIGABLE midships. HMS INDEFATIGABLE lurched out of line to starboard only to be struck squarely by a second salvo.

It appears that HMS INDEFATIGABLE received a shell in her X turret of two 12" guns, mounted amidships, which appears to have ignited cordite charges, the resultant flash shooting down to the midships magazines. An enormous explosion blew the ship apart and recent marine archaeology has shown the bow and stern sections separated and the two midships turrets lying some distance from the main wreck. The ship was wreathed in smoke but when it cleared, HMS INDEFATIGABLE was sinking by the stern and listing over to port.

She sank in seconds taking 1,017 of her crew with her.

The *Western Times of Friday 9 June 1916* reported; " The Rev G.A.Browning, M.A. (Chaplain), H.M.S. INDEFATIGABLE, was killed in the battle *(Jutland)*. He was the second son of the late Capt. Browning, R.N., and Mrs Browning, of Barton Terrace, Dawlish."

"He graduated and was a wrangler of St. John's College, Cambridge. He took Holy Orders about 15 years ago, and held his first and only curacy at Dawlish. He remained a member of the local clergy for two years, upon retirement from which he entered the Navy as Chaplain and Naval Instructor."

"He served on the BULWARK, VANGUARD, and ORION. He was appointed to the INDEFATIGABLE on the outbreak of war. At the Parish Church yesterday morning sympathetic reference was made to the rev. gentleman's death. The organist (Mr J.F.King) played the "Dead March".

Commonwealth War Graves entry: BROWNING, Guy Arrott, Revd, 31 May 1916, Jutland, aged 39, Son of Capt G A Browning, R.N., and M E Browning of Dawlish. Royal Naval Memorial, Plymouth Panel 10, Plymouth Hoe.
He is recorded on the Devon Roll of Honour.
Dawlish War memorial inscription: BROWNING G.A.   C[hap]& N.I.   H.M.S.INDEFATIGABLE

Last known address: 11 Barton Terrace, Dawlish
Next of kin: Mary Elizabeth Browning - mother
Probate was granted on 6 October 1916 to John Bruce Irving, Medical Student in sum of £3,269 0s 11d.

References: CWGC and Naval-History.net   BMD, census and Probate records.
Cambridge Alumni.   Wrecksite.eu   "JUTLAND 1916" by Steel & Hart, Publ Cassell

A ship's Chaplain would have taken on the pastoral care of members of the ship's company and may have assisted the ship's doctor in caring for those in the sick bay. His other duties included an educational role to ensure that reading and writing were improved for even the most junior personnel.

One of the junior ratings was a stoker from Dawlish who's role was to shovel coal to keep steam in the boilers at all times. He would have known nothing of how the battle was progressing, although the noise of exploding shells would be heard, until the explosion of the ship's magazine would have brought a rapid end to his life.

Alfred Thomas DEW

Born: Rewe, Nr Exeter 3 November 1891	Died: 31 May 1916, aged 24
Stoker 1st class, Royal Navy, Service No: K 22746	H.M.S.INDEFATIGABLE

Alfred Thomas Dew was one of five children of the marriage of John Dew(1860-1909) and Louisa Harriet Hodge.
Alfred's grandfather was Joseph John Dew (1836-1903) and Joseph appears with his mother, Margaret, in Rosemary Lane, St Edmund, Exeter in 1851. His mother was a laundress born in Clyst St Mary, ca 1791.
Joseph dropped his first name and John married Ann Babel(1838-1890) in St Thomas district (Exwick?) in Q3,1860. He appears as John in the 1861 census when he is working as an engineer in paper mills. They had their first son John Dew,[4] 8 months old in time for that census.
(Joseph) John Dew and Ann carried on to have a large family, John(1860-1909), George (1862-1936), Bessie(1864-1942), Samuel(1866-1941), Henry James(1868-1927), Charles (1870-1871), Walter(1972-1914), Alice(1875-1907), Charles William(1878-1907) and Albert (1879-1911).

---

4   Alfred's father was born in St Thomas district, Q4, 1860

John, aged 35, is shown as a paper maker in 1871 but a Labourer in 1881 when the family were still living in Exwick.

Ann died in 1890 and (Joseph) John Dew was a widower in 1891 and working as a mason's labourer with Bessie, Walter, Charles William and Albert living at home at Wilsons Cottages, Exwick Hill.

In the next door property his son, Samuel Dew, was living with his wife Harriet (1866-).

By 1901 (Joseph) John was 63, but still a general labourer and Bessie (36) was with him working as a laundress, with Alice (26) and Fred, described as a son aged 7. Joseph John Dew died in 1903.

(Joseph) John and Ann Dew 's first child, John Dew (1860-1909) married Louisa Harriet Hodge on 17 August 1879 in the Parish Church of St Thomas, Exeter. She was born in Exeter St Thomas, in the 4th quarter of 1859, the daughter of Thomas Hodge (1831-) and Sarah Ann Hodge(1834-).

Sarah Hodge became a widow by the age of 35 (census 1871) and living as a laundress at 1 Haven Banks, Exeter St Thomas, with Louisa Harriet Hodge and five other children.

A census entry for John Dew and Louisa in 1881 has not been found. He is also missing from the 1891 census and there is no trace until his death in Exeter St Thomas in Q4, 1909, aged 48. His principal occupation is also unknown. It appears that they must have separated before 1897, see below.

In the 1891 census Louisa Dew is head of household, married, age 30 and working as a charwoman. She lived at 10 Alphington Street, Exeter, with Annie Louisa* (b, Q4 1879, St Thomas), Frances Alice (b Q2 1882, St Thomas), William John[5] (1885-1915), Sarah E (b Cardiff, 1886) and **Alfred Thomas** (1891 – 31/5/1916).

*- Annie Louisa Dew married Alfred Dorothy on 26 January, 1900, at Powderham when he was a Licensed victualler of the Grapes Inn, South Street, Exeter. They had a child Reginald Alfred Dorothy, born 28 July 1904. Alfred Dorothy enlisted aged 38 in WW1. Annie Dorothy died 19 July 1935.

Louisa Dew next married James Morris/Morrish in Exeter in Q4, 1897 and in 1901 they are shown as living at Redhill Cottage, Powderham with Alfred Thomas Dew, 11, step-son, Frederick Morris, son, 1, and Florence Morris, 5 months. James Morris was a wagoner.

Alfred Thomas Dew was 18 when he joined the Royal Navy on 24th August, 1910 for a 12 year engagement as a Stoker, 2nd class with a service no SS 110286. His previous occupation is shown as gardener.

He joined H.M.S.INDEFATIGABLE in February 1911. He was transferred to C S Stoker 1st class on 10 June 1914 with service number K22746. There is only one known photograph, a newspaper item, (*left*, a cutting from the *Western Times* reporting the loss of local men from the INDEFATIGABLE. Alfred Dew is sitting on the right.)

---

5   William John Dew is separately recorded, dying at the Battle of Loos, 25 September 1915. See Part 1 1914-1915

His naval record shows him to be 5'4" tall and with a tattoo "Heart & true love" on left forearm.

H.M.S. INDEFATIGABLE was a battlecruiser and the_lead ship of her class. Her keel was laid down in 1909 and she was commissioned in 1911. She was an enlarged version of the earlier INVINCIBLE class with a revised protection scheme and additional length amidships to allow her two middle turrets to fire on either broadside.

When the First World War began, INDEFATIGABLE was serving with the 2nd Battlecruiser Squadron (BCS) in the Mediterranean, where she unsuccessfully pursued the battlecruiser *GOEBEN* and the light cruiser *BRESLAU* of the German Imperial Navy as they fled towards the Ottoman Empire. The ship bombarded Ottoman fortifications defending the Dardanelles on 3 November 1914, then, following a refit in Malta, returned to the United Kingdom in February where she rejoined the 2nd Battle Cruiser Squadron.

INDEFATIGABLE was sunk on 31 May 1916 during the Battle of Jutland, the largest naval battle of the war. Part of Vice Admiral Sir David Beatty's Battlecruiser Fleet, she was hit several times in the first minutes of the "Run to the South", the opening phase of the battlecruiser action. Shells from the German battlecruiser *SMS VON DER TANN* caused an explosion ripping a hole in her hull, and a second explosion hurled large pieces of the ship 200feet (60m) in the air. Only two of the crew of 1,019 survived. (ex- Wikipedia)

left, H.M.S.INDEFATIGABLE sinking

The *Western Times, Friday 9 June, 1916,* reported:

"In the recent naval battle the following Dawlish men were known to have been in the engagement: W.H.Heal, *F.J.Hill, *G.Voysey, *R.E.Brock, *Bond, H.M.S. WARRIOR; F.Morrish, H.M.S. DEFENCE, A.T.Dew, H.M.S. INDEFATIGABLE. News has been received that the above marked with an asterisk are safe. Mr A.T.Dew, we understand, had a brother killed in the battle of Loos.

Commonwealth War Graves entry: DEW, Alfred Thomas   Stoker 1st Class K/22746 31/5/1916
Age: 26   Royal Navy H.M.S. "Indefatigable."   Panel Reference 15, Plymouth Naval Memorial
Son of the late John and Louisa Dew,
Next of kin: Louise Morris(h), 12 Queen Lane, Dawlish - mother
He is recorded on the Devon Roll of Honour, but not the date and location of death
Dawlish War memorial inscription: DEW A.   A.B.   R.N.
Devon Heritage site info:

> K22746 Stoker 1st Class Alfred Thomas Dew of the Royal Navy, *HMS Indefatigable* . Son of the late John and Louisa Dew of Queen's terrace, Dawlish. Born in Exeter in the March quarter of 1890. Died 31 May 1916 aged 26 at the Battle of Jutland. *(His Naval Record and RN war Graves Roll shows date of birth 3 November 1891)*

The German High Seas Fleet, top line, engaged with the Royal Navy Grand Fleet at Jutland and H.M.S. INDEFATIGABLE was hit by gunfire from *SMS VON DER TANN* and blew up.

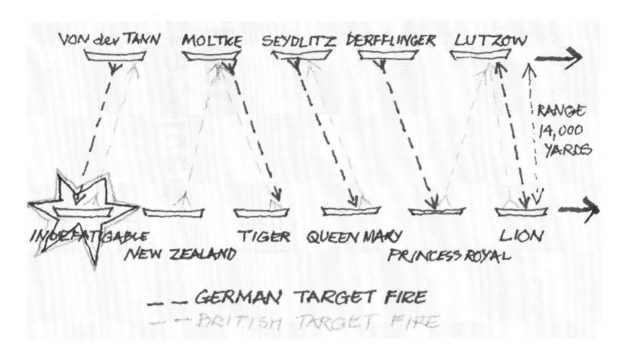

VON der TANN   MOLTKE   SEYDLITZ   DERFFLINGER   LUTZOW

RANGE 14,000 YARDS

INDEFATIGABLE   TIGER   QUEEN MARY   LION
NEW ZEALAND   PRINCESS ROYAL

_ _ GERMAN TARGET FIRE
_ _ BRITISH TARGET FIRE

William John HUTCHINGS

Born 1 April 1886, Ellacombe, Torquay   Died 31 May 1916, age 30
Able Seaman, Royal Navy   Service No: 224640 (Dev)   H.M.S.BROKE

William John Hutchings, age 14, appears in the 1901 census at 1 Alma Place, Madrepore Road, Torquay, living with his parents. Charles Thomas Hutchings (1860-1942) married Louisa Margaret (Holding) (1863 – 1948) in 1884 and they had seven children, Herbert C (1885-), William John (1886-1916), Walter G (1889-), Charles T (1891-), Henry Ernest (1893-), Lilian Louisa Bedford (1895-1960) and Winifred Margaret (1898-1903).

William joined the Royal Navy on 17 January 1903 as a Boy Seaman aged 16 ½. His service record shows that he had been working as a gardener. On his 18th birthday he signed on for a 12 year service, on 1 April 1904.

William was rated Able Seaman in June 1905 and his service record shows a VG (very good) for character in each subsequent ship. He served aboard various ships until December 1905 when he joined H.M.S.CAMBRIDGE, the Gunnery Training Ship that was a 'wooden wall' hulk moored in the Hamoaze off Devonport.

photo shows William with his wife Lilian Elizabeth Ford and their son William John Ford Hutchings.

Gunnery practise ashore took place at the Trevol ranges, Torpoint, and at sea in a number of ships. During this posting he married Lilian Elizabeth Ford in 4th quarter 1906.

Lilian Ford was a daughter and one of 16 children of John and Mary Ford of Dawlish. Their father was a tailor in 3 Park Street in 1901 and 3 Strand Hill in 1911. John and Mary Ford's grandson, Frederick George Ford, was living with them in 1901 and 1911 but he served in the Royal Marines and died in the Gallipoli campaign on 9th May 1915[6]. (see separate entry and family photograph in Part 1 – 1914-1915)

William and Lilian Hutchings had a son, William John Ford Hutchings (1908 – 1986) and in 1911 mother and son were living at 15 Elm Road, Highweek, Newton Abbot, while William was at sea. William is shown in the 1911 census as part of the Ship's Company of H.M.S.ABOUKIR, an armoured cruiser.

It appears that Lilian and her son later moved to Dawlish to live with her family.

In June 1911 William was posted to H.M.S.BLAKE which was a Destroyer Depot Ship based at Portland. His next posting in May 1914 was to the Naval Barracks, Devonport, then Portsmouth, and again to H.M.S.BLAKE (BROKE), which was then the depot ship to the 2nd Destroyer Flotilla at Rosyth. This was followed by H.M.S.HECLA taking the part of Depot Ship to the 4th Destroyer Flotilla at Scapa Flow where H.M.S.BROKE was one of twenty one destroyers, and was the Flotilla Leader (2nd in command).

H.M.S.ZULU, a Destroyer of the same general form as H.M.S.BROKE

In the major naval engagement in the North Sea, known as the Battle of Jutland, that began on 31 May 1916, there were more significant British naval losses than German, but the outcome was to persuade the German Kaiser to instruct his navy to remain in port.

Towards the end of the battle, the 4th Destroyer Flotilla encountered German forces that damaged H.M.S.TIPPERARY, the Flotilla Leader, and H.M.S.BROKE became the senior ship in the Flotilla. She was then hit by gunfire from *SMS WESTFALEN*. This blast destroyed the bridge, while the ship was in the middle of a turning manoeuvre to bring torpedo tubes to bear on the German ship. She continued to turn and collided with H.M.S.SPARROWHAWK of the flotilla.

---

6   Ford Family History has been researched by June Snell and a group family photograph, ca 1904, was included in the entry for Frederick George Ford in Part One of this series

A young officer of H.M.S.SPARROWHAWK saw the ship approaching fast and was thrown by the collision onto the other ship, where he lay for a few minutes unconscious. When he awoke he was welcomed by a colleague with the words: 'Who in hell are you?'. Now chaos reigned on both ships. Both captains assumed they were sinking, and so ordered the crew onto the other ship. Finally, both ships were freed. But just at this moment H.M.S.CONTEST, another destroyer, collided with the stern of the H.M.S.SPARROWHAWK.

In this confusion, a German battle cruiser neared the crippled H.M.S.SPARROWHAWK. Although she fired the only gun that she could, the German ship carried on, but suddenly it sank just before hitting the destroyer. What ship this was is still a complete mystery. At about this time the Captain of the *SMS LUTZOW*, Viktor Harder, ordered his crew to abandon his sinking ship and to sink her with destroyer torpedoes. The loss of this ship was the most hurtful loss for the German fleet. There is still discussion about whether the ship was still in a condition to be saved, as *SMS SEYDLITZ* survived the battle in a similar condition.

Only half an hour later, at 3.15 the destroyer H.M.S.OBEDIENT met the German 2nd squadron. She launched a torpedo, which hit the German pre-dreadnought *SMS POMMERN*, which went down in a huge explosion. In this last engagement, the German destroyer *SM V 4* was also lost. This marked the end of the battle.

About the death of William John Hutchings: The Battle of Jutland, 31 May 1916.   Fourth Destroyer Flotilla, 2 flotilla leaders (Broke damaged on 31 May, Tipperary sunk on 1 June), Able Seaman Hutchings was one of 47 killed and 36 wounded aboard H.M.S.BROKE.

Commonwealth War Graves entry:
Able Seaman,   Service No:224640   Date of Death: 31/05/1916   Age:29   Royal Navy   - H.M.S. BROKE
Plymouth naval memorial Panel 12.   Husband of Lilian Hutchings, of II, Commercial Rd., Dawlish, Devon.
UK, RN and RM War Graves Roll: generally as above, Buried at Sea.

A B Hutchings is listed on the Dawlish War memorial : HUTCHINGS W.   A.B.   R.N.
He is also included in the Devon Roll of Honour, but no date of death or location is shown.

The Devon Heritage site info:
> 224640 Able Seaman William John Hutchings of the Royal Navy, H.M.S.BROKE. Parents not known. Husband of Lilian (nee Ford) of 11 Commercial Road, Dawlish. Born nr Exeter 1 April 1886. Died 31 May 1916 aged 29 in the Battle of Jutland. (*Some of this early detail is corrected by material above.*)

FORD, WAY, MORRISH, HUTCHINGS, SHELSTON
FAMILY CONNECTIONS

Lilian Elizabeth Ford is the connection to the next casualty and to further Dawlish families including Way and Shelston, as can be found in the notes that follow.

Frank MORRISH

Born 15 September, 1873, Dawlish   Died, 31 May 1916, Battle of Jutland, aged 42
Chief Armourer, Royal Navy,   Service No: 175632   H.M.S.DEFENCE

Frank was the oldest son of William Morrish (1847-1892, born in Crediton) and Ann (nee Way, 1850-1925, born in South Tawton) of Brook Street, Dawlish.

William Morrish had been apprenticed to John Ashplant and became a blacksmith. He married Ann Way on 12 July,1871 in Bow. Later, they move south and in 1891 William was working in Dawlish.

Their oldest son, Frank, worked as a coachbuilder's apprentice. They had six more children, Lucy Jane (1872-1920), Kate A (1875-1949), Bessie Mary (1876-1946), William George (1879-1947), Mabel Grace (1882-1947), and Herbert J (1885-1937). *(see later text for Morrish family detail)*

Frank Morrish enlisted in the Royal Navy on 28 August 1893 for 12 years service, and re-enlisted on 28 August 1905 "to completion". He was 5'4" tall, with light brown hair, blue eyes and fair complexion and was described as a coach smith on his naval record.

He trained as an Armourer at H.M.S.CAMBRIDGE, the gunnery training ship and after service on various ships became an Armourer's Mate in 1899. Having a gunnery specialism puts him close to William Hutchings' career.

Frank married Emma Louisa Woodley in December 1900 in the Newton Abbot registration district. The wedding was possibly held in Teignmouth, the home of the Woodley family. Emma Louisa was the daughter of Thomas, a carpenter, and Louisa Woodley who had nine children.

By 1911, Emma Louisa Morrish was boarding at 11 Commercial Road, Teignmouth with a son, Frank Woodley Morrish (1904-1974). He was born in Devonport in August 1904[7]. His father was at that time at H.M.S.CAMBRIDGE, the naval gunnery school at Devonport.

> After the death of his parents FWM moved to London and appears in the Electoral Registers in Haringey in 43 Curzon Road (1931), 38 Crouch End Hill (1935), 57 Cedar Court, Muswell Hill (1936 &1937) and in Hendon in 1939. In the Navy List of October 1942 he is shown as a Chief Petty Officer and Temporary Lieutenant with seniority of 11 March 1941. Little more has been found until his death in Exeter[8] in December 1974.

Frank Morrish's mother, Ann, was widowed by the 1911 census when she was working as a certified midwife and living at 4 Brook Street, with daughters Kate, 35 and Mabel, 29 and an adopted son Thomas Ford, 5. His full name was Thomas Herbert Foster Ford, and was Ann's great nephew, grandson of Mary Ann Ford nee Way (her sister) and John Ford. He was the illegitimate son of their daughter Lilian. Lilian was to marry William John Hutchings who was also killed at Jutland, as described above.

---

7   GRO ref 1904, August, Devonport, vol 5b, p 325
8   GRO Ref 1974, December, Exeter,vol 31, page 0990

In the 1911 census **Frank** was an Armourer in the Royal Navy and serving aboard H.M.S.VANGUARD at Portland. He was promoted to Assistant Chief Armourer in January 1913. He joined H.M.S.DEFENCE in September 1913 and was made up to Chief Armourer.

H.M.S.DEFENCE which was a Minotaur-class Armoured Cruiser, launched in April 1907. She was 519 feet overall with a displacement of 14,600 tons and a speed of 22.5 knots. Her armament was 4-9.2in, 10-7.5in, 16-12pdr, 5-18in torpedo tubes.

DEFENCE Joined the 1st Cruiser Squadron as flagship in 1913, and took part in the hunt for Goeben and Breslau in August 1914. She was stationed off the Dardanelles in September 1913, but sent to the South Atlantic to reinforce Rear-Admiral Cradock's squadron (see the Battle of Coronel, described in Part 1); diverted to Cape of Good Hope in November 1914.

DEFENCE became flagship 1st Cruiser Squadron, Grand Fleet, in January 1915. She was sunk by gunfire of German battleship *SMS FRIEDRICH DER GROSSE* at Jutland, 31 May 1916. All hands (893 officers and men) were lost as a result of cordite charges catching fire in the ammunition passages.[9]

Extract from the Official History; " Naval Operations" by Sir Julian S. Corbett. 1923

..........Both the DEFENCE and WARRIOR had already hit the doomed *WIESBADEN*. Still Admiral Arbuthnot, in spite of straddling salvoes, held on till within 5,500 yards of his prey when he turned to starboard. Both ships were now in a hurricane of fire, which the Germans were concentrating with terrible effect to save their burning ship, and there quickly followed another of the series of appalling catastrophes which so tragically distinguish this battle from all others. Four minutes after crossing the LION's bows the DEFENCE was hit by two heavy salvoes in quick succession, and the Admiral and his flagship disappeared in a roar of flame (6.20). The WARRIOR barely escaped a similar fate.............

Commonwealth War Graves entry: MORRISH, Frank   Chief Armourer, 175632, 31/05/1916
Royal Navy, H.M.S. "Defence." Panel Reference 17.   Plymouth Naval Memorial
Long Service and Good Conduct Medal. Son of Ann Morrish, of Dawlish, and the late William Morrish; husband of Emma Louisa Morrish, of 11, Commercial Rd., Teignmouth.

Frank Morrish is recorded on the Devon Roll of Honour but date and location are not shown.
Dawlish War memorial inscription: MORRISH FRANK   C[H] AR[MR]   R.N.
He is also shown on Dawlish Boys' School Roll of Honour.

(His naval record shows his date of birth as 1871 but this appears to be an error from checks with Birth Registration and census returns. Nor does the naval record list H.M.S.Duke of Edinburgh among the 32 ships on which he served. He was 42 at his death - ed)

References: BMD and Census entries from ancestry.co.uk   naval-history.net
          northeastmedals.co.uk   Ford Family Tree(June Snell)

---

9   Conway's All the World's Fighting Ships 1860-1905 and 1906-21 & www.naval-history.net

APPENDIX - MORRISH – WAY families

William Morrish (1846-1892)[10] was born in Crediton and married **Ann** (nee Way, 1850-1925) on 12 July, 1871 in Bow church. Ann Way was born in Bow and so the family had started from a rural background. Bow is a parish in Mid Devon, about eight miles west of Crediton.

William took an apprenticeship with John Ashplant and became a blacksmith. By 1881 William and Ann had moved to Dawlish and William is described as a "Gen Labourer".
William's father, John Morrish was born in Witheridge ca 1829 and was a labourer when living with them in Commercial Road, Dawlish in 1891.

William and Ann had the following Morrish children:
Frank born 15 September 1873 in Dawlish, killed at Jutland, above.

Lucy Jane (1872-1920), was born in Q2, 1872 in Bow. She married Robert Shelston[11] (1862-1937)from Tedburn St Mary, was a gardener, in Q3, 1896 and died in June 1920 (N.A. distr[12])

Kate Annie (1875-1949), was born in Dawlish in Q3,1875. She married George Henry BELL in Exeter in Q3,1897. They had three sons Harold George W H Bell (1898-1961), Clifford Tremayne M Bell (1903-1970) and Orlando Claude T M Bell(1910-2004). Kate died in June 1949, aged 75 (ancestry tree)

Bessie Mary (1876-1946), was born in Dawlish in Q4, 1876 and married Harry Parsons in 1904. He was a Chief Armourer, Royal Navy, born in Teignmouth. She died in March 1946.

William George (1879-1947), was born in Q1,1879 in Dawlish. He married Maud Tank (1879-) in the Wesleyan Chapel, Dawlish on 20 March, 1903. Maud was one of eleven children of William James (1844-1910) and Elizabeth Vosper Tank (1842-1913) of Lower Bore Street, Bodmin. William enlisted with the Labour Corps on 13 February 1917 and served with the B.E.F. from 27/2/17 to 14/3/18. His Army record is one of few to survive the WW2 Blitz and it shows that his wife's allowance was paid to her at 11 Hamilton Street, Devonport in May 1918, and to her at 5 Higher Bore Street, Bodmin in October 1918.
After appearance at a Military Medical Board in August, 1918, W G Morrish was given a discharge for disability due to neurasthenia (otherwise referred to as shell shock). Following a further period in hospital and being sent on a month's leave, he was discharged with a pension on 8th November 1918. William and Maud had two children, Gwendoline Rose Morrish born 30 April 1904 and Lucy Louise Vesper Morrish born 29 April 1916.
William married again to Rosina Charlotte Elizabeth Sommers in Q2, 1946 in N.A. district. He died less than a year later on 24 January 1947 in Elmgrove Road. (his address was shown as 3 King Street, Dawlish)

---

10   GRO ref Crediton Q4,1846 Vol 10, p 81

11   Robert Shelston was the youngest son of Thomas and Fannie Shelston – see "True Britishers" The Shilstons and Dodds of England and Canada, publ Amazon 2020

12   The references to "N.A.district" includes Teignmouth and Dawlish, among other towns and villages in the indexing of births, marriages and deaths.

Mabel Grace (1882-1947) was born in N.A. district in Q1, 1882. She married Thomas Glass in N.A. district in Q3, 1916 and died in September 1947.

Herbert J (1885-1937)

WAY family[13]

Ann Way was one of nine children of Francis WAY (1827-1910) and Grace BAKER (1824-1880). Francis/Frank was born in North Tawton in Mid Devon and was an agricultural labourer. Grace was from a Spreyton family and became a dressmaker (1871 census).
Grace Way (1824-1880) died in Q2, 1880 in the Newton Abbot district.
Francis Way (1827-1910) married for the second time to Elizabeth Martin in Q1,1881 in Okehampton district. She had been born in St Sidwells, Exeter.
They lived at Roseberry, North Tawton at 1881 year's census with two of her sons from an earlier marriage to William Martin, a chimney sweep. The household included Francis, 53, his new wife Elizabeth, 44, William Martin, 19, a chimney sweep, Charles Martin, 13, Alfred Way, 15 and Frederick Way, 13.
By 1891 Francis had become a Grocer, at Waterloo in North Tawton and ten year's later he and his wife were living alone at the Grocer's Shop, High Street. He died in Q4, 1910.

Francis and Grace married Q1,1849 in the Okehampton district, and <u>they had the following children</u>:

Richard, born ca 1845 in Spreyton

Ann, born 1851[14] in South Tawton, married **William Morrish,** see above.   She died in Q1, 1925, aged 75.

Mary Ann, born 1852 in Bow. She worked as a cook and domestic servant of Samuel Standeland, Surgeon of Winsor House, Bow at the time of the 1871 census. She married **John Ford** in Q1, 1874, and by 1881 they were settled in Dawlish. (See the family data for Frederick George Ford who was killed at Gallipoli on 9th May 1915)
> n.b. North Tawton, Bow and Spreyton form three sides of a triangle of about 7km each and lie east of Okehampton in Central Devon.

Francis/Frank, born 1855 in Bow. He died in July 1886 .

John, born 1857 in Clannaborough, a short distance east of Bow. He married (1) Elizabeth Frances Coleman in Jan 1878 in Dawlish and had a daughter Rhoda Francis Way in 1879. He became a blacksmith in Littleham, Exmouth (1881) and married in 1889 (2) Emma Clift (1862-). They moved to Dawlish by 1891 and his daughter died in 1897, aged 18. He died in Sept 1935.

---

13   With gratitude to June Snell who has compiled a detailed account, and reproduced with permission
14   GRO ref South Tawton Q1, 1851, vol 10, p 292

William, born 1858 in Clannaborough. He worked as a Labourer and married Jane Brown in Q3,1880 (Newton Abbot district) and died in 1898.

They had four children, the eldest **William Richard Way** was born 1881 in Dawlish. He was killed on 14 February 1918 in France and Flanders and is on the Dawlish War Memorial with details on the Devon Heritage Site :

> 27046 Private William Richard Way of the 7th Battalion, the Somerset Light Infantry. Son of Jane Way and the late William Way. Born in Dawlish in 1881. Died 14 February 1918 aged 37.
>
> A soldier's Will for him left his effects to his youngest brother Frederick of 7 Queen St, Torquay.
>
> William's widow was a lodger in 3 Perrotts Buildings, Pimlico, Torquay in 1911 and working as a charwoman.

Bessey/Bessie, born in Bow in 1861, married George Shelston[15] in Q4,1882 (N.A.district). George was the brother of Robert who married Lucy Jane Morrish, see above. They are recorded in 55 Monument Street, Devonport in the 1891 census, as Bessie Shelston,(incorrectly transcribed as Brickwood) 30, married, Ellen, her daughter,1, and Alice Way, 8, born in Maryport, Cumberland, a niece of Bessie.

George Shelston was in the Royal Navy and a Petty Officer, 1st Class when the 1901 census shows them living at 12 Municipal House, Devonport with two children, Ellen G, born 1890 in Dawlish and George, born 1893 in Dawlish. They went on to have two more children, Frederick, born 1902 in Devonport and Francis, born 1905 also in Devonport.

By 1911 George was a Naval Pensioner and Public House Keeper of the Carpenter's Arms, Old Town Street, Dawlish. He died on Christmas Eve, 1913 in Dawlish and Bessie died in 1936.

Lucy, born 1864 in Bow was shown to be crippled in the left leg on the 1871 census. In 1891 she was staying/living with her sister Ann and William Morrish in Commercial Road, Dawlish and working as a dress-maker. She died in October 1891.

Alfred, born Q1 1866 in Bow. He married Mary Lavinia Jane (?)(born 1862, Calstock, Cornwall) in 1889 and in 1891 they were living at 5 Brook Street, Dawlish and by 1911 were at Park Row Cottages with Mabel Hooper, an adopted daughter (1895-). He died on 27 January 1934 and left to his widow £838-17s-10d. (Probate records) They were then living at 12 Stockton Road, Dawlish.

Frederick, born 1868 in Bow, was shown on the 1871 census. He married Ada Martin in March 1909 at St Veep, Cornwall. On the 1911 census Frederick was a Chief Cook in the Royal Navy, living at Devonport with Ada and one year-old daughter Grace. The same year the family moved to Dawlish, and they had four children in all:

Grace Way   (1910-1971), married Archibald Perring and had five children;

Hedley Martin Way   (1911-2008), married Ethel Blanchard and they had two children, Elizabeth and John - N.B. The Hedley Way Centre (recently known as the Riverside Centre in the Manor House grounds) was named in his honour;

Francis Thomas Way   (1912-2003), married Phyllis Symes in 1936 and had one son, Mervyn;

Wilfred Percival Way   (1918-1999), married Lilian Sarah Maile in 1945 and had a daughter, Jean, and a son, David.

Frederick Way died in N.A. district in June 1946.

---

15   See "True Britishers" The Shilstons and Dodds of England and Canada, publ Amazon pp7-18

William Henry MUTTERS

Born Dawlish, 1 March 1869   Died Battle of Jutland, 31 May 1916, aged 47
Private, Royal Marine Light Infantry, Service No: PLY/16964 (Dev)   H.M.S. QUEEN MARY

James Mutters (1820-1901) born in Exeter, married Mary Ann Voysey (1824-1893) born in Dawlish, in 1848. James was an agricultural labourer.
In 1851 they lived in Park Row, Dawlish with their first of nine children, Mary Jane Mutters (1850-1904).
By 1861 at the same address were Mary Jane, James (1855-), John V (1857-), Sarah Ann ** (1859-1930), and George V (1860 -).

> ** Sarah Ann Mutters married Robert Bearne (1850-1901) and their son, Arthur Henry Bearne (1882-1914) was lost at sea in the Battle of Coronel on 1 November 1914 (*see separate entry for Arthur Henry Bearne in Part 1*).

By 1871 there were four more children, Thomas (1863-), Joseph (1865-), Charlotte (1867-) and **William Henry** (1869-1916). All children were born in Dawlish.

By 1881 James Mutters was a general labourer and Mary Ann was a charwoman. Living at home with them at 6 Park Row were John V, George V, William F, all general labourers, Charlotte, an errand girl and **William H,** still at school.

> (*William F is very probably Thomas William (1863-) who appears as William Thomas Mutters after his marriage to Sarah Andrews in Q4,1884. In subsequent census entries he is recorded as William Mutters and working as a Mason's labourer and then a mason. They had four children, the youngest being Olive (1893-) who is referred to as the next of kin in the Royal Navy and Royal Marine War Graves Roll, see below.*)

William enlisted with the Royal Marines in London on 1 April 1889 at age 20. His previous occupation is shown as "Boot repairer".
He was sent first to the Royal Marines' Recruit Depot at Walmer, Kent, and then to the Plymouth Division, R.M.
He signed on for 12 years and spent much of the time at sea in pre-Dreadnought battleships, H.M.S. ANSON (7/5/1890-4/7/1893), H.M.S.EMPRESS OF INDIA (1/5/1894-11/12/1895), H.M.S.MAGNIFICENT (12/12/1895-16/8/1897), and a cruiser H.M.S.FLORA (18/8/1898-31/12/1900), South African Guardship.

On 1 January 1901 he was sent ashore at Port Stanley "per order of Commodore dated 28 Feb 01". He remained there until 22 March 1901 as his first twelve year agreement was about to expire.

While William was in the services his parents were living at 3a Manor Row (1891) on their own aged 70 and 66. James had worked as a general labourer for much of his life.

William's mother, Mary Ann, died in Q4, 1893 and his father, James, in Q1, 1901.
Census entries for William in 1901 and 1911 have proved elusive. He may not have been in this country, but the outbreak of war brings him back again onto the record book.

William enlisted once again on 31st August 1914 to join HMS QUEEN MARY (26,770 tons), the last battlecruiser built before WW1 and the sole member of her class. She was competed in 1913 and was part of the Grand Fleet based in the Firth of Forth, with easy access to the North Sea.

As part of the 1st Battlecruiser Squadron she attempted to intercept a German force that bombarded the North Sea coast of England in December 1914, but was unsuccessful. After a refit

early in 1915 she participated in the largest fleet action of the war, the Battle of Jutland.
(wikipedia and naval-history.net)(photo: www.militarian.com)

HMS Queen Mary - Lost at Jutland

For two years after the declaration of War the German High Seas Fleet made only limited sorties from Wilhelmshavn on the North Sea coast of Germany. They were contained by the threat of engagement with the British Grand Fleet which was numerically superior.

The Franco-Prussian war came to a close in 1871 with the military defeat of France, leaving Germany the most powerful mainland European power in contention with Britain. The succession of Kaiser Wilhelm II in 1888 brought new ambitions in naval expansion in the belief that only a strong navy could support a growing empire. Admiral Alfred von Tirpitz was appointed Secretary of State for Naval Affairs in 1897 and the Naval Act of 1900 aimed to create a fleet of 38 battleships in a plan for a navy of a size that could stand comparison with Britain.

At the outbreak of war Britain still had the stronger fleet and the Grand Fleet was only menaced by the threat of U-boat attack. For this reason the battleships of the 5th Battle Squadron used the safe anchorage at Scapa Flow in the Orkneys where Admiral Sir John Jellicoe flew his flag and the Battle Cruiser Squadron were held in the Firth of Forth.

In late May,1916, as news of the emergence of the German High Seas Fleet from Wilhelmshavn reached the Admiralty all ships raised steam to meet them.

Steaming in advance of Admiral Sir John Jellicoe's 5th Battle Squadron, Beatty's battlecruisers left the Firth of Forth and met Vice Admiral Franz Hipper's battlecruisers in the opening phases of the Battle of Jutland.

Engaging at 3:48 PM on May 31, the German fire proved accurate from the outset. At 3:50 PM, QUEEN MARY opened fire on *SMS SEYDLITZ* with its forward turrets. As Beatty aboard the LION closed the range, QUEEN MARY scored two hits on its opponent and disabled one of *SEYDLITZ'S* aft turrets. Around 4:15, HMS LION came under intense fire from Hipper's ships. The smoke from this obscured HMS PRINCESS ROYAL, forcing *SMS DERFFLINGER* to shift its fire to QUEEN MARY. As this new enemy engaged, the British ship continued to trade hits with *SEYDLITZ*.

At 4:26 PM, a shell from *SMS DERFFLINGER* struck QUEEN MARY detonating one or both of its forward magazines. The resulting explosion broke the battlecruiser in half near its foremast. A second shell from *DERFFLINGER* may have hit further aft. As the after part of the ship began to roll, it was rocked by a large explosion before sinking.
Of QUEEN MARY's crew, 1,266 were lost while only twenty were rescued.

Though Jutland resulted in a strategic victory for the British, it saw two battlecruisers, HMS INDEFATIGABLE and QUEEN MARY, lost with nearly all hands. An investigation into the losses led to changes in ammunition handling aboard British ships as the report showed that cordite handling practices may have contributed to the loss of the two battlecruisers.
(militaryhistory.about.com)

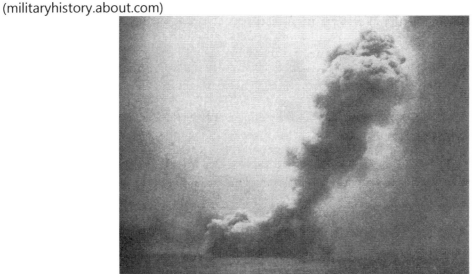

photo of the explosion of H.M.S.QUEEN MARY – IWM public domain.

Commonwealth War Graves entry:
Mutters, William Henry, Private PLY/16964, 31/05/1916, Age:47   Royal Marine Light Infantry
H.M.S. QUEEN MARY. Panel 18. Plymouth Naval Memorial. Son of James and Jane Mutters, of 41, The Strand, Teignmouth, Devon. Native of Dawlish, Devon. *(mother's name incorrect and repeated in Devon Heritage site, below - ed)*

William Henry Mutters is recorded on the Devon Roll of Honour but no date or location of death is shown.
Dawlish War memorial inscription: MUTTERS W.H.   PTE.   R.M.L.I.

Devon Heritage site info:
        PLY 16964 Private William Henry Mutters of the Royal Marine Light Infantry, H.M.S.QUEEN
        MARY. Son of James and Jane Mutter of 42 The Strand, Teignmouth. Born in Dawlish in

the September Quarter of 1868. Died 31 May 1916 aged 47. *(parentage and date of birth incorrect-ed)*

Last known address: 3a Manor Row (1891 census)

Next of kin: Olive Mutters, niece, daughter of Thomas William & Sarah Mutters, Westmead, The Bartons, Dawlish   (UK RN & RM War Graves Roll)

References:
Naval/Royal Marine service record at National Archives, Kew
Free Birth Marriage & Death records
CWGC.org
Refs from subscription sites:
UK RN & RM War Graves Roll
Census records
Forces War Records
14 family trees on Ancestry *(many with errors-ed)*

Arthur Thomas JONES

Born Llantwit Major, Glamorgan, 29 May 1887   Died 31 May 1916, aged 29
Able Seaman, R.N.   Service no: 231814   H.M.S.DEFENCE

Arthur Thomas Jones is one of the men missing from Dawlish War Memorial but this profile may show how he deserves to be there. Although he was born in South Wales, he married a Dawlish lass and left a widow and two young children when he was lost in the Battle of Jutland.

He was born to Thomas Jones (1841-1901), a coachman from Carew, Pembrokeshire, and Emma (1842-)_from Rockfield, Monmouthshire. In 1891 They were living at Llantwit Major with six children:

James, 24, (1867-) son	general labourer	born	Rockfield, Monmouthshire
William, 15, (1876-) son	stable boy		Llantwit Major, Glamorgan
Catherine, 12, (1879-) dau	scholar		"
Edwin, 8, (1883-), son	"		"
Harry, 6, (1885-), son	"		"
Arthur, 3, (1887-1916)			"

There are three other children recorded on the Swaker family tree, Elizabeth (1886-), Mary J (1871-) and Hilda J (1874-).

The family were still there, living in Colhugh Street, Llantwit Major in 1901 without Edwin or Harry, but with a grand-daughter, Anne (1900-). The father is now described as a general labourer, as was William.

Arthur Jones joined the Royal Navy at Devonport on 22 August 1904 and at the age of 17 as a Boy Seaman he was sent to H.M.S.PEMBROKE for periods of training until, at the age of 18, he signed for 12 years service.

He joined H.M.S.DEFENCE on 2 September 1913 and stayed aboard until she was destroyed with the loss of his life in the Battle of Jutland on 31 May 1916. For an account of the ship's movements and actions at Jutland, see the report for Frank Morrish, above.

Arthur Thomas Jones had married Lily Bond at the Register Office, Newton Abbot, on 7 January 1915. Their address at the time was shown as 2 Stockton Cottages, Dawlish. He would have been granted leave from H.M.S.DEFENCE for this and it is likely that the ship was berthed in Devonport on return to home waters before taking up station with the Grand Fleet.

The Bond family had lived for a while in Ireland, as Richard John Webber Bond (1849-1901) had transferred from the Royal Navy to the Coastguard service in 1877. Richard Bond was born in Dawlish on 31 March 1849 and joined the Navy. On 31 March 1867, at the age of 18, he signed for 10 years service and was rated Petty Officer, 2nd Class in 1876 at the age of 27. In the same year he married Mary Ann Evers[16]. Two of their children were born in Ireland, the others in Dawlish:

Alice, dau, (1878-) born Ireland married Thomas Samuel Rendel, 1903
Herbert Webber, son (1879-) born in Dawlish
Arthur.J. son (1883-) born in Ireland
Lily dau, (1885-1964) Dawlish

Richard Bond was rated as Boatman when attached to H.M.S. BELLEISLE in 1878. She was commissioned on 2 July 1878, and served for the next fourteen years as coastguard ship at Kingstown, Ireland. Her only activity there was firing practice four times a year, the annual squadron cruise, and one refit at Devonport.

Richard John Webber Bond left the Coastguard Service in September 1888 and died in 1890, aged [17]41. His widow was living in the home of her married daughter Alice in 1911 and her unmarried daughter Lily at 2 Frederick Cottages, Dawlish.

Arthur Thomas Jones married Lily Bond after the birth of their first child, Ethel May Jones Bond in 1914[18], but this may have been forced upon him by joining H.M.S.DEFENCE in September 1913 and then serving in the Mediterranean and the South Atlantic, as described above. They appear to have married as soon as the DEFENCE returned to home waters sixteen months later.
Their second child, Hilda Mary Jones (1917-2010), was born on 2 February 1917, after the death of her father. (Hilda married Kenneth S O Pook in 1940 and there were two children from that marriage.)
Lily Jones did not remarry and she died at Dawlish Hospital on 9 October 1964. She had been living at 35 Old Town Street, possibly with Ethel May Jones Bond (1914-1986) who was granted Probate and was a spinster.

He was not listed on Dawlish War Memorial but is now recorded on the "missing names" panel added in 2019.

---

16   GRO ref 1876, July-Sept, N.A., Vol 5b, p 305
17   GRO ref 1890, Apr-June, N.A., vol 5b, p 81
18   GRO ref 1914, Apr-June, N.A., vol 5b, p 163

Commonwealth War Graves entry: Commemorated at <u>PLYMOUTH NAVAL MEMORIAL</u>
Location: Devon, United Kingdom,   Number of casualties listed : 23228   memorial reference: 12.

He was awarded the Star medal, British War Medal and the Victory Medal.

Last known address: 2 Stockton Cottages, Dawlish

Next of kin: Lily Jones, nee Bond, at Blyth Lodge, Dawlish

References:
wikipedia – coastguard data
Naval-History.net
Marriage certificate from General Record Office
refs from subscription sites:
        National Archives, naval ratings service records
        Swaker family tree – Ancestry.co.uk
        Census entries
        Birth, marriage , death entries
        UK, Royal Navy and Royal Marines War Graves Roll
        UK, Naval Medal and Award Rolls

The general conclusion of the Battle of Jutland is that it was a victory for the Royal Navy as it led the Kaiser to order his High Seas Fleet to remain in port at Wilhelmshavn, recognising the greater numerical strength of the Royal Navy's surface ships.
The German navy then invested in submarines for warfare against cargo vessels bringing materials to Britain, and this policy was to bring the United States into the war in 1917 when her shipping was being torpedoed.

June 1916

George Henry GIBBINGS

Born Q1 1886, Dawlish   Died 17th June 1916, aged 30
Sergeant, Service No: 3854 / 7304   Devonshire Regt, 1st/6th Battn

George Henry F T Gibbings was the oldest child of Henry Frank and Mary Ann Gibbings (nee Bennett) who lived in Chapel Street, Dawlish.
Henry F Gibbings (1855-1928) was the son of William Gibbings (1811-1862), a baker, and Jane Potter Loutten (1818-1875). They were both born in North Tawton and had moved to Teignmouth ca. 1840 where all their children were born.

Henry Frank Gibbings married Mary Ann Bennett in 1877[19]. Mary Ann Bennett (1859-) was the daughter of John and Sarah Bennett. John Bennett (1826-) was a farm labourer, born in Bristol, South Gloucestershire. His wife, Sarah, was born in Rockbeare and they may have lived in Welford, Glos, before moving to Dawlish ca. 1853 where all their children were born. Mary Ann Bennett was baptised at Welford on the 19th June 1859.

In 1881, Henry F Gibbings is shown as a 'companion to a gentleman' and recorded at Oak Glen, Eastcliff, Dawlish in the household of Mary Ann Grace, 77 and her son Edwin Grace, 44, gentleman. By 1891 Henry and Mary Ann Gibbings were settled at Chapel Street, Dawlish with Loveday.A.E. Gibbings, daughter, 10, **George Henry F**, son, 5, and John. B. 3, all born in Dawlish. Henry F Gibbings was a cellarman and his wife a laundress.

In 1901, George was 15 and working as a Yard boy on a cattle farm. The family of Henry Gibbings, 45, Mary, 42, George, 15, John, 13, Gertrude, 7, William, 5, Archibald, 3, and Millicam, 2, were living at Manor Row, Dawlish.
The census return for 1911 shows Mary Ann Gibbings living at 5 Regent Avenue with her sister, Louisa and five children. Since her marriage at the age of 18 she had ten children of which eight survived by 1911. It is not clear where her husband was at that time.

George's birth is shown in the March Quarter of 1886[20].
In January 1903 George enlisted at Teignmouth with the 2nd Battalion of the Devonshire Regiment, the regular army.
George Henry Gibbings married Florence Batters in Devonport in [21] 1907.
By 1911 he was a Lance Corporal in barracks in Malta.
The 2nd Battalion was in Cairo, Egypt when war broke out in August 1914 and it returned to England on the 1st October, leaving for France and arriving at Le Havre on 6th November 1914.

At some point George was returned home after a breakdown in his health and he was then attached to the 1st/6th Battalion, the Devonshire Regiment. This was one of Kitchener's New Army battalions of volunteers that were trained before being sent into active service. In this case they were sent to India.

---

19   GRO ref N.A.,1877, Q2, vol 5b, p276
20   GRO ref Newton Abbot district, 1886, Q1, Vol 5b, p116
21   GRO ref Devonport, 1907, Q2, Vol 5b, p701

An extract from the *Dawlish Gazette of 24th June 1916* records some of his early life:

"He was the eldest son of Mr and Mrs H F Gibbings of Manor Row, Dawlish. The sad news (of his death) was received by the deceased's wife at Devonport in a communication from the War Office, expressing regret and sympathy with her in her loss. Sergt. Gibbings is of course well known in "Dawlish. All his young days were spent in the town. A good-natured, obliging man, a steady, trustworthy soldier, his friends were many and his enemies nil."

His service records do not exist, as far as can be established.

The following press item reveals some elements of his army experience:
Exeter and Plymouth Gazette of Friday 23 June 1916
"Mr Frank Gibbings of Manor Row, Dawlish, received news yesterday of the death of his eldest son, **Sergt. George Gibbings**. When war broke out deceased was serving in Egypt. He returned to England with the regiment and was sent to France. After a few months active service there he was invalided home in consequence of a breakdown in health.
He recovered, and subsequently went to Mesopotamia. He contracted enteric fever, and died in a Bombay hospital on June 17th. He was 30 years of age and had served in the army 13 years.
He leaves a widow, but no children. Much sympathy is expressed with the widow, the parents and members of the family."

The Death Grant of £13.14s.4d and the War Gratuity of £11.10s.0d were paid to his "Widow and sole legatee" and his rank was shown as Sergeant.
The Victory Medal and the British War Medal were sent to his widow and his rank was shown as Acting sergeant with a Regimental number 7304.

He was buried at the Kirkee Cemetery and is shown on the 1914-18 Memorial, Mumbai(Bombay), Maharashtra, India.

His eldest sister, Gertrude Maggie Gibbings, married Alfred Coker of the Royal Engineers in the Dawlish Wesley Church and was reported as a quiet wedding in the *Dawlish Gazette* of 30th September 1916.

Commonwealth War Graves entry:
GIBBINGS, George Henry   Corporal 3854,   17/06/1916
Age 31   Devonshire Regiment   1st/6th Bn.   Panel Face C.   Kirkee 1914-1918 Memorial, India.   Son of Frank Henry and Mary Gibbings, of Dawlish, Devon; husband of Florence Gibbings, of 1, Lansdowne Place, The Hoe, Plymouth.

Devon Roll of Honour - He is not included on the Devon Roll of Honour for Dawlish.
Dawlish War memorial inscription: GIBBINGS G.H.   SERGT.   DEVON REGT.
He is shown on the Dawlish Boys' School Roll of Honour.

1/6th Battalion Territorial Force, the Devonshire Regiment.
04.08.0914 Stationed at Barnstaple as part of the Wessex Division.
05.08.1914 Moved to Plymouth and then to Salisbury Plain and attached to the Devon & Cornwall Brigade.
09.10.1914 Embarked for India from Southampton arriving at Karachi 11.11.1914.
30.12.1915 Moved to Basra and joined the 36th Indian Brigade. This was formed in December

1915 in Mesopotamia. It was heavily involved in the attempts to relieve the 6th Poona Division besieged in Kut, including the attack on the Dujaila Redoubt (8 March 1916).

In May 1916 the Brigade joined the newly formed 14th Indian Division and remained with it until June 1918.

(The Long, Long Trail)

References:

Free Birth Marriage Death records	Dawlish Gazette – 24th June 1916 in Dawlish
Museum	
Refs via subscription sites:	Census records
Forces War Records	UK, WW1 Service Medal and Award Rolls
UK, Soldiers Died in the Great War 1914-1919	
UK, Army Registers of Soldiers' Effects 1901-1929	
Exeter & Plymouth Gazette in National Newspaper Archive	

July 1916

William BROWNING

Born Dawlish, Q2,1897   Died 1 July 1916, aged 19
Private 11255   8th Battalion, Devonshire Regiment

William Browning was the second son of James Browning (1864-1918) and Fanny Langdon (1859-1954).

James Browning was born in Throwleigh where his father, William, had been an agricultural labourer,   married to Eliza. Both of their parents had been born in Sampford Courtenay.

In 1881 James was 16 and an "indoor servant" to a farmer, William French of Charlwood, Ashcombe.

By 1891 William and Eliza had moved to Queen Lane, Dawlish where he was described as a "dairyman" and James, 27, was an agricultural labourer.

James married Fanny Langdon in 1893[22] and they had six children between then and 1911, although two died.

Fanny Langdon was born to John Langdon, a shoemaker, and Elizabeth Langdon in Liskeard, Cornwall. After leaving school she moved away taking work as a domestic servant and in 1891 was Cook to the household of Georgina Pike at 1 Oak Park Villas, East Cliff, Dawlish.

Their surviving children were James (1895-), William (1897-1916), Dorothy Eliza (1898-1960) and John Langdon (1904-1990).

In 1901, the family were living at 6 Commercial Road, Dawlish and James was now working as a Town Porter for the GWR.

By 1911 the whole family had moved to 2 Brunswick Terrace, Torre, Torquay where James, 46, was once again a farm labourer, James, 16, was a grocer's apprentice, **William**, 14, was an errand boy and the younger children were at school.

---

22   GRO ref Newton Abbot district, 1897, Q2, Vol 5b, p324

There is little to find about William's Army career, but it is known that he served in France and he arrived there on the 8th December 1915.

The Devonshire Regiment would have been refreshed by new trainees after the losses of the Battle of Loos (25 September 1915) and they were to take part in the Somme offensive of 1st July 1916, where many young men lost their lives, as did William Browning.

In the opening phase the British assault broke into, and gradually moved beyond, the first of the German defensive complexes on the Somme. Success on the first day in the area between Montauban and Mametz led to a redirection of effort to that area, for the initial attack was defeated with huge losses north of Mametz. There was a stiff fight for Trones Wood and costly, hastily planned and piecemeal attacks that eventually took La Boisselle, Contalmaison and Mametz Wood.

Mametz was within the German lines until 1 July 1916 when it was captured by the 7th Division, and Mametz Wood, north-east of the village, was cleared on the days following 7th July. The 8th and 9th Battalions of the Devonshire Regiments, which were part of the 7th Division, attacked on 1 July 1916 from a point on the south-west side of Albert-Maricourt road, due south of Mametz village, by a plantation called Mansel Copse. On 4 July they returned to this location and established a cemetery, burying their dead in a section of their old front line trench. All but two of the burials belong to these battalions.

Devonshire Cemetery contains 163 Commonwealth burials of the First World War, ten of which are unidentified.

Commonwealth War Graves entry: W.Browning   Private 11255   Died 1.7.16   Devonshire Regiment, 8th Battalion.

William Browning is not recorded on the Devon Roll of Honour for Dawlish, nor is he on the Dawlish Boys' School Roll of Honour despite being born here and spending his early years in Dawlish.

He is shown on the St Marychurch, War Memorial, Torquay.
Devon Heritage site info: The following appears on the St Marychurch, Torquay War Memorial description.

W. BROWNING	11255 Private William Browning of the 8th battalion, the Devonshire Regiment. Son of James and Fanny Brough of Chelston. Born in Dawlish in 1897. Died 1 July 1916 aged 19.

The headstones placed in the Devonshire Cemetery at Mametz by the Commonwealth War Graves Commission do not mark actual graves. These men were buried where they had fallen late on in the evening of July 1st 1916 by a working party led by the Padre; the headstones were added later.

153 men of all ranks are commemorated in the Devonshire Cemetery, all but two being members of the 8th and 9th Battalions of the Devonshire Regiment. Driver Fred Lambert and Sergeant D. Wright, both of the Royal Field Artillery, were interred here later.

21 of the men from the 8th Battalion who lie here are believed to have been born in Devon. A further 44 Devon-born men from the 9th Battalion are also buried in the Mametz Cemetery. (Devon Heritage)

William Browning was awarded the 1915 Star, Victory Medal and British War Medal

References: BMD and census records.   CWGC site
UK, WW1, Service Medal and Award Rolls, and Medal Roll Index Cards

CWGC Headstone in the Devonshire Cemetery, Mametz

Ernest John BOWDEN

Born Kenton, Q3, 1892   Died 1ˢᵗ July 1916, aged 23

L/Corporal, Service No: 8687   2ⁿᵈ Battallion, Devonshire Regt

Ernest John Bowden and Sidney Charles Bowden (1897-1919) were brothers from a Dawlish family, and both were killed in WW1.

Their grandparents were John and Mary Bowden who were living at 'Orchard' in the vicinity of Langdon/Shutterton in 1851. John Bowden (1813-1884) was an agricultural labourer, born in Dawlish, and his wife Mary (1814-) was born in Ideford. They had five children by 1851:

Martha	(1838-)	dau, 13		born	Dawlish
John	(1850-)	son, 11	ploughboy		"
Anne	(1842-)	dau, 9	scholar		"
James*	(1846-)	son, 4			"
Sarah J	(1850-)	dau, 1			"

By 1861 John and Mary Bowden had moved to Park Row, Dawlish with:

James*	(1846-)	son, 14	scholar	"
Sarah Jane	(1850-)	dau, 11	"	"
Richard	(1854-)	son, 7	"	"
Thomas	(1855-)	son, 6	"	"
John	(1860-)	son, 1 mo		"

James Bowden* was born in Dawlish in summer 1846[23] and he first married Mary Hill (1844-1882) in 1871[24]. She appears in the 1851 census as Mary Heel (sic), daughter of John and Ann Heel but later census entries revert to the spelling Hill. (See text on James Henry Hill, p84)

In 1881 James (37) and Mary Bowden (39) were living at 4 Church Street with three children:

William J	(1876-)	son, 5	Dawlish
Alfred George	(1876-1964)	son, 4	"
Mary J	(1879-1958)	dau, 2	"

James was shown as a labourer.

Mary Bowden (nee Hill) died in early 1882 [25] leaving James with three young children.

James next married Elizabeth Packer, born in Thorverton, in the second quarter of 1884[26].

In 1891 they were living at 27 High Street, Kenton with three children:

Mary J	(1879- 1958) dau, 12	Scholar	born in Dawlish	
Frederick W	(1885-1964) son, 6	"		Teignmouth
Henry J	(1887-) son, 4	"		"

Ernest John was born in St Thomas registration district (Kenton) in 1892[27].

By 1901 the family had moved to 42 High Street, Dawlish and had one more child, Sidney Charles (1897-1919).

In 1911, the census return for 75 High Street shows that James and Elizabeth Bowden (nee Packer) declared five children, but that one had died. The children from their marriage were Frederick William, Henry John, Ernest John, Sidney Charles and one other. Frederick is also shown as a widower, aged 26, and there is another daughter (of Frederick's marriage?) Beatrice (1906-).

39

---

23   GRO ref 1846, Sept, N.A., vol 10, p 142

24   GRO ref 1871, July-Sept, N.A., vol 5b, p 212

25   GRO ref 1882, Jan-Mar, N.A., vol 5b, p 86

26   GRO ref 1884,Q2, Newton Abbot district, vol 5b, p279

27   GRO ref 1892, Sept, St Thomas, vol 5b, p 74

Sidney Charles Bowden was 15 and an agricultural labourer, but by 1912 he had joined the Coldstream Guards and was wounded and paralysed in action on 1ˢᵗ October 1914 at Ypres. He was discharged in 1916 and died on 19 January 1919 and is buried in Dawlish cemetery. *(See separate entry in Part Three)*

Ernest John Bowden was not with his family in 1911. He was already enlisted in the 2ⁿᵈ Battalion, Devonshire Regiment and in barracks in Malta.

The record shows him as a Private aged 21. That may indicate that he enlisted with a false age but as his service record has not survived there is no way to tell. There is little to show of his service beyond knowing that he disembarked in France on 24 March 1915 and served there until his death on the first day of the Battle of the Somme.

The 2ⁿᵈ Battalion took part in the Battle of Albert, 1-13 July 1916. In this opening phase of the Somme offensive, the British assault broke into and gradually moved beyond the first of the German defensive complexes on the Somme.

Success on the first day in the area between Montauban and Mametz led to a redirection of effort to that area, for the initial attack was defeated with huge losses north of Mametz. There was a stiff fight for Trones Wood and costly, hastily planned and piecemeal attacks that eventually took La Boisselle, Contalmaison and Mametz Wood.

The Register of Soldiers' Effects show that Ernest J Bowden was presumed dead on 1 July 1916 and that a Death Grant of £8.13s.7d was paid to Phoebe Harris "sole legatee". The War Gratuity of £10.10s.0d was similarly paid. Phoebe Harris does not appear among relations and there is no sign of a marriage having taken place.

Commonwealth War Graves entry:
BOWDEN, Ernest John   Lance Corporal,   8687,   01/07/1916
Age: 23   Devonshire Regiment, 2nd Bn.   Pier and Face 1 C. Thiepval Memorial.
Son of James and Elizabeth Bowden, of 63, Manor Row, Brook St., Dawlish, Devon.

Ernest John Bowden is recorded on the Devon Roll of Honour.
Dawlish War memorial inscription: BOWDEN E.J.   L/CORPL.   DEVON REGT.
He is also among those recorded on the Dawlish Boys' School Roll of Honour.
Devon Heritage site info:
> 8687 Lance Corporal Ernest John Bowden of the 2ⁿᵈ Battalion, the Devonshire regiment. Son of James and Elizabeth Bowden of the High Street, Dawlish; brother of Sidney (q.v) Born in Kenton in 1893. Died 1 July 1916 aged 23. *(the birth date appears incorrect-ed)*

Last known address: 42 High Street, Dawlish (1901 census)
Next of kin: James Bowden, father, 75 High Street, Dawlish (1911 census)

References:
Free Birth, Marriage, & Death refs
Refs from subscription sites: Forces War Records.   Census data
UK, Army Register of Soldiers' Effects

Edward DOBLE

Born: Q2 1888, Withycombe Raleigh   Died 10th July 1916, Mesopotamia, aged 28

Gunner 57979   Royal Field Artillery

Edward Doble was from a family long established in Withycombe Raleigh, next to Exmouth and within the registration district of St Thomas. It was his marriage which brought him across the Exe to Dawlish.

His grandfather was Robert Doble, (1815- Q2,1857) a brickmaker, living in Withycombe with his wife, Agnes, nee Burgoin, (1815-Q4, 1882) and seven children in 1851. They were William (1833-1908) a sailor, Robert (1837-1912), Henry (1840-), Elizabeth (1843-1916), James Thomas Burgoyne Doble (1844-)(incorrectly transcribed by Ancestry as Jennie), Frederick Charles (1847-1927) and Edward Richard Burgoyne Doble (1849-).

Edward's father was James Thomas Burgoyne Doble, and his family story is complex:

- James T B Doble was born in St Thomas Q4, 1844 and married Rebecca Cox (1840-1879) of Wool, Dorset, in St Thomas registration district in Q4 1864.

By 1871 they had three children, Stephen Robert James Cox Doble (1863-), Agnes Charlotte (1867-), and William (1870-) and were living at 6 Perriman Row, Withycombe. James T B Doble is recorded in 1861 as a brickmaker's assistant, and in 1871 as a Brick Moulder, a trade which spread through the family.

- Agnes Charlotte Doble, daughter of James and Rececca Doble, was born in St Thomas district in Q4 1867 and became a domestic servant in the Lockyer household at Ingleside, Withycombe Raleigh at the 1901 census. In 1911 she was unmarried and living with her widower father, James.

- William Doble (1870-) became a Coastguard and in 1901, aged 29, he was at Challaboro' Coastguard Station with Agnes, 23. It is probable that she was Agnes Mary Rice (1877-1924) and born in Wrafton, Barnstaple. In 1911 he had been promoted to Petty Officer in the Coastguard Service and he and Agnes were at 5 Coastguard Station, Cob Road, Lyme Regis.

- Later in the decade James and Rebecca Doble had Jessie B (1875-) and Henry Burgoyne(1874-).

A connection with Bristol may explain the appearance of Henry Burgoyne Doble, Jessie Doble and William Doble in the Baptism register at St Marks, Easton, Glos on the same date, 1st November 1875.

- Private Henry Burgoyne/Burgoin Doble had been a groom when he enlisted with the Devon Regiment and then served in India, Malta and South Africa. He was awarded the Indian Medal 1895 with clasp, Punjab 1894-89, Queen's South African medal with clasp "Defence of Ladysmith", and King's South African medal with two clasps.

He was discharged at Malta in March 1911 and re-enlisted on the 10th July 1915 from 15 Dacre Road, Eastbourne, where he lived with his wife Mary Eliza Doble (Married 15/5/15), and served in the 1st Garrison Battalion of the Norfolk Regiment.

- Frederick Charles Doble was born in St Thomas district in Q1,1847 and married Selina Alice Carter of Dawlish in Q2,1868. In 1871 he was a brick and tile maker and living at Lympstone with his wife and one child, Frederick (1870-) and his brother Alfred.

F C Doble died in Sherborne district in March 1927.

- Edward Richard Burgoyne Doble was born in Q2, 1849 and married Charity Summers on 13 July 1873 in Gateshead, Durham. He was listed as a confectioner at 25 Radnor Street, Manchester in the 1901 census.

When Robert Doble died in 1857, Agnes was a widow.

By 1861 the three older sons had moved away and there were two more children at home, Jessie (1854-1937) and Alfred (1857-1947). Agnes was listed as a lacemaker, a craft local to East Devon.

- Alfred Doble (1857-1947) married Emma Gibbings in St Thomas district in 1902. He was shown as a boarding-house keeper in 1911 and the Probate record shows that he died on 18 March 1947 while living at Bella Vista, 3 Stoke Villas, Withycombe Raleigh.

They had a son, Ernest Alfred Doble who married Mary Susan Gibbings in 1905 and was a hairdresser in Torquay. A E Doble died on 16 August 1909 and his widow was living with Alfred and Emma in 1911 with her daughter Phyllis Marjorie Doble (1906-), born in Torquay.

There is a death of Rebecca Doble registered in Loughborough, Leics, in Q2,1879.

The census of 1881 does not easily reveal James' family, but there is a record of James Doble, 35, born in Exmouth, working as a general labourer on the railroad and lodging at the Market House Inn, Taunton. The census also shows Charlotte, 13, William, Henry and Jessie forming a household in Parkers Lane, Withycombe Raleigh.

By 1891 James T B Doble is once again a brickmaker with a new wife, Elizabeth, 34, living at 6 Jubilee Cottages, Withycombe where James was to stay for the next twenty years.

There were two children from his first marriage and two new children and three step-children,

The children were Charlotte (1871-), Henry (1874-), from his first wife, and **Edward** 3 (1888-1916), and Walter 1 (1890-) from his new marriage.

The step-children were Henry Perryman 16 (1875-), Thomas Perryman 15 (1876-) and Ellen Perryman 12 (1879-). Henry Perryman may be the birth registration of George Henry Perryman, born in Bristol, Glos, in Q4, 1875. It has been asssumed that Elizabeth Perryman was James' new wife.

James and Elizabeth had four children, **Edward** (1888-1916), Walter (1890-), Sidney (1893-) and Wallace (1894-1918).

Elizabeth Doble died in 1906. The 1911 census shows James, 65, a widower and a domestic gardener, and that he had eight children, all being alive at that date. Living with him were Charlotte, 40, unmarried, Henry, 36, an army pensioner, Walter, 21, a domestic chauffeur, and Wallace, 17, a domestic gardener.

" 44949 Private Wallace Doble of the 9th Battalion, the Northumberland Fusiliers; formerly 15064 of the Army Cyclist Corps.

Son of James and Charlotte Doble. Born in Withycombe in 1894. Died 9 April 1918 aged 24." (record in Devon Heritage referring to the Exmouth War Memorial inscription)(the reference to mother, Charlotte, is believed to be an eroneous assumption based on the 1911 census entry – ed).

Wallace enlisted at Abergavenny, Monmouthshire (UK Soldiers died in the Great War 1914-1919) and was the husband of Lena Doble (Plant) of 10 Greenswood Avenue, Mile End, Stockport.

[A great grand-daughter lives in Australia]

- Sidney Doble(1893-) was Mentioned in Despatches in the London Gazette of 1ˢᵗ January 1917 "in recognition of distinguished services during the War" when he was an Acting Leading Stoker, Royal Navy, K 3948. (family record)

Edward became a road contractor's labourer and after his mother's death in 1906 he married Alice Maud Way (1883-1938) in Q3, 1907. She had been born in Cockermouth, Cumberland. She is recorded in the 1891 census, living with her aunt Bessie Way, and in 1901 as a servant to Mark Cornelius' household at Marine Parade, Dawlish.

- Alice Maud Mary Way was a grand-daughter of Francis and Grace Way who had nine children.
A son, Francis/Frank Way married Sarah Jane Tucker of Dawlish in Q1,1880. They had two children, Alice Maud Mary, born in Cockermouth district, 1883, and Albert Henry George Way, born in Dawlish in 1884.
- Albert Henry George Way was born on 26 July 1884 and at some point went to Canada from where he joined the Canadian Over-Seas Expeditionary Force on 27 January 1916. His Attestation Paper shows his next of kin as (Alice) Maud Mary Way, his sister.

- Bessey/Bessie Way was born in Bow in 1861 and married George Shelston in Q4,1882 (N.A.district). They were shown at 55 Monument Street, Devonport in the 1891 census as Bessie Shelston,(incorrectly transcribed as Brickwood) 30, married, Ellen, her daughter,1, and Alice Way, 8, born in Maryport, Cumberland, a niece of Bessie.

The Way family were settled in Dawlish (See appendix to Frank Morrish history pages, above) and it is no surprise that Edward and Alice Maud moved there.
There were two children by 1911 when they were living at 2 Alma Cottages, Manor Hill, Dawlish. (They had four children but two had died by the 1911 census.) They were Francis Edward James Doble (1908-1940) and Walter George Doble (1910-1978). A further child, Albert Frederick W Doble (1912- 1983) was born after the census. All were born in Dawlish.

- Francis Edward James Doble married Clare M Sewell (1907-1964) in Q3 1931 in Worcester district and they had a son Anthony Vine Doble (1934-2012). [Plant Family Tree/Ancestry] A further son, Francis Edward John Doble was born in 1940, shortly after the death of his father.
George Doble served in WW2 in Burma, and later ran a shop in Honiton. [A grandson lives in South Africa]
There are descendants living in South Africa, Australia and the UK.

It is recorded that Edward Doble enlisted at Newton Abbot, but there are no indications as to the date. There were a number of Divisions engaged in Mesopotamia and there will have been Royal Field Artillery detachments with them. Following the withdrawal from Gallipoli in January 1916 there was further bad news with the siege of Kut, which had become a major concern for the armies fighting the Ottoman army. They had been advancing up the Euphrates from Basra to protect the oil fields and met Turkish forces, acting with German advisers.

The British garrison at Kut were encircled by Ottoman forces and in a state of siege for five months before starvation forced their surrender. After five rescue attempts in which relief forces lost 20,000 men, the British garrison surrendered and 13,000 men marched out of Kut to imprisonment. Two thirds of the soldiers died on the march to Baghdad.

Basra was an important logistical base at which ships unloaded supplies to be sent north on shallow draught vessels. Here a Royal Field Artillery contingent is being transferred to barges at Basra, ca 1915. (National Army Museum)

New hospitals were also set up to better care for the sick and wounded. Gunner Edward Doble died at the 33rd British General Hospital of heatstroke.

Edward Doble is recorded on the Devon Roll of Honour
Dawlish War memorial inscription: DOBLE E.   BOMB^{R} R.F.A.
He is also named on Exmouth War Memorial as "57979 Gunner Edward Doble of the Royal Horse Artillery and the Royal Field Artillery. Son of James and Elizabeth Doble; husband of Maud Doble. Born in Withycombe in the June Quarter of 1888. Died 10 July 1916 aged 28."

Commonwealth War Graves entry: DOBLE, E   Gunner   57979,   10/07/1916
Royal Field Artillery   Grave Ref: VI. P. 9.   Basra War Cemetery   During the First World War, Basra was occupied by the 6th (Poona) Division in November 1914, from which date the town became the base of the Mesopotamian Expeditionary Force. A number of cemeteries were used by the MEF in and around Basra.

Next of kin: Alice Maud Doble (nee Way) (1884-) widow. The Death grant and War Gratuity were paid to her.

References: CWGC record   Free BMD records
Private memo on the Way family by June Snell
True Britishers by Trillo, Edwards & Thomson, publ Amazon 2020
Mons, Anzac and Kut by Aubrey
Refs from susbscription websites:
Forces War Records   Family trees -Ancestry.co.uk
census records.   UK, Army Registers of Soldiers' Effects (21 entries)

Charles LAKE

Born Crediton, 25 April 1884   Died 22ND August 1916, aged 32
Petty Officer, Royal Navy, Service No: 206229 (Dev)   H.M.SUBMARINE E 16

Charles was the youngest child of James Lake (1836-1914), born in Sandford, who married Ann Cleave (1838-1892). James was an agricultural labourer in the 1891 census when they lived at 96 Jollys(?), Crediton.
They had three children, all born in Crediton; Caroline M (1872-) a boot machinist, Walter G (1876-) a tinplate worker, and **Charles Lake** (1884-1916).

Charles joined the Royal Navy as a Boy Seaman on 28th September 1899 and on reaching the age of 18 on 25 April 1902, became an Ordinary Seaman when he signed on for 12 years service. He was based in Devonport.
He married Mary Ann Cundy (1882-) of Dawlish in Q1 1906 in Devonport.
Mary Ann was the daughter of Richard Cundy, a builder, and Hannah who lived at 3 King Street, Dawlish (1891 census).

Charles and Mary Ann had three children, born in Dawlish; Frank (1907-), Joyce (1909-1984), and Leonard (1912-1913).
In the 1911 census record, Mary Ann Lake was living with her widowed mother, Hannah Cundy, at 8 King Street, with her first two children, Walter Lake, her brother-in-law, and two Cundy grandchildren of Hannah. Charles was recorded staying with a relative, George Thomas Trewin at 99 Victory St, Keyham, Devonport while he was on the books of H.M.S.VIVID, the Devonport Naval Barracks.
Charles Lake was rated Leading Seaman in April 1912 and then Petty Officer in May 1913. On concluding his 12 years service, he signed on again on 6 April 1914 – to completion.

In September 1915 he was posted to H.M.S.ARROGANT, acting as Depot ship to the 4th Submarine Flotilla at Dover, and in November 1915 he went on to H.M.S.MAIDSTONE, a submarine depot ship at Harwich. His character was shown as VG (very good) throughout his naval service.

Submarine E 16 was commissioned on 27 February 1915 and sank U-boat U6 off Stavanger, Norway on 15 September 1915. E 16 was based at Harwich and was one of 33 submarines there. Harwich was an important naval base for control of the southern North Sea and the entrance to the English Channel. Following the Battle of Jutland, the command of approaches to the German naval base at Wilhelmshaven assumed greater importance. However, the shallow waters of the North Sea made it possible to lay minefields as a deterrent to enemy shipping and it appears likely that submarine E 16 was sunk by hitting a mine in an unrecorded minefield.

Submarine E 16 was mined in the Heligoland Bight and sunk off the German Coast. There were no survivors among the crew of 3 officers and 28 ratings.

Commonwealth War Graves entry: LAKE, Charles Petty Officer 206229 22/08/1916
Age: 32 Royal Navy H.M. S/M. "E16." Panel Ref:11. Plymouth Naval Memorial
Son of James and Ann Lake, of Crediton, Devon; husband of Mary Ann Lake, of 8, King St., Dawlish, Devon

Dawlish War memorial inscription: LAKE CHARLES P.O. SUB[M] E.16
Charles Lake is listed on the Devon Roll of Honour, but the location (North Sea) is not shown.

Devon Heritage site info:
    206229 Petty Officer Charles Lake of the Royal Navy., H.M.SUBMARINE E.16. Son of James and Ann Lake of Crediton,; husband of Mary Ann Lake of 8 King Street, Dawlish. Born 25 April 1884. Died 22 August 1916 aged 32. The wreck of E 16 was discovered in Heligoland in 42 metres of water in 2001.

Last known address: 99 Victory Street (East), Keyham, Devonport (census 1911)

Next of kin: Mary Ann Lake, wife, of 8 King Street, Dawlish

References: Wikipedia.org   naval-history.net
wrecksite.eu   (HMS E-16)
Subscription site ancestry.co.uk for:
census records, family trees

Sidney Charles LUCAS

Born Dawlish 1892	Died 30th August 1916, aged 24
Lance Corporal, 3/6029	Devonshire Regiment, 1st Battalion.

Sidney Charles Lucas was from a local family. His grandfather, Cephas Lucas, was born in Mamhead and married Eliza, born in Exeter. He was an under-gardener and they were living in a cottage at Ashcombe in 1861 where their children had been born; Edward (1849-1915), William Henry (1852-1933), Rebecca Sarah (1854-1932), James Frederick (1857-1908), Eliza Ann (1860-1941) and Harriet Ann (1863-1940).

Sidney's father was William Henry Lucas who had married Emily Brown (1857-1895) in 1879 and they had six children, all born in Dawlish;

> Henry James (Harry)(1879-1947),
> Emily Daisy (1881-1960),
> Maud Louisa (1884-1909),
> William (1886-),
> Edith Beatrice (1889-1960)
> **Sidney Charles (1892-1916).**

Their father was variously shown as an agricultural labourer and a domestic gardener.

The family were living in Manor Row, Dawlish in 1881 but moved to Chapel Street (No 14 in 1891). Their mother died in 1895 at the age of 38, when Sidney was three years old.

In 1901 William Henry Lucas, a widower, was still living at No 13 Chapel Street with all of his children. The older daughters were shown as "laundress", Harry was a "general labourer", William "shop porter" and **Sidney** still at school. *(Chapel Street has since been renamed Albert Street)*

> - Harry (Henry James Lucas) married Elizabeth Pearce of Dawlish in Q3, 1907 and they lived at 3 Chapel Street, Dawlish while he was a mason's labourer.
> In the 1911 census **Sidney Charles Lucas** is living with them and working as a general labourer.

> - Emily Daisy Lucas married John Tibbs in Q2, 1904 and was living at 1 Clifford Street, Chudleigh when she died in 1960. She was paid Sidney Lucas' Death Grant of £12. 0s. 0d by the War Office in 1917. A son, Cyril John Tibbs (1913-) became a master butcher and was named in her will.

> - Edith Beatrice Lucas moved to work as a domestic servant in Pontypridd, Rhondda (in 1911 census) and later that year married Henry W Fletcher. Mrs Edith B Fletcher received the residual Sidney Lucas' War Gratuity of £16.11s. 7d in 1919. She died in Pontypridd district in 1960.

It is not known when **Sidney** enlisted at Exeter with the First Devons. This was one of the permanent battalions of the Devonshire Regiment that left its posting in Jersey, the Channel Islands, and was sent to France on 21st August 1914. On arrival they were reinforced by around 500 reservists from Exeter. The "Medal Rolls Index" card shows that he arrived in France on 20 September 1914, and so may have been among those reservists.

In September 1914, during their first spell in the line, they suffered 100 casualties from shelling. In October, on the La Bassee Canal, they supported the badly mauled 1st Dorsets and helped capture Givenchy Ridge. The Devons performed well during a bitter three-week battle but lost two thirds of their officers and a third of their men. From November they occupied Messines Ridge in rain and sleet, often knee- or waist-deep in mud and icy water.

On 21st April 1915 they occupied Hill 60, which had been captured on 17th April. Counter-attacks and heavy shelling cost them more than 200 casualties.

On 31st July 1915 they moved to the Somme.

When the Somme offensive began on 1st July 1916 the Devons were at Arras but returned to the Somme, to consolidate the line around Longueval. Shellfire and German counter-attacks cost them 265 casualties. In September they made two very successful advances near Guillemont at a cost of 376 casualties. (keepmilitarymuseum.org)

On 1 July 1916, supported by a French attack to the south, thirteen divisions of Commonwealth forces launched an offensive on a line from north of Gommecourt to Maricourt. Despite a preliminary bombardment lasting seven days, the German defences were barely touched and the attack met unexpectedly fierce resistance. Losses were catastrophic and with only minimal advances on the southern flank, the initial attack on the Somme front was a failure.

In the following weeks, huge resources of manpower and equipment were deployed in an attempt to exploit the modest successes of the first day. In this period Lance Corporal Sidney Charles Lucas was killed in action, on 30th August, 1916.

The German Army resisted tenaciously and repeated attacks and counter attacks meant a major battle for every village, copse and farmhouse gained. At the end of September, Thiepval was finally captured. The village had been an original objective of 1 July. Attacks north and east continued throughout October and into November in increasingly difficult weather conditions. The Battle of the Somme finally ended on 18 November with the onset of winter.

Commonwealth War Graves entry: Lucas, Sidney Charles   Lance Corporal   3/6029
30/08/1916   Devonshire Regiment, 1st Bn.   Panel Ref: Pier and Face 1 C. Thiepval Memorial
The Dawlish War memorial inscription is   LUCAS S   CPL   DEVON REGT
He is listed on the Devon Roll of Honour and on the Dawlish Boys' School Roll of Honour.

The Devon Heritage site shows him as 3/6029 Corporal Sidney Charles Lucas of the 1st Battalion, the Devonshire Regiment. Son of William Lucas of 3 Chapel Street, Dawlish. Born in Dawlish in 1892. Died 30 August 1916, aged 24.

The "Medal Rolls Index" cards shows him awarded the 1914 Star, the British War Medal and the Victory Medal while his rank is shown as Private. However, the index "UK, Soldiers died in the Great War" indicates that he was an Acting Corporal at his death.

References: Free Birth Marriage Death records
Subscription websites for: census records   Military records
familytrees (ancestry.co.uk)

Etienne Geoffrey MILWARD

Born 23 January 1896, Bromsgrove   Died 2 September 1916, aged 20

Temporary Captain   Duke of Cornwall's Light Infantry, 7th Battalion

Etienne was the grandson of Robert Harding Milward (1839-1903), a solicitor practising in Bromsgrove, Worcestershire. Robert Milward and Harriet Harding married and had ten children, the second son being Geoffrey (or Jeffrey) Lionel Milward who also studied Law and became a Barrister.

From the *Exeter and Plymouth Gazette of Friday 19 April 1895,*

> "On Wednesday the marriage of Miss Katherine Sparkes, daughter of Mr. Weston Joseph Sparkes, of Oak Cliff, Dawlish with Mr Geoffrey Lionel Milward, of The Linthurst(sic), Bromsgrove, Barrister, took place at the Parish Church of St Michael's (*now St Gregory's*) Dawlish."

Etienne Geoffrey Milward was born 23 January 1896 at Ayresdale North, Birmingham, father- Geoffrey Lionel Milward, mother- Katherine Anne Georgie Milward formerly Sparkes, Occupation of father -Barrister at Law." (Copy Birth Certificate)

It is not clear when Geoffrey Lionel Milward was working in Cairo, but a census entry for E G Milward in 1901 at Upper Ilsley, Warwicks, (where he is shown, age 5, living with a cousin) suggests that the boy stayed in England for schooling. It appears that his parents' marriage was unhappy.

His mother's death: -

> From the *Gloucestershire Echo of Saturday 29 February 1908,*

> "**SUICIDE OF A BARRISTER'S WIFE** - A verdict of "Suicide during temporary insanity" was returned on Friday at an inquest at Chelsea on the body of Mrs. Katherine Milward, sister-in-law to Sir Ernest Cable, an Indian merchant, in whose residence in Cadogan Gardens the deceased was on Wednesday found dead. She was identified by her husband, Mr Geoffrey Lionel Milward, Barrister, formerly practising at Cairo, who said he had lived apart from his wife for some time. Evidence was given that two blue poison bottles were found in the deceased's room, and a doctor stated that death was due to carbolic acid poisoning." (She was aged 45 -ed)

Etienne was 12 year's old when his mother took her life in this manner.

Etienne enrolled later at the University of London and matriculated as a student at the January 1913 examination and was placed in the Second Division having satisfied the examiners in English, Mathematics, Latin, French and Heat, Light and Sound. (*Main subject unknown -ed)*

In August 1914, soon after the outbreak of war, Etienne Milward applied for a Temporary Commission and this was granted on 15th August.

In applying for a Temporary Commission for the duration of the War he gave his address as Oak Cliff, Starcross, Devon (*It is most probably Oak Cliff at Dawlish Warren, now the centre of a holiday homes business*).

> His application was counter-signed by H W Sparkes as Guardian. It also contained a "Certificate of Moral Character" from Charles Francis Benthall, Vicar of Cofton St Mary, Starcross who certified that he had known Etienne Geoffrey Milward for "the last five

years". It may therefore be assumed that he had spent much of his time at Starcross in the care of the Sparkes family, after the death of his mother.

Herbert Weston Sheppard Sparkes (1859-1923) was the eldest son among six children of Weston J Sparkes (1827-1903), a Solicitor, and his wife Eliza (1821-). H W Sparkes was the brother of Etienne's mother, Katherine Anne Georgie Sparkes (1863-1908), and after her death appears to have acted as guardian to Etienne G Milward.

Duke of Cornwall's Light Infantry, 7th (Service) Battalion

Formed at Bodmin in September 1914 as part of K2 and came under command of 61st Brigade in 20th (Light) Division.

Moved to Aldershot and Woking but by November 1914 was at Pirbright. Moved to Witley in February 1915 and Amesbury next month.

Landed at Boulogne on 25 July 1915.

(Harry Patch (1898-2009), last British survivor of trench warfare, served with the 7th DCLI.)

On 26 July 1915 the 20th (Light) Division completed concentration in the Saint-Omer area, all units having crossed to France during the preceding few days. Early trench familiarisation and training took place in the Fleurbaix area.

Lieut E G Milward was first wounded on 6th September 1915 and a telegram to H W Sparkes shows that he was "admitted to Endsleigh Place Hospital, Endsleigh Gardens, London on 9th September, 1915 suffering from gunshot wounds".

> The 20th Light Division was later engaged in the Battle of Delville Wood between 15th July 1916 and 3rd September. Delville Wood was fought over countless times and became choked with the dead of both sides. The Division was also engaged in the following Battle of Guillemont between 3 and 6 September,1916.

Etienne Geoffrey Milward was holding the temporary rank of Captain in the Duke of Cornwall's Light Infantry, 7th Battalion when he died of wounds on 2 September 1916.

A "Field Service" report originates from No 21 Casualty Clearing Station showing cause of death as "died of wounds received in Action."

A War Office telegram was sent on 3 September to "W Sparkes, Oak Cliff" telling him of the death from wounds.

On 4th September 1916 H.W.Sparkes wrote to the Secretary of State for War.

"Sir,   I have the honour to acknowledge the receipt of your telegram reading as per copy enclosed.

> 2.   I beg to observe that the initials of my adopted son(nephew) are E.(Etienne) G.(Geoffrey) Milward,- not **H.**E.G.Milward- as quoted in this telegram but I assume there is no doubt about identity.

> 3.   My wife and I beg to tender our appreciation of the expression of sympathy expressed by the War Office.

> 4.   That in May last he was gazetted Tempy(sic) Captain and acted as the Senior Captain of his Company when 20 ½ years old bears testimony to his being a gallant and efficient soldier of the King – R.I.P.

> 5.   I beg the favour of being acquainted in due course with such particulars as can be properly vouchsafed of the manner of his end.

I have the honour to be, Sir, your most obedient servant
H.W.Sparkes"
(There is no surviving correspondence in the National Archives file of a response to item 5 - ed)

Etienne's father, Geoffrey Milward, and his uncle, H W Sparkes, both applied to the War Office for his effects to be forwarded to them. They were also competing to settle a Mess Bill for 126 Francs, the equivalent of £4.10s.4d to clear the deceased's account. His effects amounted to:

1 Identity Disc
1 Whistle
1 Fountain pen
2 Collar badges
6 Stars
10 Buttons
1 Stud
1 Tobacco pouch
1Key   and were sent to Cox & Co, Shipping Agency Ltd, 16 Charing Cross, London.

The National Probate Calendar shows that his estate was administered by Geoffrey Lionel Milward, who had written to the War Office on November 19th, 1916;
"....According to instructions received, immediately applied for his effects to be sent to me here. Having received no answers to my application and his effects have not arrived, I pray you therefore, to order that my son's belongings may be sent to me without further delay.
Four months is a long time for a father, who is now a childless widower, to wait.
I have the honour to be, Sir, your obedient servant
Geoffrey Milward."

A letter was sent by Geoffrey Milward's solicitor in November 1917 advising the War Office that an application had been made for the administration of E G Milward's estate, and requesting that monies due should be sent to them. At some point the cover sheet for the War Office file has H W Sparkes showing as guardian and next of kin, later struck out and Geoffrey Milward is shown.

Etienne Geoffrey Milward does not appear on the Devon Roll of Honour for Dawlish but is recorded on the Birmingham Roll of Honour.
Commonwealth War Graves entry: Milward E G   Captain   Date of Death: 02/09/1916
Duke of Cornwall's Light Infantry 7th Bn.   Grave Reference: II. B. 35.
LA NEUVILLE BRITISH CEMETERY, CORBIE

Cofton War memorial inscription: Etienne G Milward   Duke of Cornwall's Lt Inf   2 Sept

(There is no record for Cofton War Memorial on the Devon Heritage site.)
 It may be assumed that the inscription at Cofton was requested by his uncle and guardian, H W Sparkes.

Last known address: 9 Manor Road, Edgbaston

Next of kin: Geoffrey Lionel Milward, father

References: Birth Certificate   Newspaper references (quoted)
BMD and census records   National Archive, Kew – Officer's record and correspondence file
www.longlongtrail.co.uk
Refs via subscription websites:
Ancestry.co.uk family tree   UK, Soldiers died in the Great War
National Probate Calendar

Wilfrid Miles noted in the British Official History that the defence of Guillemont was judged by some observers, to be the best performance of the war by the German army on the Western Front. A pause in Anglo-French attacks at the end of August to organise bigger combined attacks, and postponements for bad weather, coincided with the largest counter-attack by the German army in the Battle of the Somme. Joffre, Foch and Haig abandoned attempts to organise large combined attacks in favour of sequenced army attacks and the capture of the German defences from Cléry on the north bank of the Somme to Guillemont from 3 – 6 September brought the French Sixth and British Fourth armies onto ground which overlooked the German third position. Rain, congestion and reliefs of tired divisions then forced a pause in French attacks until 12 September.
Ex- Wikipedia

Carl RADFORD

Born Dawlish, Q2, 1896   Died 3 September 1916, aged 20
Lance Serjeant , 14757   12th Battalion, Gloucestershire Regiment

Carl Radford was the fourth son of Henry Radford (1864-1934) and Mary Ann Matthews (1864-1964).

Henry was born in Dawlish to Richard and Elizabeth Radford who lived in Church Street, Dawlish (1871 census). Richard had been an agricultural labourer and his wife a "washerwoman."
Henry Radford was a "mason" (1901) and then a "plasterer"(1911) and their four children, born in Dawlish, survived to adulthood; Stanley (1889-1965), Claude (1891-1962), Percy (1892-1974) and **Carl** (1896-1916). By 1911 the parents had been married 23 years and were living at Swan Cottage, Dawlish.

Carl was working as a grocer's apprentice at Dawlish Co-Operative Stores at the age of 15, and then moved to the Co-operative in Bristol. The *Dawlish Gazette report of 23rd September 1916* said that he was "a smart young fellow".

Carl Radford is shown as enlisting in the Gloucestershire Regiment at Weston-Super-Mare and entering France on the 21st November 1915. He was home on leave in the Spring of 1916 but was on the sick list with 'shell shock' for a while on his return.

He was killed in one of the assaults in the Battle of the Somme which started on 1 July 1916. His grave is in the cemetery at Guillemont and it would connect him with the "Battle of Guillemont" which took place between the 3rd and 6th September. The defence of Guillemont was judged by some to be the best performance of the War by the German Army on the Western Front.

Carl Radford's rapid progress to Lance Sergeant at the age of 20 suggests a capable soldier, or a rapid depletion of NCOs in his regiment. His three brothers were also serving, one in India with the Devonshire Regiment, one with the R.A.M.C. in France and the other in munitions work which had its own dangers.

The Commonwealth War Graves entry is:
       Radford C,   Lance Serjeant   14757   03/09/1916   Age: 20
       Gloucestershire Regiment, 12th Bn.
       Grave Ref: XIII. I. 9.   Guillemont Road Cemetery, Guillemont

Headstone inscription "**God shall wipe away all tears**"

Son of Henry and Mary A. Radford, of Bridge Cottage, Church St., Dawlish, Devon.
Carl Radford appears in the Devon Roll of Honour for Dawlish and on the Dawlish Boys' School Roll of Honour.
Dawlish War memorial inscription:
RADFORD C.   L/SERGT.   GLOUC. REGT.

Next of kin: Henry Radford, father.

UK, Army Registers of Soldiers' Effects shows that   Death grant of £8.5s.3d and the War Gratuity of £10 were paid to his mother, Mary, Sole Legatee.

Medal Rolls Index Cards show him awarded the 15 Star, British War Medal and the Victory Medal.

References: CWGC and census records
Warren Family tree (Ancestry)

The **Battle of Guillemont** (3–6 September 1916) was an attack by the Fourth Army on the village of Guillemont. The village is on the D 20 running east to Combles and the D 64 south-west to Montauban. Longueval and Delville Wood lie to the north-west and Ginchy to the north-east. The village lay on the right flank of the British sector, near the boundary with the French Sixth Army. The Fourth Army had advanced close to Guillemont during the Battle of Bazentin Ridge(14–17 July) and the capture of the village was the culmination of British attacks which began on 22/23 July to advance on the right flank of the Fourth Army, to eliminate a salient further north at Delville Wood. German defences ringed the wood and had observation over the French Sixth Army area to the south towards the Somme.

Preparatory to a general attack intended for mid-September, from the Somme north to Courcelette (beyond the Albert–Bapaume road) the French Sixth Army, the Fourth Army and Reserve Army conducted numerous attacks to capture the rest of the German second line and to gain observation over the German third line. The German defences around Guillemont were based on the remaining parts of the second line and numerous fortified villages and farms.

    Ex- Wikipedia

Henry Alfred Hogarth BREN

Born Leeds 21 February 1892   Died France 9 September 1916, aged 24
Lieutenant   Prince of Wales' Leinster Regiment
(Royal Canadians 4th Battalion (Special Reserve)

Henry Alfred Hogarth Bren came from a family of churchmen and missionaries and this is reflected in his memorial in Holcombe Church.

IN LOVING MEMORY OF
HENRY ALFRED HOGARTH BREN
LIEUT LEINSTER REGIMENT
EXHIBITIONER OF ORIEL COLLEGE OXFORD
WHO FELL AT THE STORMING OF GUILLEMONT AND
GINCHY 9 SEPTEMBER 1916 AGED 24
With Christ which is far better

Henry's grandfather, Rev'd Robert Bren (1823-1885) was born in Reading. He married Sarah Jordan Brown (1824-1906) and they went to Ceylon (now Sri Lanka) where he worked as a missionary from 1849 to 1858. Their children, Robert (1850-1938), Sarah J (1853-) and Henry Alfred (1855-1930) were all born there.

By 1861 Rev'd Robert Bren was curate of Papworth Agnes church, Cambridgeshire. In 1871 the family had moved to Clarence House, London Road, Reading, St Giles, where he was shown as a clergyman, C of E, and a tutor for the Church Missionary Society. They had 9 students of Theology lodging with them in 1881. Robert died in Reading on the 6th October 1885. His widow and daughter continued to live there and his widow and son, Rev'd Robert Bren, proved his Will.

Henry's father, Henry Alfred Bren was born in Kopay, Jaffna, Ceylon. He became the curate of St. John's Church, Reading in 1881 before returning abroad, where he met Georgiana Elizabeth Cole, 1861-1938. Georgiana was born in Notting Hill, London. They were married on 30.10.1885 in Nasik, Bombay (now Mumbai), India.

Their first child, Robert Bren (1889-1957) was born in Bombay and soon afterwards they returned to Britain where Elsie Muriel Georgiana Bren (1890-1972) was born in Reading, Berkshire.

Henry Alfred Bren and family left Reading and moved to Leeds where they were living at 4 Reginald Terrace, Potter Newton, for the 1891 census and after the birth of **Henry Alfred Hogarth Bren**.

Rev'd Henry Alfred Bren was appointed Principal of St Paul's Church of England Training College, Swindon Road, Cheltenham and settled there with his family by the 1901 census.

His eldest son, Robert, followed him into the church. Robert was an undergraduate at Oxford and studied Theology before he married Gladys Mary Dawson on 22 June 1918. He enlisted in July 1918 at the age of 30 in London when their address was 13 Crystal Palace Park Road, Sydenham. He had been a member of the Inns of Court O.T.C. He was discharged from military service in February 1919. They had a son, Robert (Robin) Henry Dawson Bren (1919-) who emigrated to New Zealand in 1946 after service in the RAF in WW2.

The younger son, Henry Alfred Hogarth Bren appears to have been resident at the College in Cheltenham in 1911. He matriculated from Oriel College, Oxford in November 1911.

At the time of the 1911 census his mother and siblings, Robert and Elsie M G Bren, are shown at 'Nasik', Holcombe, and that remained their family home until Georgiana Elizabeth Bren's death on 6 January 1938. Note that the house bore the name of the district where the parents married in 1885. It is the first on the left as you enter Fordens Lane from the Dawlish to Teignmouth road.

On the outbreak of war Henry A H Bren joined the Public School's Battalion of the Middlesex Regiment and he was a Private in that regiment when he applied for Appointment to a Commission in the Special Reserve of Officers, stating a preference for the 4th Battalion of the Leinster Regiment (Special Reserve).

He was awarded a Temporary Commission as 2nd.Lieutenant on 7th November 1914. His medical record shows him as being tall for the times at 6' 1/2".

Henry was stationed in Gough Barracks, Curragh, Co. Kildare, Ireland.

In October 1915 he was admitted to the Military Hospital in Curragh suffering from nasal obstruction and tonsillitis. On 27th January 1916 he was discharged as fit for general duties. From there he embarked for France.

From 3rd to 6th June 1916, he fought in the 16th Irish Division at the Battle of Guillemont, which formed part of the Battle of the Somme.

On 31st July 1916 he was suffering from hay fever, and was admitted to the 7th Stationary Hospital in Boulogne. He was discharged on 12th August 1916, arriving in Etaples, Pas de Calais, the following day. He remained there until 19th.August and rejoined his unit on the following day.

The 7th Leinsters were part of the 47th Brigade which launched an attack on Guillemont on the 2nd September 1916. This was successful, taking the Germans by surprise, and Guillemont village was captured.

On the 9th September the 7th Battalion took part in the assault on Ginchy to the north of Guillemont. As the attackers moved forward they were mown down by machine-gun fire from a trench that was thought to have been abandoned. The next day the battalion was withdrawn from the front, having been reduced to 15 officers and 289 other ranks from a total of around 1,000. Ginchy was captured but at the cost to the 16th (Irish) Division of 4,300 casualties at Guillemont and Ginchy.

Rev'd H A Bren received a telegram at St Paul's College, Cheltenham dated 16th September 1916, stating:

> "Regret to inform you that Lieut H A H Bren Leinster Regiment was missing September 9. This does not necessarily mean killed or wounded. Further reports will be sent when received. Kindly notify Casualties' War Office full name of officer's father."

A further telegram reached Rev H Bren, St Paul's College, Cheltenham, dated 4th October,

"Deeply regret to inform you that Lieut H A H Bren Leinster Regiment previously reported missing 9 October (*clearly error for September -ed*) now reported killed in action. The Army Council expresses their sympathy."

Revd H A Bren moved to Holcombe to retire. He is shown as resident at Holcombe in the 1919 and 1923 Kelly's Directories for Dawlish, living at 'Nasik', Fordens Lane. He died on 3 January 1930.

Wilfrid Miles noted in the British Official History that the defence of Guillemont was judged by some observers, to be the best performance of the war by the German army on the Western Front.
A pause in Anglo-French attacks at the end of August to organise bigger combined attacks, and postponements for bad weather, coincided with the largest counter-attack by the German army in the Battle of the Somme.
Joffre, Foch and Haig abandoned attempts to organise large combined attacks in favour of sequenced army attacks and the capture of the German defences from Cléry on the north bank of the Somme to Guillemont from 3 – 6 September brought the French Sixth and British Fourth armies onto ground which overlooked the German third position.
  (wikipedia)

Commonwealth War Graves entry:

Bren, Henry Alfred Hogarth, Lieutenant, died 9/9/16 aged 24, Leinster Regiment, 4th Battalion attached to 7th Battalion. Son of Revd Henry Alfred Bren and Mrs Bren of
"Nasik", Holcombe, Dawlish, Devon. Recorded on Thiepval Memorial Pier and Face 16c.
Thiepval Memorial, The Somme, 80300 Authuille, France.

The Ginchy roundel on the Thiepval Memorial, *left*

Bren, Henry Alfred Hogarth, Lieutenant, Prince of Wales's Leinster Regiment (Royal Canadians) 4th Battalion, killed in action - Ireland's Memorial Records 1914-1918

Dawlish War memorial inscription:
3 Memorial tablets at St George's Church, Holcombe, Dawlish EX7 0JT

Last known address: "Nasik", Holcombe, Dawlish

Next of kin: Father, Revd Henry Alfred Bren (ret'd)

Holcombe Church memorials.
CWGC records
Free Birth, MReferences:
arriage & Death records
The Battle of Guillemont (3–6 September 1916) see Wikipedia.
Officer records at the National Archive, Kew
refs via subscription websites:
Census records
National Probate Calendar records
UK, Soldiers Died in the Great War
Ireland's Memorial Records
Patricia Bren (New Zealand) correspondence
Birt family tree (ancestry)

October 1916

Allan MOSS

| Born East India, ca 1857 | Died 10 October 1916, aged 59 |
| Major | Worcestershire Regiment, 2nd Battalion |

Allan Moss was the eldest of ten children of Thomas Moss (1828-1903) and Helen Lucretia Billings (1834-1913).

Thomas had been born at Cawnpore, India and was working as a civil engineer. He married Helen L Billings in 1853 in Meerut, West Bengal and she was born in East India.
They are first shown on UK census returns in 1881 when Helen Lucretia Moss was head of household in Marygate, St Olave, York, with their children, including Allan, 24, who is shown as a Lieutenant in the 36th Regiment.
The children were Allan, Clara (1861-1937), Thomas (1863-), Jessie (1865-), Gerald (1868-), Helen (1870-) and Ralph (1873-). Many of the children had been born in Allahabad, Uttar Pradesh, India.

By 1901 Thomas Moss had rejoined his family and they were living at 7 Barton Crescent, Dawlish, and he is shown as a Retired Civil Engineer, Public Works Dept, India. His wife and two unmarried daughters, Jessie and Helen were at home.
Thomas Moss died on 27 June 1903 and he left £6,211.10s.11d *(equivalent in 2020 £772,301)* to his widow. In 1911 the widow Helen was 76 and living with the daughters Jessie and Helen and two servants. The census entry shows that one of ten children had died by that date.
Helen Lucretia died on 19 April 1913 and her daughter Jessie, spinster, was left £412.10s.od.

The Misses Moss are listed in Kelly's 1914 Directory for Dawlish among "Residents" at 7 Barton Crescent.

Allan Moss was a career soldier in the 36th Regiment who was commissioned as a Lieutenant on 10 April 1876, at the age of 19. He was posted a Captain on 1st January 1884 and a Major on 2nd March 1891.

36th Regiment

The 36th Regiment became the 36th (Herefordshire) Regiment and it moved to India in 1863. After the manoeuvres in 1872 the regiment returned to Rawalpindi until relieved in 1875, when they marched to Meean Meer. In October, 1875 the regiment marched for Bombay where on November 13th they sailed for home in H.M.S. Euphrates. They landed at Devonport, after trans-shipping at Portsmouth, in December.

ENGLAND

The 36th formed part of the 2nd Brigade of the 1st Division. Back in Raglan Barracks in 1876 the regiment was inspected by the G.O.C. Western District and the Commander-in-Chief commented favourably in his report. The officers of the regiment in this year placed a mural brass in Hereford Cathedral to the memory of the 9 Officers, 20 Sergeants, 17 Corporals, 2 Drummers and 307 Privates who died in India during the regiment's service there from 1863 to 1875.

In April, 1878 the Army Reserve was mobilised because of a scare of war with Russia. The 36th received men from both the Hereford and Worcester Militia.

In December a draft of 126 volunteers embarked for South Africa to join the 99th and take part in the Zulu War. In 1878 the 36th took second place in the regiments at home for immunity from crime.

In July 1881 the Regiment returned again to Ireland and Cork.

General Order No. 41 of 1881 completely reorganised the Army. The Minister of War, Mr. Cardwell, is generally given the credit—or blame. The 36th now lost their old number and title and became the 2nd Battalion of The Worcestershire Regiment.

2ND BATTALION, THE WORCESTERSHIRE REGIMENT

These reforms meant that the 36th lost their green facings, and when new colours were needed they would be white, for white was the colour for the facings of all English non-royal regiments. The 36th adopted the Valise Star from the 29th—a new pattern with "WR" in the centre. This was also later changed for the Lion of the 29th.

The 36th remained in Ireland until 1883 when they crossed to Jersey in the Channel Islands. There they served for two years until moving to Portsmouth late in 1885. The next move was to Pembroke Dock at the end of 1887.

IRELAND AND ALDERSHOT

In 1889 the battalion returned yet again to Ireland and spent two years in Limerick and then moved to Curragh Camp in 1891. Ireland must have been a very pleasant place to soldier in then —plenty of sport off duty and plenty of room for serious soldiering. The army was still forming squares and advancing in columns as if they would never have to face anything more lethal than an assegai, but that solid discipline which was to stand it in such good stead in South Africa and Flanders was being built up. In 1893 the 2nd battalion moved from Curragh Camp to Aldershot. Soldiering at Aldershot in those days was hard work. It was too near the Horse Guards. Generals were forever ordering field days on Lafflans plain and these field days were carried out in scarlet and blue cloth helmets and ended, generally, with a grand march past of friend and foe.

MALTA AND BERMUDA

It was now the turn of the 2nd battalion to go abroad and they sailed for Malta, and disembarked in November 1895. There were eight regiments in the garrison and there was great competition on parade and at sport. The band and drums were the pride of Malta. Captain Hovell (known as "Mad Jack") was commanding "A" Company in Malta. He was a very strong swimmer and once swam round the island Gozo. Every man of his company had to be able to swim a mile, play water polo, march well, be a marksman, do semaphore and know the morse code, and use a pick and shovel. When the battalion moved from Malta to Bermuda in 1897 the competition was lacking but the same high standard was maintained.

Late in 1899 the war in South Africa had broken out and the battalion was under orders for Halifax, Nova Scotia. A telegram was sent to the War Office requesting that the battalion be sent to South Africa. This was granted and the battalion sailed for England in November. They disembarked at Cape Town on January 12th, 1900. The battalion formed part of the 12th Infantry Brigade under General Clements, (late 24th Foot) and on January 25th came under fire during a reconnaissance in force. The war mainly consisted of long marches and short engagements. When peace was signed at Pretoria on May 31st, 1901 the battalion had acquitted themselves well and proved the efficiency of the sound training they had received in Ireland, Aldershot, Malta and Bermuda. The battalion went from South Africa to Ceylon.

THE YEARS BETWEEN 1902-1914.
BLOOMFONTEIN — COLOMBO — AHMEDNAGAR — JHANSI — ALDERSHOT.

1903 saw the Battalion in Bloomfontein, where it remained on garrison duties until 1904. In October, 1904, the Battalion embarked at Durban for Ceylon, where Headquarters were at Colombo, and detachments at Kandy and Trincomali. A grand station with plenty of sport and social life.

Two years in Ceylon passed quickly, and in 1906 they sailed for India, where they were to spend the next six years in Ahmednagar and Jhansi.

After 18 years abroad, in 1913, the Battalion embarked for home and arrived in Aldershot in March, where it remained until the outbreak of the first Great War.

At 4.0 p.m. on August 4th, 1914, the signal for mobilisation was hoisted at Command Headquarters. It was war!

(extracted from http://www.worcestershireregiment.com/h_36th_Foot_history.php

It is not known at what point in this regimental story **Major Allan Moss** retired, but it is clear that he had done so by 1908.

In 1908 **Allan Moss** is shown on the retired list but on the outbreak of war he re-enlisted and was serving on the staff of the cable censor in the Worcestershire Regiment. At the time of his death he was living at 8 Den Crescent, Teignmouth and was buried in Dawlish cemetery. A private headstone was erected by his family.

He does not appear to have married.

His death is recorded as being from heart failure. The probate record shows that he left £3,593-16s-4d to Lieutenant Colonel Claude Moss.

Commonwealth War Graves entry:

Moss A, Major, 10/10/1916, age 59, Worcestershire Regiment, Son of Thomas and Helen Lucretia Moss

Grave Registration Document: Buried in Dawlish cemetery – grave ref 2151

"Retired, but I understand joined up again." "Died of heart failure."

He does not appear on the Devon Roll of Honour for Dawlish, nor is he shown on the Dawlish War Memorial

Last known address: 8 Den Crescent, Teignmouth

Next of kin: Miss Jessie Moss

References:
CWGC
Free birth marriage death records
http://www.worcestershireregiment.com/
h_36th_Foot_history.php
Via subscription: ancestry.co.uk
Census records
National Probate Calendar
UK, Hart's Annual Army List 1908
Lutyens family tree

November 1916

William Alfred Victor ELLIOTT

Born Dawlish Q2,1897   Died 3 November 1916, aged 19
Private 27916   Duke of Cornwall's Light Infantry

William A V Elliott was the eldest child of Alfred and Agnes Hannah Elliott.

Alfred Elliott (1867-) was the second son of William Elliott (1842-) and Jane Brooks (1841-). William Elliott was a Boot and shoe maker living in Kenton in 1871 and 1881.
Alfred was born in Kenton but moved to Dawlish and in 1901 was established at Priory Terrace, High Street with his wife and William A V Elliott who was three years old. Alfred Elliott was a grocer working on his own account.
By 1911 the family had moved to Homeleigh House, Exeter Road, Dawlish and their second son, Bertram Charles Elliott had been born (1904-).
William A V Ellliott was first apprenticed as a tailor to Mr Cowling in the Strand. Later he moved to work in Torquay and it was there that he enlisted in February 1916. It seems likely that he was one of the first to be called up following the introduction of conscription by a Bill in Parliament in January 1916. The remnants of his Service Record show that he had been living at 27 Sunbury Terrace, Brixham and that he was unmarried.
His attestation record is dated 19th February 1916 and the parent unit was the Duke of Cornwall's Light Infantry. He was mobilized on 13th March 1916 as a "Special Reservist in Class III, Garrison Service Home, mech transport."
He was posted on 19th May 1916 and retained at depot, 95th Training Reserve Battalion when he was given the Service Number TR/7/12212.

His death is recorded as the result of a "Bomb Accident" on 2nd November, reported in the *Dawlish Gazette* newspaper as "the accidental bursting of a hand grenade." He was sent to hospital but died on the following day. The War Office called for a Court of Inquiry and the documents were filed with the soldier's records, but have not been seen. The CWGC site indicates that he may have been posted at Chisledon Camp, Wiltshire, and that is also shown on his grave *(below)*.
He was buried in Dawlish Cemetery in a grave commemorating also his mother, Agnes Hannah Elliott who died in November 1923. It is a low frame of granite set below a large cupressus in the south eastern part of the old cemetery. It is possible that his father died in Central Devon in 1951, aged 83.

Below the inscription are the words *"Until the day breaks".*

The Western Times of Friday 17 November reported the funeral. "The funeral of Pte.W.Elliottt, D.C.L.I., whose death occurred at a bombing school, somewhere in England, through an accident, took place at Dawlish Cemetery on Thursday afternoon, the Rev.W.E.Withers, Wesleyan Minister, officiating. The chief mourners were: Mr A. Elliott (father), Master B.Elliott (brother), Miss F.Mallett,

Mr Elliott (grandfather), Mr and Mrs F.Elliott, Mr and Mrs E.Elliott, Mr. W.Kemp, Mr T.Cowling, Rev.W.E.Withers. There were some beautiful floral tributes. In addition to those of relatives and friends was one from the Wesleyan Church and Sunday School, with whom the deceased was associated for many years."

Commonwealth War Graves entry:
  ELLIOTT, WILLIAM ALFRED VICTOR,   Private,   27916
03/11/1916, Age: 19   Duke of Cornwall's Light Infantry, 11th Bn.
Grave Ref: 2689. Dawlish Cemetery
Son of Alfred and Agnes H. Elliott, of Homeleigh House, Dawlish.

He is listed on the Devon Roll of Honour for Dawlish, and on the Dawlish Boys' School Roll of Honour.
Dawlish War memorial inscription: ELLIOTT W.A.V.   Pte   D.C.L.I.

Last known address: 27 Sunbury Terrace, Brixham, Devon
Next of kin: Father, Alfred Elliott, Homeleigh House, Dawlish

References:
Free Birth Marriage Death records   Data via subscription service:
Uk, Soldier's Service Records (remnants)   Census records
Elliott family tree 2011 (Ancestry.co.uk)   National Newspaper Archive

His mother Agnes Hannah Elliott inscribed on the border of the family grave.

Bertram Charles HONOUR

Born Holcombe, Q4, 1890   Died 18 November 1916, aged 26
Private 4170   Devonshire Regiment, 2nd/4th Battalion

Bertram Charles Honour was a grand child of Henry Honour (1794-1888) (a Chelsea Pensioner, born in St Albans) who married Mary Spiers(1819-), born in Scotland, and they came to live in Holcombe village, near Dawlish.

They had six children, Robert H (1846-), Agnes (1848-1911), Thomas (1850-1929), Charles J (1854-), Charlotte (1856-) and Caroline (1860-).

We are interested in Thomas Alexander Honour who was born in Plymouth in the October/December quarter of 1850. His parents, Henry and Mary, were living then at the rear of 19 Lower Batter Street, St Andrew's, Plymouth.

They moved to Holcombe village ca 1853, to judge by the places of birth of the last three children.

In the 1871 census return Henry states that he was a pensioner of the 53rd Regiment in Chelsea, that his wife was a needlework seamstress and that the sons Thomas and Charles were sailors.

> *(Thomas Honour appears in various documents as Thomas Alexander, Thomas Charles and Thomas H Honour, but these may be transcription errors, or that Charles was also Thomas Charles.)*

By 1881 only two children were still living at home, Charlotte, 24, unmarried and Charles, 26, a "mariner."

Henry and Mary Honour's cottage in Holcombe was close to that of Charles Abraham Ware Jarman and Agnes Ann (Honour), their eldest daughter. Charles and Agnes Jarman had a large family of eleven children, one of whom, Charlotte Jarman (1875-), married Frederick Bright.

By this marriage, the large local Jarman family cemented relationships between the Honour, Kerswell and Bright families. Unlike many 19th century families, the Bright parents had two sons only and they were both killed in the Great War. This experience was equally the case for Thomas Alexander and Emily Drusilla Honour wiping out their family name in cruel tragedy.

Thomas Alexander Honour married Emily Drusilla Jarman (1847-1916) in Holcombe in the July/September quarter of 1883.

Bertram Charles Honour was the first son of Thomas and Emily, being born in Holcombe in the October/December quarter of 1890.

His brother, Reginald Alexander Honour, was born on the 26th June 1894. *(His death is recorded on 17 October 1918 in Part Three)*

Thomas was still shown as a sailor in the 1901 census, at the age of 49, while the boys Bertram and Reginald were scholars. In 1911 the rural life of Holcombe had attracted Thomas ashore as a farm labourer and both the boys were gardeners. Emily Drusilla Honour died in the April/June quarter of 1916, just months before Bertram.

There are no surviving Service Records for Bertram beyond a British Army WW1 Medal Roll Index Card that shows that he was awarded a British War Medal.

From other sources we can see the movements of the **2/4th Battalion, Devonshire Regiment.**

It was formed at Exeter in September 1914 as a Second Line battalion; became part of 2nd Devon and Cornwall Brigade, 2nd Wessex Division.

12 December 1914: sailed for India and came under orders of the Southern Brigade, 9th (Secunderabad) Division. (www.longlongtrail) from January 1915 to October 1917 when they sailed for Egypt (The Regimental Warpath 1914-1918).

The **9th (Secunderabad) Division** was an infantry division of the British Indian Army. It was part of the Southern Army and was formed in 1904 after Lord Kitchener was appointed Commander-in-Chief, India between 1902 and 1909.

The Division remained in India on internal security duties during World War One, but some of its brigades were transferred to serve with other units. (Wikipedia)

The Dawlish Gazette of 2nd December 1916 reported: "Sympathy will be felt with Mr Tom Honour, of Holcombe, in the death, in India from fever, of his eldest son, Pte. Bertram Honour, of the Devons (T.P.). The deceased went out to India not long since with a contingent which comprised a number of Dawlishians. He was an excellent fellow and esteemed by his comrades. Before joining up he was gardener at Derncleugh, Holcombe."

His Death Grant of £12.8s.4d and the War Gratuity of £10.8s.4d were paid to his father, Thomas. On his death on 3 November 1929, Thomas Alexander Honour left £284.9s.8d to Charlotte Discombe, his sister, who had married Frederick Richard Discombe in 1888.

Commonwealth War Graves entry: HONOUR, BERTRAM CHARLES   Private   4170
18/11/1916   Age: 26   Devonshire Regiment, 2nd/4th Bn.
Son of Mr. and Mrs. Thomas Honour, of Holcombe, Dawlish, Devon. Buried in St. Thomas' Mount Church Cemetery.
Panel Ref: Face 9. Madras 1914-1918 War Memorial, Chennai. Madras War Cemetery is about 5 kilometres from the airport and 14 kilometres from the central railway station. The cemetery can easily be located on the right hand side of the road 1 kilometre from St. Thomas Mount. (CWGC)

It is not known if there is a record in the Devon Roll of Honour for Holcombe.
B.C.Honour is listed on the Dawlish Boys' School Roll of Honour.

Holcombe War memorial inscription, located on the west face of St George's, Holcombe:
"Pte Bertram C Honour   2nd/4th Devons"
Last known address: Holcombe, Dawlish
Next of kin: Father, Thomas Alexander Honour

References: Free BMD records   Honour family records
Refs via subscription site (Ancestry.co.uk)
Census records from 1851 to 1911   International Find a Grave Index
UK, Soldiers Died in the Great War   British Army WW1 Medal Roll Index Card
National Probate Calendar   MaureenSmale family tree

Henry LEAMAN

Born Dawlish, Q3, 1885[28]   Died of wounds, 21 December 1916, aged 31
Sapper 498299 / 3477   Royal Engineers, 1st/3rd Field Company

Henry's grandfather Edward Leaman (1831-1916) was born in South Brent and was established in Torquay in 1871 with his wife Mary Elizabeth (formerly Ward)(1836-) and six children. They went on to have eight children[29] including William Thomas Leaman, born in 1858.

William Leaman (1858-1933) married Ellen Allford (1855-1910) in the June quarter of 1876. She was one of seven children of Job and Susan Allford living at Hele Cottage, St Marychurch in 1861. The Leaman family were well known in Dawlish. William Thomas Leaman had been elected onto the Urban District Council and was vice-chairman.

He had worked in Torquay until he took a job as stoker at the gas works, progressing to manager by 1901. In 1901, the census return lists the children as Louisa (1881-), Charles (1883-), Mary E (1884-), **Henry (1885-1916)**, Steven (1887-1918 -*see separate WW1 record*), Evelyn Maud (1890-1916), Floria (1893-), Edith (1895-), Frederick (1896-), and Herbert (1898-).

Henry was the third son who, after leaving school and working as a groom, took a job with the railway in Bristol for about ten years before war broke out. The oldest child, William Edwyn Leaman (1878-1960) was not listed at home. He, later, was the partial beneficiary of William Thomas Leaman's death on 11 April 1933, when he was described as a 'railway engine driver'.

Their mother, Ellen Leaman, died on 15 May 1910.

William Leaman became a magistrate (Kelly's Directory, 1930) and sat on the Dawlish Urban Tribunal. They had fourteen children of which three had died by the date of census of 1911.

Henry Leaman married Blanche Irene Jefferies (1884-) in Bristol in April to June quarter of 1909, and they had a daughter Hilda Blanche Leaman in September quarter of 1910, while living at 10 Golden Street, Wells Road, Knowle, Bristol. There were two further children.

Henry followed a stoking tradition as a 'railway engine stoker', and is thought to have worked for the GWR locomotive department at Bristol for about ten years.

A report in the *Exeter and Plymouth Gazette of 2 January 1917* says that he left "a widow and three young children".

Henry Leaman enlisted in the Royal Engineers at Bristol and has a service record number of 498299. There is a further service record number of 3477 used in the Medal Roll index, and this is also given in Register of Soldiers' Effects.

He came home on leave in June 1916 for the funeral of his younger sister Eva (Evelyn Maud Leaman) who died of consumption at the age of 26. She had been the organist to the Wesleyan church in Dawlish.

The funeral also brought his older brother Charles Edward Leaman home on leave from the Royal Engineers. He had married Susan Jane Elliott in Dawlish in 1903, and he died in 1940. Three other Leaman brothers served in WW1; Stephen Leaman was killed in 1918 while serving with the Royal Welch Fusiliers, leaving a widow, Elizabeth, and a child, Edith; Frederick Allford Leaman served as

---

28   Birth GRO ref 1885, Q3, N.A. vol 5b, p110
29   Cox family tree- Ancestry.co.uk

an acting Corporal with the Royal Army Service Corps and Herbert Leaman also was a sapper with the Royal Engineers. They both survived the war, and Herbert married Doris Jane Ferris in 1926.

It is quite common that servicemen transferred from one unit to another and it appears that Henry was first attached to the 1st/3rd Field Company and then to the 2/1st South Midland Field Company of Royal Engineers which included contingents from Gloucestershire.

The Royal Engineers attachments to Divisions provided a range of support functions such as transport by horse, lorry or train, and telephone and other communications. Henry had been a groom and a railway engine stoker and found a natural place in the Royal Engineers.

The history of 48th (South Midland) Division

The South Midland Division was a formation of the Territorial Force. It was formed as a result of the reforms of the army carried out in 1908 under the Secretary of State for War, Richard Burdon Haldane, and was one of 14 Divisions of the peacetime Territorial Force.

1914

The units of the Division had just departed for annual summer camp when emergency orders recalled them to the home base. All units were mobilised for full time war service on 5 August 1914 and moved to concentrate in the Chelmsford area by mid August 1914.

1915

On 13 March the Division was warned that it would go on overseas service and entrainment began a week later. Divisional HQ and the Gloucester & Worcester and South Midland Brigades went via Folkestone-Boulogne while all other units went from Southampton to Le Havre. By 3 April the Division had concentrated near Cassel. The Division then remained in France and Flanders until late 1917 and took part in the following engagements:

1916

The Battle of the Somme which included the following phases:

The Battle of Albert; The Division held the line between the 56th (London) and the 31st Divisions, both of which were heavily engaged at Gommecourt and Serre respectively on 1 July 1916.

The Battle of Bazentin Ridge in which the Division captured Ovillers; The Battle of Pozieres Ridge; The Battle of the Ancre Heights; The Battle of the Ancre continued until November 18th, 1916 with lesser engagements in the weeks following.

Henry Leaman is shown to have died of shrapnel wounds on 21st December 1916.

He is recorded on the Devon Roll of Honour for Dawlish.

The Dawlish Boys' School Roll of Honour lists an H C Leaman, Lance Corporal, Devon Regt but no casualty of that description can be found and it may be an erroneous entry for H Leaman.

Dawlish War memorial inscription: LEAMAN H.   SPR   S.MID. R.E.

Devon Heritage site info:

> '498299 Sapper Henry Leaman of the Royal Engineers. Died 21 December 1916. Son of William and Ellen Leaman of the Gas Works, Dawlish (his father was the manager).; brother of Stephen. Born in Dawlish in 1886. Died 21 December 1916 aged 30.'

Commonwealth War Graves entry: Leaman, H   Sapper,   498299,   21/12/1916,   Royal Engineers, 1st/3rd Field Coy.   Grave Reference K. 15.   Aveluy Communal Cemetery Extension

Last known address: 10 Golden Street, Wells Road, Knowle, Bristol

Next of kin: widow, Blanche Irene Leaman.

References:

CWGC records   1914-1918.net   *Exeter & Plymouth Gazette*

Refs via susbcription website: National Probate Calendar – William Thomas Leaman.

Census data   UK, Soldiers Died in the Great War   UK, Register of Soldiers' Effects

Cox family tree (Ancestry.co.uk) and Leaman family tree (Ancestry.co.uk)

Grave of William Henry Leaman on which his sons Harry and Stephen are named, in Dawlish Cemetery

Leonard Walter BLACKBURN,

Born Carshalton, Surrey, Q1,1898   Died Dawlish 29th December 1916, aged 18
Rifleman   5827   London Regiment (London Rifle Brigade), 5th Battalion.

Leonard Walter Blackburn was the second son of Joseph and Sarah Blackburn.
Joseph (1850-) was born in Norfolk and Sarah (1858-) was from Essex and they were living in Carshalton (Sutton registration district) when their children were born from 1886 to 1900. Joseph was a house painter.

It is likely that Leonard enlisted early in 1916 and was attached to the 3rd/5th Battalion which moved to Exeter and then to Dawlish for training. It appears that he died here.

Battalions of the Territorial Force, The London Regiment

The London Regiment was unusual. Not only were all of its battalions of the Territorial Force (although the first four were affiliated to the other City of London regiment, the all-regular Royal Fusiliers) but each battalion was regarded as a Corps in its own right.

3/5th Battalion

Formed at Bunhill Row on 26 November 1914.
By April 1915, at Tadworth. Moved in October to billets at Sutton, then to Fovant in January 1916.
8 April 1916: became 5th Reserve Bn. Moved to Exeter in November 1916, then Dawlish in December. Moved to Blackdown in April 1917, where it then remained.

3/6th, 3/7th and 3/8th Battalions

Formed in early 1915. By April 1915, at Tadworth. Moved in October to billets at Surbiton / Orpington / Blackheath respectively, then to Fovant in January 1916.
8 April 1916: became 6th, 7th and 8th Reserve Bns. Moved to Newton Abbott / Dartmouth / Paignton in autumn 1916, then Dawlish in December. Moved to Blackdown in April 1917, where they then remained.
(1914-1918.net)

The Exeter and Plymouth Gazette of 2 January 1917, reported his funeral in Dawlish:

> Rifleman L.W.Blackburn, London Rifle Brigade, was buried with full military honours yesterday at the cemetery. The coffin, covered with the Union Jack, was carried from the Cottage Hospital to Park Road where 'A' Company, to which deceased belonged, was drawn up with the band of the battalion.
> A firing party, under Sergt Lloyd, was drawn from the same company.............The mourners were the parents and sister. There were many floral tokens including one from officers and men of 'A' Company.

Commonwealth War Graves entry: BLACKBURN, LEONARD WALTER   Rifleman 5827
29/12/1916   Age: 18   London Regiment (London Rifle Brigade), 5th Bn.
Grave Ref: 780.   Dawlish Cemetery
Son of Joseph and Sarah Blackburn, of Norfolk Cottage, Gander Green Lane, Sutton, Surrey.

References: Forces War Records CWGC BMD and census records
Died at Home (FWR) Death recorded in Newton Abbot, Q4, 1916 Vol 5b, p 150

Dawlish Gazette of 6th January 1917:

MILITARY FUNERAL AT DAWLISH

"A military funeral, always an impressive event, took place at Dawlish on Monday last, when the mortal remains of Rifleman L W Blackburn, of the L.R.B., were interred at the Cemetery.

The circumstances of the young soldier's death, away from home and kinsfolk, after very brief illness, had aroused the keen sympathies of the community. The cortege left the Cottage Hospital at 2.30, and was headed by a firing party, under Sergt Lloyd, followed by the platoon to which deceased belonged, and then the fine L.R.B. band, which played beautiful funereal music to a slow march. The procession went direct to the Cemetery, where the whole of the service was conducted by the Rev Elsen Doddrell, Chaplain to the Battalion. A large crowd of people attended the funeral.

The coffin was covered with the Union Jack, with the deceased's hat and rifle laid on it.

The mourners were Mr and Mrs Blackburn (father and mother) and Mrs Blackford (sister)."

"Floral tributes included one from "A" Company and another from the Matron and staff of the Cottage Hospital.

At the close of the service, three volleys were fired over the grave. The band then played a verse of "Thy will be done." Beautifully rendered, pianissimo, it was perhaps the most touching part of an affecting service. The sounding of the "Last Post" (the soldiers' requiem) by a party of buglers under Bugle-Major Molde, concluded the ceremony."

It might be noted in passing that there was no mention of the contrast between the seasonal celebration of Christmas or the passing into the New Year of 1917. In describing in detail the solemnity of the funeral the correspondent gave due emphasis to the loss of a soldier's life, even one with no local family.

January 1917

Samuel Alfred CHAPPLE

Born Q4,1890 in Ilfracombe, N Devon   Died, Tidworth, 8 January 1917, aged 26

Private 4550   Devonshire Regiment, 4th (Reserve) Battalion (Territorials)

Samuel came from an Ilfracombe family. His grandfather, Samuel Chapple (1838-1866), married Elizabeth Hancock (1838-) in Q1,1853. Their son, Samuel Edward Chapple, was born on 29th August 1853 in Berrynarbor in North Devon and went on to marry Ellen Blackmore in Q1,1880.

Samuel Edward Chapple signed on for ten years service in the Royal Navy from 29th August 1871 at age 18 and was released on 31st August 1881 in the rating of Able Seaman, no 72334. He was at Funchal, Madeira in 1871 and Pembroke Dock in 1881. On his return he became an Insurance Agent.

Samuel and Ellen Chapple were living at 14 Victoria Road, Ilfracombe in 1891 with their children John Henry (1883-), Ellen May (1885-1929), Elizabeth (1886-), Lily (1888-) and **Samuel Alfred** [30](1890-1917).

There is a record of Samuel Chapple at Holy Trinity Church of England School for Boys in Ilfracombe in 1896 and 1897.

In 1901 they had moved to 28 Oxford Street with another child, Herbert (1893-), William Blackmore, 84, an uncle and retired mason, and Frederick Blackmore, 28, a nephew and printer.

It is not clear when Samuel Alfred Chapple left North Devon after 1901, but his appearance on the Dawlish Boys' School Roll of Honour and the Devon Roll of Honour for Dawlish suggests that he may have been sent to a relative in Dawlish, yet to be identified, and attended school there in his early teens.

There is then a record at Holy Trinity School, Ilfracombe, of Samuel Chapple attending evening class during 1908, being listed as a hairdresser and taking a class in French.

In 1911, Samuel and Ellen were at 28 Oxford Grove, Ilfracombe, with their other son Herbert, who was shown as a Hairdresser, and a grandson Kingsley, (1905-).

Also in the 1911 Census there is a record of Alfred Chapple, aged 20, boarding with the Trewin household at 21 Palace Avenue, Paignton when he was shown as a hairdresser's assistant.

> A possible confusion arises with another Samuel Chaple/Chapple. In the 1851 census a Samuel Chaple, aged 13, was a farmer's servant at Burland, Marwood, Barnstaple. A marriage occurred between Samuel Chapple and Lucy Lerwill in Q1, 1889 (Barnstaple, Vol 5b, p 766).
>
> In 1891 Lucy Chapple (1852-1935) was shown at 2 Barum Cottages, Ilfracombe in the home of Mary Lerwill, 73, a widow, and nine others including, Samuel Chapple, 4, grand-son, Lucy Chapple, 2, grand-daughter and Frederick John Chapple, 4 months, grand-son.
>
> By 1901 Lucy Chapple was a widow, aged 49 and working as a laundress at 14 Highfield Road, Ilfracombe, with Samuel, son,14, Lucy, daughter, 12, and Charles Chapple, 21, nephew and labourer.
>
> Samuel Chapple enlisted with the 4th Devon Regiment, service no 4917, on 19th February 1907 at the age of 18 and 6 months (birth date ca August, 1888) and was granted a free discharge on 21st December 1909. (this shows his elder brother to be named Jack, younger brother, Frederick, younger sister, Lucy)

---

30   GRO birth ref Q4, 1890, Ilfracombe, vol 5b, p419

In 1915 Samuel Alfred Chapple married[31] Florence Emily Thomas (1888-1968?) in Teignmouth. Florence Thomas was the daughter of George B W Thomas and Ellen Tidball and they lived at 46 Parson Street, West Teignmouth in 1891. They had moved to 23 Fore Street in 1901 and were still there 10 years later. The father, George Buckler Wood Thomas, was born in London and his wife, Ellen Emma, was from Kent. He was a self-employed house decorator and they had two daughters, Ellen Emma Beatrice (1886-) and Florence Emily, born in 1888[32]. Ellen had work as a dressmaker and Florence as a milliner.

After Florence's marriage to Samuel they moved to Dawlish. The record of "UK, Soldiers Died in the Great War 1914-1919" gives Samuel's residence as Dawlish and that would also account for his appearance on the Dawlish War Memorial. After his death his widow appears to have returned to her family home which is the address given for her on the Commonwealth War Graves Commission site.

The Devonshire Regiment, 4th (Reserve) Battalion was part of the 43rd (Wessex) Division, an existing Territorial Force division drawn primarily from the south-western counties of England. It had Divisional Headquarters in Exeter. In late July 1914 the Division was on Salisbury Plain at its annual training camp when it received instructions that it was to take precautionary measure should war be declared on Germany.

On 3rd August the infantry brigades were ordered to defend the ports on the south-western coast and were in transit to these posts when orders to mobilise were received, following the declaration of war on 4th August. Those men who volunteered for foreign service began to move into camps for training.

On 10th August the Division concentrated on Salisbury Plain with Divisional Headquarters opening at Tidworth on 13th August. Those who volunteered for service abroad were sent to India, while the training facility remained at Tidworth.

It is not known when Samuel enlisted but his death occurred in hospital at Tidworth, Wiltshire, which suggests that he may have been conscripted and was in training at the time. The Death Grant of £2. 9s. 1d and the War Gratuity of £3.0s.0d were paid to his widow, Florence Emily Chapple.

He was buried in Teignmouth cemetery.

There is a marriage record of Florence E Chapple to Philip Summers in Barnstaple in 1930[33] and of a death[34] of Florence E Summers in Gloucester City district in 1968, aged 81.

Commonwealth War Graves entry:
CHAPPLE, SAMUEL ALFRED   Private   4550   08/01/1917   Age: 26
        Devonshire Regiment, 4th (Reserve) Bn.
        Grave Ref: EE. 84.   Teignmouth Cemetery
        Son of Mr. and Mrs. S. Chapple, of Ilfracombe; husband of Florence Emily Chapple, of 23, Fore St., Teignmouth.

---

31   Marriage GRO ref 1915, Jan to Mar, N.A. vol 5b, p263

32   Birth GRO ref 1888, Q1, N.A. vol 5b, p106

33   GRO Marriage record Barnstaple, 1930, Q2, Vol 5b, p 1156

34   GRO death record Gloucester, Mar 1968, vol 7b, p 521

Samuel Alfred Chapple is shown on the Dawlish section of the Devon Roll of Honour. He is also shown on the Dawlish Boys' School Roll of Honour, implying that he was a schoolboy in Dawlish between 1901 and 1908.

Dawlish War memorial inscription: CHAPPLE S.A.   PTE   DEVON REGT
He is named also on the Teignmouth War memorial.

Devon Heritage site information repeats the entry of the CWGC site, above
Next of kin: Mrs Florence Emily Chapple

References:
Free Birth Marriage Death records
Heather Roche – Teign Heritage Centre, Teignmouth Museum
refs via subscription sites:
Census records
UK, Soldiers Died in the Great War 1914-1919
UK, Army Registers of Soldiers' Effects
Forces War Records
redmore family tree (ancestry.co.uk) and Bellia Family tree

Thomas Alfred SMITH

Born Dartmouth 1877   died France, 13 January 1917, aged 39
Private   22145   Devonshire Regiment, 9th (Service) Battalion

Thomas Alfred Smith was the grandson of William Smith (1803-) and Lumley Hunt Jago (1801-1873). William was a carpenter and joiner, born close by Dartmouth at Dittisham.
In 1861 they were living "above town" in St Saviour's, Dartmouth with two sons, Richard Egg Smith, 23, a carpenter, and Thomas H Smith, 14, a joiner(learner).

Richard Egg Smith (1838-) married Louisa Alford Bell (1844-1883) in April 1863 in the Wesleyan Chapel, Totnes [35].
Louisa Bell was the daughter of John Bell (1811-), a ship's carpenter in Dartmouth. He was a widower by 1861 when he had six children including Louisa, 17 and Hannah, 11.

By 1881, Richard and Louisa were living in Smith Street, Dartmouth and they had six children, William John (1864-), Emma Louisa (1866-), Richard George (1869 -), Amy Alford (1872-), Mary Ann (1874-), and **Thomas Alfred (1877-1917).** A further child, Sarah Jane, was born after the census in 1882 and a year before the death of her mother.
In 1891, Richard E Smith was still working as a carpenter, was aged 53 and living at Smith Street, Dartmouth with Amy, 19, Mary Ann, 17, Thomas, 14, and Sarah Jane, 8. Thomas was working as a Baker's assistant. From this time the family appears to disintegrate and it has not been possible to identify with certainty the death of the father.

Thomas Smith enlisted at Bedford with the Bedfordshire Regiment on 5th December 1893 (family record sources) when he was nearly 17 but he declared his age at 18 years and 1 month. He is shown as a labourer and was 5' 7 3/4" tall, weighing 127 lbs (9 stone). He completed twelve years service on the 4th December 1905 having taken courses in Transport Duties (1895) and Butchery (1901). He transferred to the Army Reserve from 3rd January 1906 for a period of four years. His father and siblings are shown as next of kin.

John Wood Lambshead (1853-1934) was an agricultural labourer in Dawlish when he married Hannah Bell (1850-1939) of Dartmouth, sister of Louisa.
They had three children, Hannah Bell (1883- ?), Edith Jane (1884-1925) and William John Lambshead (1885-1964).

Thomas Alfred Smith married Hannah Bell (Lambshead) on 24th August 1907 in St Gregory's Church, Dawlish. They were cousins, their respective mothers being sisters. In the following year one child was born prematurely and died. This is recorded in the *Devon and Exeter Gazette of Friday 8th May 1908* in which a report appeared of an inquest. "An inquest was held here *(Dawlish)* touching the death of the infant son of Thomas Alfred Smith, employed at Dartmouth Naval College. Dr C. Ll. H. Tripp attributed death to inanition *(want of nourishment)* from premature birth. The jury returned a verdict accordingly."

The 1911 census show Thomas in the Royal Naval College, Dartmouth as a boot cleaner, married and 34 years old. His wife "Annie Smith", 28, was with her parents, John Wood Lambshead, 57,

---

35   GRO marriage ref Totnes,1863, Q2, vol 5b, p 379

and Hannah Alford Bell Lambshead, 60, of 4 Brook Street, Dawlish. Another child to Thomas and Annie is Edith Janie Smith (1909-), shown on the 1911 Census. A further child has been recorded, born after the census, as Hannah Louisa Smith (1911-1989).

John Wood Lambshead was at this time working for the railway company as a labourer.

Thomas's second military record is sketchy. The Army Medals Roll index card gives no more than his regiment and number, but appears to place him in the 1st Battalion, Devonshire Regiment. There is no date given for his arrival in France. Other references place him in the 9th (Service) Battalion, Devonshire Regiment, which was composed mainly of Kitchener's volunteers. The 9th Battalion had been engaged in the assault on Mametz Wood on 1st July 1916 and the Battle of Guillemont on 3rd September (Battles of the Somme, 1916).

A Casualty Clearing Station entry shows that he was admitted on 5th January 1917 with "Pyrexia of unknown origin", which is a fever for which there is no certain diagnosis. He died in hospital on 13th January.

A Death Grant of £4.10s.6d and a War Gratuity of £3.10s.0d were paid to his widow.

He was awarded the British War Medal and the Victory Medal.

Commonwealth War Graves entry: SMITH, ALFRED THOMAS   Private   22145
13/01/1917   Age: 41   Devonshire Regiment, 9th Bn.

Grave Ref: VII. F. 17.   Puchevillers British Cemetery, Somme, France

Son of Richard Egg Smith and Louisa Alford Smith, of Dartmouth, Devon; husband of Hannah Bell Smith, of 5. Stoneland Cottages, Dawlish, Devon.

The headstone is engraved "A devoted husband and father. Greatly Missed."

Devon Heritage site info: 22145 Private Thomas Alfred Smith of the 9th Battalion, the Devonshire Regiment. Son of Richard Smith and the late Louise Smith of Dartmouth. Born in Dartmouth 9 February 1886. (Date of birth does not correspond with family census data) Died 15 January 1917 aged 31.(date of death does not correspond to other references). Served out a Royal Navy contract before enlisting in the Devonshire Regiment. (This may be a reference to employment at Royal Naval College Dartmouth?)

He is recorded on the Devon Roll of Honour, but date of death not given (13/1/1917 – CWGC)

Dawlish War memorial inscription: SMITH T.A.   PTE.   DEVON REGT.

Last known address: 5 Stonelands Cottages, Dawlish
Next of kin: Hannah Bell Smith, widow
References: CWGC   Free Birth Marriage & Death records
Family reference data
Subscription website references: Forces War Records for hospital admissions
Ancestry.co.uk for census data,   Medal Rolls,
UK, Soldiers died in the Great War (death date in error, shown as 15 January 1917)
UK, Army Register of Soldiers' Effects.

This limited biography illustrates the problems in providing certainty of information for common surnames. While other references have been consulted there are often minor discrepancies than may not correspond with the official records. Wherever possible the original document has been consulted whether on paper or in digital form.

Arthur Charles BURCH

Born Dawlish, 5 January 1882   Died 17 February 1917, aged 35

Private 26681   Wiltshire Regiment 1st Battalion

Arthur Charles Burch was a first cousin of William Henry Burch, the last Dawlish casualty before the Armistice in 1918. Their common grandfather was William Burch, a gardener born in Lympstone on Christmas Eve, 1825. He was a son of Thomas and Sarah Burch.

William Burch married Anna Maria Garrish (1831-) of Chagford early in 1853[36] and the census of 1911 records that they had 11 children, of which 3 had died. They were living at Manor Place, Dawlish (1861) and 16 Park Row (1871). Census records for this family over the years from 1861 suggests that their children were:

> William Burch, born in Dawlish 3 October 1853, joined the Royal Navy at age 18 for 10 years, extended for a further 10 years and retired as a Petty Officer 1st Class and naval pensioner on 5th October 1891. Married Ann, six years his senior, no children.
>
> George John Burch, born in Dawlish 20 July 1856, joined the Royal Navy as a Boy Seaman at age 16 ½ and served two 10 year terms to retire as a Petty Officer, 1st Class on 20 July 1894.
>
> Sarah Ann Burch, born Dawlish 1857-
>
> Ellen Burch, born Dawlish 1858-
>
> Mary Jane Burch, Born Dawlish 1860, married Stephens
>
> Eliza Burch, born Dawlish 1862- *(taken from a family tree, this may be Bessie)*
>
> **Bessie Burch**, born Dawlish 1862 – also known as Eliza, the **mother of Arthur Charles Burch**
>
> Annie M Burch, born Dawlish 1865-
>
> Selina Burch, born Dawlish 1865-
>
> Henry Garrish Burch, born Dawlish 1867- , father of William Henry Burch, (above) 1897-1918
>
> Thomas Burch, born Dawlish 1871-
>
> Emma Jane Burch, 1872-1956

In 1881 Bessie Burch was 19 and a housemaid to Sarah Lindsey, a boarding house keeper at 10 West Cliff Hill, Dawlish. **Arthur** was born in the following year[37] and while Bessie was his mother no father is shown and so is given his mother's surname. The Parish Register shows that he was baptised in St Gregory the Great, Dawlish, on 26 March 1882 (alongside his name is the abbreviation "illi", presumably indicating that his mother was not married and no father has been named).

Arthur retains the surname of Burch when he appears in the 1891 census at Rose Cottage, High Street, Dawlish in the household of his grandparents, William and Ann Maria. Three of their children were still living at home, Bessie, 28, working as a laundress, Henry, 24, a painter, and Emma, 20, a housemaid.

In 1891 also, Bessie Burch married George Newman[38] when Arthur was aged 9.

---

36   Marriage record GRO ref N.A., 1853 Jan-Mar, vol 5b, p 238

37   Birth record GRO ref Q1, 1882, Newton Abbot district Vol 5b, page 114

38   Marriage record GRO ref 1891 Apr-June, N.A. Vol 5b, p195

Arthur left home and joined the Royal Navy as a boy seaman on 22nd July 1897 at age 15. He has a record in the UK, Registers of Seamen's Services, No 194753, which gives his trade as a plumber. He joined H.M.S.IMPREGNABLE and then H.M.S.LION before he was invalided out of the service on 3 October 1898. There is no indication of the nature of his incapacity.

In 1901 he was boarding with the Long family at 22 Victoria Terrace, Portland when his occupation was shown as "Fireman on steam, Navvy, Public Works".

John Long (1847-1924) and his wife Arabella (1857-) had seven children at home in 1901 and their eldest daughter Louise (1882-) was of a similar age to Arthur, the lodger. Arthur and Louisa were married in 1907 [39].

It is not known whether Arthur Charles Burch joined the army by choice or by conscription, for the expectation might be that he would rejoin the Royal Navy.

The WW1 Service Medal and Award Rolls show that he had been enlisted with the 5th Dorset Regiment, as a Private, No 18625 before joining the Duke of Edinburgh's (Wiltshire) Regiment, 1st Battalion, Private No 26681.

From the Wiltshire Regiment War Diary

15th February 1917, Romarin, France

"Except for wire cutting, bombardments by artillery and trench mortars preparatory to the impending daylight raid, these days passed without incident as far as this Battn's Sector was concerned. There was very little retaliation on the enemy's part in response to our periodical bombardments. On the night of the 15th/16th, however, the enemy was busy repairing the gaps cut in his wire, and to ensure that adequate gaps were made the wire cutting programme had to be prolonged until the last possible moment. On the 16th there were two casualties: wounded, still at duty, 12093 Pte Miller, J (A Coy). Wounded, 9191 L/Cpl Strong, G."

17 February 1917

"The raid was carried out in conjunction with a party of the 10th Cheshire Regt. (200 in strength) the objective allotted to the Brigade being the enemy's defences N and S of FACTORY FARM, the farm itself included. Zero hour was 10.40a.m. The enemy seemed to be taken quite by surprise and his trenches were gained with but slight loss. All objectives were seized, with the exception of FACTORY FARM, where stout resistance was offered. Elsewhere very few of the enemy were found. It is believed that about 20 Germans were killed in this Battn's objective, exclusive of casualties caused by shell fire. Two prisoners were taken, and no identification was secured. 1 died of wounds, 1 missing. The majority of these were caused by hostile machine gun fire, which was brought to bear upon the parties as they returned to our line."

Arthur Charles Burch is shown to have been Killed in action and was buried at the Berkshire Cemetery, Hainaut, Belgium.

The UK, Army Registers of Soldiers' Effects show that a Death grant of £2.6s.9d and a War Gratuity of £3.0s.0d were paid to his widow Louisa. The latter payment was made in 1919 by which time she had remarried to Frederick Sylvester Wilson (1888-1966) at St Peter's, Portland, Dorset on 21 April 1919.

The British War Medal and the Victory Medal were awarded and sent to his widow.

---

39   Marriage record GRO ref Weymouth, June 1907, Vol 5a, p 665

The Berkshire Cemetery, Hainaut – from CWGC website

Arthur Charles Burch is not included on the Devon Roll of Honour, but he appears on Dawlish Boys' School Roll of Honour.

Dawlish War memorial inscription: BURCH A.C.   PTE.   WILTSHIRE REGT. (side panel, west face)

Devon Heritage site info: No information is shown for the entries on the west facing panel.

Last known address: Portland, Dorset
Next of kin: Bessie Newman, mother

References: CWGC.org.uk   Wiltshire Regiment war diary
St Gregory the Great, Baptism Register
Subscription websites for the following:
Ancestry.co.uk family trees and UK Census records 1861- 1911
UK, Registers of Seamen's Services   UK, WW1 Service Medal & Award Rolls 1914-20
UK, Army Registers of Soldiers' Effects   UK, Soldiers died in the Great War

George PIKE

Born Starcross, 10 June 1890   Died 19 February 1917, aged 26
Able Seaman, 236053   H.M.S.THUNDERER

George was third son of Harry and Emily Pike. Harry's family came from Kenton, and he was the son of John Pike (1821-) and Sarah (1823-). Harry was an agricultural worker who had been born at Kenton and his mother was from Okehampton. Harry Pike (1863-1935) and Emily Pike (1861-1896) had married[40] in 1885 in St Thomas' district.

Emily was one of eleven children of Henry and Louisa Pike from Okehampton. There is no known connection between the two Pike families.

In 1891, Harry and Emily were living at 1 Staplake Cottage, Starcross with three children;
    Henry James (1887-)
    William (1889-)
    George (1890-1917)
There were three more children before Emily died[41] in the December quarter of 1896.
    Amelia (1892-)
    Annie (1894-)
    Edith   (1895 -)

The 1901 census shows Harry Pike as a widower with five children at the same address, William, George, Amelia, Annie, and Edith.

> There is a Naval service record for a Henry James Pike, born in Exeter on 20 May 1887, who joined the Royal Navy as a Stoker, 2nd Class on 19 November 1908, aged 21. His previous occupation was farm labourer. He transferred to General Service as a Stoker 1st Class on 11 October 1909 and was invalided on 1 August 1923 by which time he had served as a Petty Officer Stoker, and the last seagoing posting was to H.M.S.KING GEORGE V.

George Pike joined the Royal Navy as a Boy Seaman on the 13th March 1906. On reaching 18 years of age he signed on for 12 years' service.

In 1911 he was an Able Seaman (A.B.) and is shown as a Visitor at Staplake Cottage, Starcross where his older brother William was a boarder with Thomas Knowles. Their family appears to have separated and their father was a lodger with Charles Manning at 2 Chapel Street, Dawlish.

George was drafted to H.M.S.THUNDERER in June 1912, part of the first Ship's Company and stayed until he was posted to R.N. Barracks, Devonport (H.M.S.VIVID) on 1st October 1915. He appears to have shown himself well and was 'Passed educationally for Petty Officer on 2 June 1914'.

George Pike married Rose Mary Shorland in July 1915.

> Rose Mary Shorland was the daughter of William and Mary Ann Shorland and was born at Powderham. They had ten children but William, a farm labourer, died ca 1890, and Mary Ann is a widow in the 1891 census. It appears that Mary Ann remarried to Henry Cann, for in 1901 she is living with two children, Frank, 19, an agricultural labourer, and Rose M Shorland, 12, at 1 Shapter's Court, Old Town Street, Dawlish.

> By 1911, Rose Mary Shorland was living as a servant at 9 Queen Street, Dawlish.

---

40   Marriage GRO ref St Thomas, 1885, Oct-Dec, Vol 5b, p 100
41   Death GRO ref St Thomas,1896, Oct-Dec, vol 5b, p47

George and Rose Mary Pike had no children and she died a widow on 5th June 1943 at 38 Brook Street, Dawlish, leaving her effects to Walter Shorland, a farm labourer.

George was invalided out of the service on 11th December 1915 (the indistinct handwritten note on his service record appears to show 'pulmonary tuberculosis') . It seems likely that he died in hospital in Exeter as that is the reference on the Devon Roll of Honour.

The Devon Roll of Honour states Pike, George, A.B.   H.M.S.THUNDERER, 19 Feb 1917, Exeter

Dawlish War memorial inscription: PIKE G.   A.B.   H.M.S.THUNDERER

Devon Heritage site info:

236053 Able Seaman George Pike of the Royal Navy, H.M.S.THUNDERER. Husband of Rose Mary Pike of 38 Brook Street, Dawlish. Born in Dawlish 10 June 1890. Died 19 February 1917 aged 26. Buried in Dawlish Cemetery.

Commonwealth War Graves entry: PIKE,   GEORGE   Able Seaman   236053   19/02/1917   Age: 26   Royal Navy H.M.S. "Thunderer."   Grave Ref: 779.   Dawlish Cemetery   Husband of Rose Mary Pike, of 38, Brook St., Dawlish.

Last known address: 38 Brook Street, Dawlish

Next of kin: Rose Mary Pike, wife, (1889-1943)

H.M.S.THUNDERER was the third Orion class battleship built for the Royal Navy and was the last vessel to be constructed by Thames Iron Works and completed in June 1912. She was the last and largest warship ever built on the River Thames. By a margin of £1000 she was the most expensive battleship of the 1909 Construction programme built, and after her completion her builders declared bankruptcy. She proved to be the slowest (by a knot) of the Orion class on trials.

During World War 1, THUNDERER served in the 2nd Battle Squadron of the Grand Fleet. In December 1914 she was refitted. She was present with 2BS at the Battle of Jutland, 31 May 1916, firing 37 13.5" shells. She suffered no damage.

As a result of the Washington Naval Convention she was decomissioned in 1921. From 1922 she served as a cadet ship, the sole surviving ship of her class until she was sold for scrap in December 1926.

References:
Naval Service record (National Archives, Kew)
http://www.forumeerstewereldoorlog.nl
refs via subscription sites: Census records.   Forces War records.
Pike and Shorland family trees – ancestry.co.uk

Edward Maurice SCOTT

Born 8 November 1893, Woking, Surrey   Died 24 February 1917, Iraq, aged 23
Private 240474   The Buffs (East Kent Regiment) 1st/5th Battalion

Edward Maurice Scott was the son of Samuel Arthur Scott (1857-1904) and Mathilde Caroline Elise Scott (1855-1946). He was born in 1893[42] and Baptised at St Mary's, Horsell, Woking on 28 March 1894.

His mother, Mathilde Caroline Elise Typke, was the eldest child of Herman Typke (1820-1909), born in Berlin, Prussia, a naturalised British subject, and Caroline Typke (1829-1904) born in Switzerland. Herman was a watchmaker employing four people in his London business and lived at 3 Wimpole Street, Marylebone in 1881.

Samuel and Mathilde married[43] in 1883 in Marylebone and by 1891 they had moved to New Malden and had two children, Samuel G (1886-) and Joyce Eda (1891-).
Samuel became a bank clerk and by 1901 the family had moved again to Pine Cottage, Star Hill, Woking. They had four children at home, Samuel G, Joyce Eda, **Edward M (1893-1917)** and John Douglas (1895-).

At some point after 1901 Samuel Arthur Scott and his wife moved to Dawlish, possibly for his health. A Death Certificate shows that he died on the 20th September 1904 at No 15 Brunswick Place, Dawlish. His wife, Mathilde, informed the registrar and it shows that Arthur was 49 and a pensioned banker's clerk. He died of leucocythemia, pneumonia 14 days, and heart failure. Mathilde continued to live in Dawlish and is there with her daughter Joyce Eda Scott in the 1911 census. At that time the younger boys were at boarding school, Woodfield House, Wolverley, Nr Kidderminster. (Edward) Maurice Scott was 17 and (John) Douglas Scott was 16.
Mathilde (Matilda) died in the Chichester registration district in the September quarter of 1946, aged 91. Her sisters Anna Clara Elise Typke and Ida Elise Typke died in the same registration district in 1949 and 1937, and further research may show that they supported each other in old age.

There is a record that Edward enlisted in the Buffs at Ashford, Kent, but there is no record of the date.

1/5th (The Weald of Kent) Battalion Territorial Force

04.08.1914 Formed at Ashford as part of the Kent Brigade of the Home Counties Division, then moved to Dover, Canterbury and then Sandwich.
30.10.1914 Embarked for India from Southampton where the Home Counties Division was broken up.
December 1915, Landed at Basra and joined the 35th Indian Brigade of the 7th Indian Division.
February 1916 Became corps troops and formed composite unit with 2 companies of the 1/4th Hampshire Battalion.
12.05.1916 Transferred to the **35th Indian Brigade** of the 14th Indian Division.

---

42   Birth record GRO ref Guildford District, Jan-Mar 1894,Vol 2a, p58
43   Marriage record GRO ref 1883, July-September, Marylebone, Vol 1a, p 1027

The brigade remained with the division for the rest of the war and took part in a large number of small actions: the Advance to the Hai and Capture of the Khudaira Bend 14 December 1916 – 19 January 1917, the Capture of the Hai Salient 25 January – 5 February 1917, the Capture of the Dahra Bend 9 – 16 February, the Capture of Sannaiyat 17 – 24 February, the Passage of the Tigris 23 – 24 February. The re-capture of Kut, 24th February (ex-Wikipedia).

Sir Frederick Maude reported on the operations which led to the capture of Sannaiyat on 24th February 1917, opening the passage of the Tigris. Edward Scott died on that day.
"The capture of the Sannaiyat position, which the Turks believed to be impregnable, had only been accomplished after a fierce struggle, in which our infantry, closely supported by our artillery, displayed great gallantry and endurance against a brave and determined enemy. The latter had again suffered severely. Many trenches were choked with corpses, and the open ground where counter-attacks had taken place was strewn with them.
Early in the morning of February 25th the cavalry and Lieut.-Gen, Marshall's force moved northwest in pursuit of the enemy, whose rearguards had retired in the night."

Edward Maurice Scott is shown as 'killed in action' and a Death Grant of £1.16s.7d was paid to his mother, Mathilde. The amount suggests that he had not long been serving with the regiment at the time of his death.
A larger War Gratuity was split £5.10s.0d to his mother and £2.15s.0d each to his brothers Samuel and John Douglas.

Commonwealth War Graves entry: SCOTT, EDWARD MAURICE   Private   240474
24/02/1917   Age: 23   The Buffs (East Kent Regiment), 1st/5th Bn.
Grave Ref: XXIX. B. 105/116.   Amara War Cemetery, Iraq.
Son of the late Samuel A. Scott, and of Mathilde C. E. Scott, formerly of Woking, Surrey.

E M Scott appears on the Devon Roll of Honour but date and place of death are not shown.

Dawlish War memorial inscription: SCOTT E.M.   PTE.   THE BUFFS

Last known address: 15 Brunswick Place, Dawlish
Next of kin: Mother, Mathilde Scott

References:
Copy of Death Certificate for Samuel Arthur Scott
Subscription website for;
Census records
UK, Army Registers of Soldiers' Effects
Baptism record (St Mary, Horsell, Woking)
http://www.nationalarchives.gov.uk/pathways/firstworldwar/battles/mesopotamia.htm
http://www.firstworldwar.com/source/baghdad_maude.htm

March 1917

Francis George LARCOMBE

Born Williton, Somerset 1884   Died France, 30th March 1917, aged 33
Lance Corporal, No 26094   Devonshire Regiment, 2nd Battalion

Francis George Larcombe was one of four children of John Clarke Larcombe and Georgiana Mary Wood. John C Larcombe (1858-1909) was a Gamekeeper, born in Nettlecombe, Somerset, and Georgiana (1859-1941) was a Certificated Schoolmistress born in Chepstow, Monmouthshire. They had married in 1881[44].

In 1891, John and Georgiana Larcombe were living at a cottage in Lowton, Pitminster, Somerset with two children, Annie C (1882-) and Francis G (1884-1917). In the following year Henry John Larcombe was born and in 1895 they had another daughter, Laura Mary Larcombe.
In 1901 (Francis) George was 17 and a cowherd on Slade Farm, Dulverton.

Francis George Larcombe married Ellen Susan Millman (1884-) in 1909[45] at St Thomas the Martyr, Exeter. Ellen Susan Larcombe was a dress maker. Ellen came from a large Exeter family living in St Thomas and was the daughter of Frederick J and Ellen M Millman.

Francis George Larcombe became a Freemason and member of the Salem Lodge in Barton Terrace, Dawlish. He is remembered there on their Roll of Honour.
Francis became Head Gamekeeper of the Luscombe Estate, Dawlish and in 1911 the family was recorded as living at Beech Grove Lodge, Dawlish with their first child, Ellen (1910-) and a lodger, the Under Gamekeeper, John Beer. They had a second child, John[46] in 1912.
> John later married Madeline Sumner (1913-1974) in Frome, Somerset in 1940 and died in that district in 1990, aged 78. He was a highway engineer, as recorded in the Probate record of 25 May 1954 from the Will of Francis George Larcombe.

Francis' mother Georgiana Larcombe was now, in 1911, a widow and living at Marsh Green, Rockbeare, with her second son, Henry John Larcombe, a farmer, and her youngest daughter Laura Mary Larcombe (1895-). Georgiana died in 1941[47].

It is not known when **Francis** enlisted nor where, neither do Medal Rolls Index Cards give the date of his entry into France. It might be supposed that he joined when conscription took effect in 1916, since the Death Grant paid to his widow was £1.17s.2d, a modest sum. *The Dawlish Gazette of 14th April 1917* mentions that he had only been on active service for three months when he died.

In March 1917 the Germans were falling back to the newer and deeply defended Hindenburg Line. General Haig gave orders for a general advance all along the line to start on March 17th. This was conducted with caution as the retreating Germans had left booby traps and hidden machine gun nests to delay the pursuing troops. After a long period of trench warfare the open battlefield was a new experience. The 2nd Devons had another new experience encountering German cavalry, which was eventually driven back. On the 25th there was a night attack on the village of Lieramont

---

44   Marriage GRO ref Williton district, 1881, July-Sept, Vol 5c,   p 413
45   Marriage GRO Ref St Thomas district, July- Sept 1909, Vol 5b, p116
46   Birth record GRO ref 1912, July- Sept, Newton Abbot district, vol 5b, p 158
47   Death record GRO ref Middleton, Lancs, Dec 1941, Vol 8d, p 750

which was defended by thick wire and infantry. Two days later cavalry patrols found Lieramont evacuated and the 2nd Devons moved up to occupy it.

The enemy was beginning to stiffen resistance and an attack on Heudicourt on the 29th-30th March failed. A fresh assault was ordered on the 30th and the 2nd Devons followed a barrage that lifted at 4.15pm to attack from the south. There was sharp fighting with rifle and machine-gun resistance, but by 6.45pm all objectives had been secured.

Francis George Larcombe is shown to have been killed in action on the 30th March.
Commonwealth War Graves entry: LARCOMBE, F G   Lance Corporal   26094   30/03/1917
Age: 33   Devonshire Regiment, 2nd Bn.   Grave Ref: 1. Heudicourt Communal Cemetery, Somme, France
Son of Mrs. Larcombe, of Marsh Green, Exeter, and the late John Larcombe; husband of Ellen Susan Larcombe, of Beech Grove Lodge, Luscombe, Dawlish.

He appears on the Devon Roll of Honour, but no date or place of death shown.
Dawlish War memorial inscription: LARCOMBE F.G.   L/CORPL.   DEVON REGT.

Last known address: Beech Grove Lodge, Luscombe, Dawlish
Next of kin: Ellen Susan Larcombe, widow
Death announcement in *The Dawlish Gazette of 28th April, 1917*
"LARCOMBE
Mrs Larcombe has received the official announcement that
her husband, Corpl F.G.Larcombe, fell in action March 30th, 1917
The blow was great, the shock severe,
To part with one we loved so dear"

The Service of Commemoration on the centenary of his death was held in the Private Chapel at Luscombe Castle by kind permission of Mr David Hoare.
References:
Free Birth Marriage Death records

The Devonshire Regiment, pages 237-240 (Dawlish Library reference collection)
Records from Ancestry.co.uk subscription website:
    Census data for 1891,1901 and 1911
    Porter-Popham File 2015 family tree (ancestry.co.uk)
    UK, Army Registers of Soldiers' Effects
    Probate records for Francis George Larcombe 1917 and John Larcombe 1954

James Henry Hill

Born Dawlish, 1st April 1891   Died April 10th, 1917, aged 26

Private 10014   Royal Army Medical Corps

James Henry Hill was the son of Henry John Hill and great grandson of John and Ann Heel/Hill. The surname appears spelled Heel in 1851, but later census entries adopt the spelling Hill. John (1808-1871), a farm labourer, was born in Moreton, Devon.

The 1841 census return shows John and Ann Hill, living at Heavy Gate, Dawlish, with their first child Elizabeth,2, and her younger brother John (1840-).

The 1851 census shows the family as living in Merrifuls(?) Row, Dawlish.

The family was:

John Heel (sic), Head	Marr	40	(1808-1871)	Farm labourer, born	Moreton
Ann "	wife	33	(1818-)		born Dawlish
Samuel "	son	9	(1842-)		"
Mary "	dau	7	(1844-)		"
Henry "	**son**	**6**	**(1845-)**	grandfather to James Henry	"
William "	son	3	(1848-1924)		"
Emily Sarah	dau	9 mo	(1850-)		"

From later census data the further children were in 1861

Thomas "	son	(1852-)
Sarah Jane "	dau	(1855-)
William "	son	(1859-)

Henry does not appear with the family in 1861 but was a farm servant, aged 15, at Southwood Farm, Dawlish for Henry W Holman.

Henry Hill (1845-) married Elizabeth Cox (nee Coombes) in 1870. Both Henry and Elizabeth were born in Dawlish. Elizabeth was a widow, born to James and Eliza Coombe/s in Dawlish ca 1846.

> There is another link between the two families when Henry Coombes (1840-66) married Elizabeth Hill (1839-) in 1863. Henry Coombes died in 1866 and Elizabeth Coombes then married Thomas Stoyle in 1869 (q.v. Walter Stoyle in Dawlish WW1, died 13/03/1915)
> The surname is spelled variously Coomb/Coombe/-Coombes in different documents.
> The Coombes family lived in Old Town Street, Dawlish (1851 census) and comprised:

James Coombes	Head, marr,	37	Labourer	born	Newton
Eliza "	wife,	36			Alphington
Joshua "	son	13			Dawlish
Henry (1840-1866)	son	11	(to marry Elizabeth Hill)		Dawlish
Eliza	dau	8			Newton
Elizabeth (1846-)	dau	6	(to marry Henry Hill)		Dawlish
John	son	2			"

Elizabeth Coombes had first married Charles Cox on 7th November, 1868[48], but the marriage was short-lived as he died and was buried on 17th May 1869, aged 24[49]. Charles Cox is possibly the agricultural labourer working for James Carpenter at Higher Rixdale Farm in 1861 and is shown as

---

48   Marriage ref GRO 1868, Oct-Dec, East Stonehouse, vol 5b, p 131

being born in Dawlish which would explain the link to Elizabeth Coombes. He later joined the Royal Marines and was a Private based in East Stonehouse (Plymouth).

Henry Hill and Elizabeth Cox were married in the Zion Chapel, East Teignmouth on 22nd May 1870 and his profession is shown as 'Marine', but he was unable to sign his name, leaving his mark 'X' only. The witnesses were Thomas Stoyle and Mary Hill.

In 1871 they are living at 41 St Paul's Street, East Stonehouse, Plymouth and Henry was a Private in the Royal Marines. They had two children at the census, Henry John Hill and William T Hill.

Henry and Elizabeth Hill had a total of nine children all of which survived to the 1911 census, by which time they had been married 41 years. The children were all born in Dawlish and were:

Henry John 1867-1921	**father to James Henry,** married Bessie Dawe (see below)
William T 1870-	became an Ostler (1891)
Charles Henry 1873-	married Amy Nixon and they had six children
Frederick J 1876-	became a Telegraph Messenger, G.P.O.
Thomas 1878-	moved to London, Shoreditch, (see above)
Albert J 1880-	became a butcher's assistant (1901)
Lily 1882-	became a laundress (1901)
Ethel 1885-	" "
Arthur 1887-	

By 1881 Henry (1845-) must have completed his time as a Marine because he appears as a mason's labourer in Dawlish with his wife and three of the children, William, Frederick and Albert, living in Stockton Road. Henry later took work as a Water Bailiff (1901).

Henry, 66, and Elizabeth, 65, appear again in the 1911 census living at Queen House, Old Town Street, where they had been for 20 years. Only their daughter Ethel, 26, and a grandson, Cyril (1903-) who had been born on St Mary's, Scilly Isles, were living with them. The three adults were engaged in laundry work.

Their eldest son, Henry John Hill (1867-1921) married Bessie Dawe (1860-1953) on 30 August 1890 in the parish Church, Dawlish. Bessie was the sister of Clara Kate Blackmore, nee Dawe (1863-1932), who was the mother of Charles Henry Blackmore (1890- 29/08/1917) q.v.

They lived at 7 Badlake Hill and Henry John Hill was a house painter and Bessie a dressmaker. **James Henry Hill** was born on the 1st April 1891 at Badlake Hill. An aunt, Clara Blackmore (*para,above*), was present at the birth. There were four further children but only three in all survived to the 1911 census:

James Henry,	1891-1917, subject of this profile
Frances Edward	(1894-1970) and
Russell	(1897-24/11/1920), who was also to appear on Dawlish War
Memorial.	

In 1901 Henry John and Bessie Hill were living at 8 Hatcher Street and ten years later were at Stuart House, 31 Strand, with Frances Edward Hill, now a plumber, and Russell, still at school.

James Henry Hill enlisted at Leicester and the Medal Roll Index Card shows that he first served in H.S. on 31-10-14. The 'H.S.' may refer to Hospital Ship because a report in the *Dawlish Gazette of*

---

49   Death record GRO ref, 1869, May, Newton Abbot, vol 5b, p 92

2 January 1915 shows that he contributed to an entertainment for men of the 3rd Devons, based in the town.

> "Others contributing were Pte Jim Hill, (Son of Mr H Hill, Dawlish, who belongs to the R.A.M.C. of the Regular Army, and is now attached to No 1 Base, 'Carisbrook Castle', hospital ship)".

The ferrying of wounded men from France to Britain was carried out by marked Hospital Ships, a number of which ran between Le Havre and Southampton, whence men would be taken by train to other larger hospitals including Netley, overlooking Southampton Water. R.A.M.C. personnel would be allocated to a number of different ships according to need.

Later in 1915, on the 19th June, James Henry Hill married[50] Ethel Flora Grumbridge (1891-1943?) in the Parish Church, Dawlish. It is not known if there were children of this marriage.

In 1917 Private James Henry Hill, R.A.M.C. was serving aboard the Hospital Ship SALTA which struck a mine and sank off Le Havre. The following account is recorded in www.wrecksite.eu

> "In 1915 SS SALTA was requisitioned by the Admiralty as a hospital ship. On April 10th, 1917, while in convoy with 3 other hospital ships in front of Le Havre, the pilot didn't follow the 'follow me' sign from HMS Diamond and pulled to port to let the other ships pass first. This proved fatal as she immediately struck a mine laid by the German submarine UC-26 (Matthias Graf von Schmettow) and sank in 9 minutes, 1/2 mile North of the Whistle Buoy.
>
> Despite the rescue effort of 2 destroyers, 4 trawlers and a pilot vessel, only 74 from the 250 on board are saved. P-26 in an attempt to help, also struck a mine and was broken in two pieces. 40 of the crew of 59 from P-26 were rescued by P-19."

Commonwealth War Graves entry: HILL, JAMES HENRY   Private   10014   10/04/1917
Age: 26   Royal Army Medical Corps, attd. H.M.H.S. "Salta."   Grave Ref: "Salta" Memorial.
<u>Ste. Marie Cemetery, Le Havre</u>.
A memorial in Plot 62 marks the graves of 24 casualties from the hospital ship 'Salta' and her patrol boat, sunk by a mine on 10 April 1917. The memorial also commemorates by name the soldiers, nurses and merchant seamen lost from the 'Salta' whose bodies were not recovered.

Son of Henry John and Bessie Hill, of Stuart House, Strand, Dawlish, Devon.

He is recorded on the Devon Roll of Honour, but no date or place of death are shown

Dawlish War memorial inscription: HILL JAMES   Pte.   R.A.M.C.

Devon Heritage site info:
10014 Private James Henry Hill of the Royal Army Medical Corps, attached to H M Hospital Ship *Salta*. Son of Henry John and Bessie Hill, of Stuart House, Strand, Dawlish. Born in Dawlish in the September quarter of 1893 (*incorrect-ed*). Died 10 April 1917 aged 26.

---

50   Marriage record GRO ref 1915 April-June, Newton Abbot Vol 5b, p 301

A headstone in Dawlish cemetery was erected to his wife:

In loving memory of
ETHEL (F GRUMBRIDGE)
who died Jan 8th 1943 (? inscription eroded)
Aged (?)

Also of J H Hill
Her devoted husband
who lost his life in the sinking
of H.M.Hospital Ship 'SALTA'
April 10th 1917, Aged 26
Next of kin: Widow, Ethel Hill
References:
GRO Birth and Marriage Certificates
wrecksite.eu
Hocking C., Dictionary of Disasters at
Sea during the age of Steam.
Way family tree by June Snell
via   subscription   website
(Ancestry.co.uk):
UK, Soldiers died in the Great War
UK, Army Registers of Soldiers' Effects
Medal Roll Index Cards
UK, WW1 Service Medal & Award Rolls
Adams family tree

.   .   .   .

The start of the 20th century saw Britain at the zenith of its imperial power.

Her flag flew over 24% of the world surface and 412 million people.

But the signs of decline had begun, with productivity falling behind Germany and the USA, and above all, Britain remained a class ridden society.

Great riches were enjoyed by the ruling elite, whilst the living standards of farm workers and artisans had begun to fall behind others, such as the Dutch, although still somewhat better than the French peasantry.

Australia was shown as a beacon of hope, a new confident nation that asserted it's right to self rule in 1901, and offered a fresh start to a young man, who may have hungered for new opportunities.

It was legally defined by the Privy Council in 1898 as "Terra Nullius" - a land empty of people - conveniently ignoring the fact of Aboriginal inhabitants, and laying vast swathes of land open for settlement.

The opening of the Suez canal and the development of steam ships had cut the journey down to just 35 days, and at some point George Carter West became one of those brave young men that cut their ties with home and family and settled in the new city of Brisbane.

George Carter WEST

Born Dawlish, Q2, 1877   Died France, 15th April 1917, aged 39
Gunner 543   2nd Divn, Heavy Trench Mortars, Australian Field Artillery

George Carter West was the son of Frederick Pike West and cousin of Albert Henry West (q.v.), who was to die in Flanders near Ypres on the 4th October 1917.

Their joint grandparents were Edward and Fanny West. Edward West (1813-1874) was born in Kenton and was a gardener. He married Fanny Pike who was born in Exeter(1817-1892), on 30th August 1835.

In 1861, the grandparents lived at 9 Regent Street, Dawlish with six children:

William Charles West (1841-1921)
Mary Ann West (1846-1924)
Frederick Pike West (1849-1923)   father of George Carter West
Thomas Pike West (1851-1931)   father of Albert Henry West
George Edward West (1854-1902)   worked for the Post Office, Dawlish,1911
Robert John West (1856-1919)

The eldest daughter, Frances West (1839-1893) was living away as a servant, a position she held in various households over the following thirty years.

In 1871 they were living at 15 Regent Street and Frederick was then 22 and working as a coachman.

Frederick P West married[51] Nancy Carter (1850-1901) in 1873.

By 1881, Frederick and Nancy were living at Bay View Cottage, Richmond Place and had five children, Roseina, 7, Edward, 6, Sydney, 2, and Emily, 11 months.

George Carter West had been born in Dawlish in 1877[52]. At the time of 1881 census George C West, 4, was a visitor to William and Kate Carter at North Street, Otterton. William was a butcher and the son of a farmer, and it is interesting to note that George learned butchery before joining the army. No clear relationship has been found between Nancy West (nee Carter) and William Carter but they were both born in Harpford.

By 1891, Frederick and Nancy had moved to Manor Place. Frederick followed his father as a gardener and his eldest son, Edward, now 16, had been invalided out of the Royal Navy. There were three more children, Charles D, 8, Herbert P, 6, and Keturah H,2.

There are no entries to be found for George in 1891 or 1901 but *The Dawlish Gazette of 5th May 1917* records his service as a cavalry man in the South African War. He served a 12 year term in the 20th Hussars, probably from ca. 1894-1906 for soon after this he sailed for Australia.

Nancy West died early in 1901 and does not appear with Frederick in the census at 5 Manor Hill, with Rose, 27, a domestic/cook, Emily, 20, Herbert, 16, a labourer, and Lena, 12. There is no mention of the invalid Edward J West (1875-).

---

51   Marriage record Newton Abbot 1873 Jan-Mar vol 5b, p 168
52   Birth record N.A.district, April-June, Vol 5b, page 116

In 1911 Frederick is shown as living at 5 Manor Place which is the address given for his next of kin on George's enlistment. Only Herbert, 26, ex-naval invalid, and Helena (Lena), 22, were still at home.

George C West went to Australia in 1906 and it appears that he worked as a butcher at "Meat-works" in Brisbane before he joined up eight years later.

His enlistment papers show that he joined the Australian Imperial Force on 14th December 1914 at Townsville, Queensland for the duration of the War. His civilian trade was as a butcher.

When the United Kingdom declared war on Germany at the start of World War 1, the Australian government followed without hesitation. By the end of the war, almost 20% of those who served in the Australian forces had been born in the United Kingdom, even though nearly all enlistments had occurred in Australia.
The Australian government had pledged to supply 20,000 men, organised as one infantry division and one light horse brigade plus supporting units.

Departing from Western Australia on 1 November 1914, the Australian Infantry Force (AIF) was sent initially to British-controlled Egypt to pre-empt any attack by the Ottoman Empire, and with a view to opening another front against the Central Powers. The AIF had four infantry brigades with the first three making up the 1st Division. The 4th Brigade was joined with the sole New Zealand infantry brigade to form the New Zealand and Australian Division.

George C West served first with the infantry in the 9th Battalion 3rd Rifle Brigade. He was appointed on 8th February 1915 to the 3rd Rein *(sic)* 9th Infantry. He was a Private and attached to the 25th Battalion, 7th Brigade when he embarked at Brisbane by H.M.A.T.AENEAS[53] on 29th June 1915. West embarked at Alexandria on 4th September 1915 to join the M.E.F. on the Gallipoli peninsula. He was promoted to Corporal on the 11th September and appears on the casualty list on the 19th at Beauchops Hill.

Australian soldiers landing at ANZAC Cove
The combined Australian and New Zealand Army Corps (ANZAC), commanded by British General William Birdwood, went into action when Allied forces landed on the Gallipoli peninsula on 25 April 1915. The Battle of Gallipoli would last for eight months of bloody stalemate. By the end of the campaign, Australian casualties were 8,700 killed and 19,000 wounded or sick. Allied forces were withdrawn from the beaches of Gallipoli by the first week of January 1916, without further casualties.

West was taken to hospital at Mudros and thence to Alexandria where he arrived on 9th January 1916. He left Alexandria on the 14th March to sail to join the British Expeditionary Force (BEF) on the Western Front and disembarked at Marseilles on 19th March. At some point he held the rank of Sergeant.

On 11th June 1916 he transferred from the 25th Battalion to the 2nd Division Heavy Trench Mortar Battery. West was disciplined with a reprimand on the 21st July for quitting the ranks without permission while on the march.

---

53   H.M.A.T. His Majesty's Australian Transport

On 4th October 1916 he reverted to the rank of Gunner at his own request and became a batman.

On 24th February 1917 he was detached for duty with the 5th Infantry Brigade HQ. He was batman to Captain Christie at a Brigade HQ at Bullecourt when, on 15th April, a shell landed on the HQ and he was killed outright. *The Dawlish Gazette of 2nd June 1917* reported, "Lieutenant Stanley Gritten of the Australian Imperial Brigade has written to Miss Lena West detailing the circumstances of the death of her brother, Corpl. George West, second son of Mr Frederick West of 5 Manor Place, Dawlish. He says that on the 15th April he was suddenly called upon to assist in repelling an enemy attack. While thus engaged a large shell burst close by and your brother was killed instantly by a fragment which hit him on the forehead. All West's comrades join with me in expressing their deep and sincere sympathy with you and your family in your great loss. Your brother met his death while nobly doing his duty, and the General wishes you to accept his sympathy."

A fellow soldier, Gunner Higgins, stated that *"He was called 'Westie'. He was about the gamest man I ever saw and the best N.C.O. in the Battery. All the boys will tell you that."*

His father, Frederick, by then aged 68, received a package on 14th June 1917 conveying the effects of "543 Gnr West G.C., V2 A.T.M.Bty, A.I.F."

G C West is shown on the Devon Roll of Honour, but with an incorrect date of death. He is also on the Dawlish Boys' School Roll of Honour.

Dawlish War memorial inscription: WEST G.C.   CORPL.   AUSTRAL; I.F.

Devon Heritage site info: G.C.WEST 543 Gunner George Carter West of the 2nd Division, The Trench Mortar Battery of the Australian Field Artillery. Parents not yet identified. Born in the June Quarter of 1877. Died 15 April 1917 aged 40. He was an Australian Citizen.

Commonwealth War Graves entry: WEST, G C Gunner 543   15/04/1917   Australian Field Artillery 2nd Div. T.M.Battery   FRANCE - VILLERS-BRETONNEUX MEMORIAL The memorial is the Australian National Memorial erected to commemorate all Australian soldiers who fought in France and Belgium during the First World War, to their dead, and especially to name those of the dead whose graves are not known. *(photo below, from CWGC.org.uk)*

Next of kin: Father, Frederick P West, 5 Manor Place, Old Town Street, Dawlish

References:

Free Birth Marriage Death index   Australian War Memorial, Red Cross Records
Declaration by Gnr Higgins Aust Corps, H.T.M.Battery
Via subscription website, Ancestry.co.uk: Australia WW1 Service Records, 1914-1920   -
WEST, George Carter   Census records England

The Battle of Arras, April - May 1917

The Battle of Arras claimed the lives of other Dawlish soldiers, and was set in context by Revd Roger Whitehead when giving the tribute to the next casualty at the Service of Commemoration.

"In late 1916 it was clear to the commanders on both sides that the war was in effect in stalemate on the Western front.

For the British, the Battle of the Somme had been a hugely expensive failure; the same had been true for the French at the Battle of Verdun. But in both countries there was increasing pressure from public opinion for an end to the war – an end that had to be victorious. On the Entente side, the French Prime Minister and the Defence Minister were forced to resign under public pressure for victory. In Britain, Lloyd George was also under pressure but less so.

In Russia, the growing discontent with the war and its less than competent delivery was causing unrest which was to lead to the Russians admitting that they could not support the Entente on the Western front – and, of course, it led on to the fall of the Tsar and the withdrawal of Russia from the war.

The United States was increasingly being drawn to take sides, especially as a result of German U-boat attacks on American shipping, and in April 2017 the USA declared war on Germany, though it was nearly a year before it could organise an army to fight in Europe. So, the Entente planned a major French offensive in the south and a diversionary British offensive around Arras further north to relieve pressure on the French.

On the German side, Hindenburg's tactics were defence in depth. A series of defensive lines were created, one behind the other, with no less than two rear battlefields being created to absorb and repulse the attack if necessary. Hindenburg's expressed aim was that "the attackers would fight themselves to a standstill and then the reserves would be neutralised". However, lack of materials and a cold winter (which delayed the hardening of concrete) meant that not all the preparatory work was completed.

In preparing for their offensive, the British had learned lessons from the Somme. This included the use of aerial surveillance by the Royal Flying Corps (often at great human cost because the German planes were superior) and the formation of the 1st Field Survey Company, Royal Engineers, which was able to detect the emplacements of German heavy guns from their sound and flashes.

This enabled British artillery to be targeted on the heavy guns, and at the start of the battle of Arras it was reckoned that 80% of German heavy guns were neutralised.

The British had also learned to use 'creeping bombardments' in which the artillery laid down a wall of firepower in front of the advancing infantry to protect them from machine gun fire, allowing, what the manuals called, "fire and manoeuvre". In preparing for the war many miles of underground shelters were built so that up to 24,500 men could be safely sheltered in gas proof underground areas lit by electricity, and their ammunition and other needs could be brought to the front by trams.

The first day of the attack was a major success. The British gained more ground in a day than at any time in the war up to that day, and with relatively small casualties. However the German defences held and the battle descended into the same trench warfare that had marked the

Western front for 2½ years with very many casualties. It did not divert enough German troops from the south for the French to win the Battle of Ainse.

Although historians generally consider the battle a British victory, in the wider context of the front, it had very little impact on the strategic or tactical situation.

Ludendorff later commented: "No doubt exceedingly important strategic objects lay behind the British attack but I have never been able to discover what they were".

Hubert John BRIGHT

Born Holcombe 1ˢᵗ January 1897   Died France 17 April 1917, aged 20
Corporal 25800   Machine Gun Corps

At first sight Hubert John Bright has no clear connection to Dawlish for his parents moved from home to home wherever there was work. His grandfather, John Bright (1845-1906), was a farmer who was born in Colyton and married Jane Dunster from Dunkerswell. They had a large family and Frederick Bright(1875-1932) was their fourth son, born in Colyton.

Hubert's father, Frederick Bright married Charlotte Jarman(1874-1946) of Holcombe[54] in 1896.

Twin boys were born in Holcombe on New Year's Day 1897, Hubert John and Reginald Charles Bright (died 19ᵗʰ February 1918, q.v.). Their births were registered by Agnes Jarman who could have been the older sister of Charlotte, their mother, or Agnes the wife of Charles Jarman. (The Jarman family profile is recorded in the note on Thomas Frederick Jarman who died on 22 June 1915, q.v.)

The census of 1901 shows that Frederick and Charlotte Bright were living at Kerswell Cottage, Kenn with four children, the twins Hubert John and Reginald Charles, 4, Frederick Leonard, 2 born in Honiton and Florence Agnes Rose, 1 month and born in Exminster. Frederick was 26 and an agricultural labourer. The third son, Frederick Leonard, born in 1898, served in World War One and returned to the Culm Valley with pulmonary TB. He married May Salter and they had a daughter called Sylvia. Frederick was in and out of hospital and eventually died in an Exeter sanatorium on July 24th 1928.

Hubert was Reginald's twin. Whatever similarities they may have had as children, they were to take different paths in life. Today we can barely comprehend that, a hundred years ago, boys became virtual men at the age of 14, the year they left school. There were no teenagers, just young adults. Few allowances were made for what we would term today adolescent behaviour. The reality of life was that their father was an agricultural labourer who moved from place to place. In a family of nine, living in a four-roomed cottage, the boys were expected to leave home as soon as they left school and find work, any work. Reginald found work as a gardener and was living with his aunt and grandfather at the Post Office in Holcombe, Dawlish. Three years later, he had become a farm boy and may have returned to live with his parents in Clayhidon.

Frederick and Charlotte roamed across East Devon to find work as the recorded places of birth of their further children show Frederick and Charlotte Bright had at least five homes in 15 years of

---

54   GRO ref 1896 Oct-Dec, Honiton, Vol 5b, p29

marriage and more places were to follow in the years leading up to the start of the Great War. (Tribute from Clayhydon) By 1911 they were living at Burrows Farm, a few miles south of Bolham Water in the parish of Clayhidon, with their children (Frederick) Leonard, 13 born in Awliscombe, (Florence) Agnes, 10 born in Exminster, Mary (Jane), 7 born in Dalwood, Winifred, 5 also born in Dalwood, and Thomas, 3 born in Honiton. They had a niece, Vera Jarman, 2, staying with them. The census data from 1911 shows that they had seven children in all, and all still living. A further child, Harry George, was born in 1912.

Hubert left home to live in nearby Honiton as servant to a Thomasine Richards, a widow aged 63 who ran a printing business. He was engaged in general porting work. This would have been the first time that he had lived in a town of any sort. The experience may have tempted him to explore further afield. Trains then, as now, ran from Honiton to Waterloo. Evidence suggests that Hubert found a job as a manservant in London, where he may have stayed with a relative, Robert Bright. He next appears on the public record as having enlisted in the Army at Walworth, South London.

Frederick and Charlotte had moved again to Egypt Cottage, Hemyock when the War Office corresponded at Hubert's death. Frederick died in the Wellington, Somerset, district in 1932[55] aged 58.

Hubert John Bright's initial posting was to the Rifle Brigade, service number Z/502. At some point he transferred to the Machine Gun Corps, Infantry battalion, service number 25800. He entered France on the 11th January 1915.

In 1914, all infantry battalions were equipped with a machine gun section of two guns, which was increased to four in February 1915. The sections were equipped with Maxim guns, served by a subaltern and 12 men. The obsolescent Maxim had a maximum rate of fire of 500 rounds per minute, so was the equivalent of around 40 well-trained riflemen. However, production of the weapons could not keep up with the rapidly expanding army and the BEF was still 237 guns short of the full establishment in July 1915. The British Vickers company could, at most, produce 200 new weapons per week, and struggled to do that. Contracts were placed with firms in the USA, which were to produce the Vickers designs under licence.

On 2 September 1915 a definite proposal was made to the War Office for the formation of a single specialist Machine Gun Company per infantry brigade, by withdrawing the guns and gun teams from the battalions. They would be replaced at battalion level by the light Lewis machine guns and thus the firepower of each brigade would be substantially increased. The Machine Gun Corps was created by Royal Warrant on October 14 followed by an Army Order on 22 October 1915. The companies formed in each brigade would transfer to the new Corps. The MGC would eventually consist of infantry Machine Gun Companies, cavalry Machine Gun Squadrons and Motor Machine Gun Batteries. The pace of reorganisation depended largely on the rate of supply of the Lewis guns but it was completed before the Battle of the Somme in 1916. A Base Depot for the Corps was established at Camiers.

Shortly after the formation of the MGC, the Maxim guns were replaced by the Vickers, which became a standard gun for the next five decades. The Vickers machine gun is fired from a tripod and is cooled by water held in a jacket around the barrel. The gun weighed 28.5 pounds, the water another 10 and the tripod weighed 20 pounds.

---

55   GRO death ref 1932, Oct- Dec, Wellington, Somerset, Vol 5c, page 327

Bullets were assembled into a canvas belt, which held 250 rounds and would last 30 seconds at the maximum rate of fire of 500 rounds per minute. Two men were required to carry the equipment and two the ammunition. A Vickers machine gun team also had two spare men.

The 17th Machine Gun Company was part of the 17th Brigade and formed part of the 24th Division. It fought in the Battle of Arras, from 9th April to 16th May. "From this, even without records, we can reliably deduce his original unit as being the 3rd.Rifle Brigade.... in October 1915, transferred with 3rd.Rifle Brigade to 24th.Division. In 1916 the 17th Brigade suffered in the German attack at Wulverghem and then joined the Somme offensive, seeing action in the battles of Delville Wood and Guillemont.

We do not know whether Hubert served with the 3rd.Rifle Brigade or 17th.M.G.C. during these battles but both were part of 17th Brigade and he would have been at all of them with either unit. In April the following year, the Brigade was involved in seizing Vimy Ridge as part of the Battle of Arras. It was here that Hubert was killed."

The British effort was a relatively broad frontal assault between Vimy in the north-west and Bullecourt in the south-east. When the battle officially ended on 16 May, British Empire troops had made significant advances but had been unable to achieve a breakthrough. New tactics and the equipment to exploit them had been used, showing that the British had absorbed the lessons of the Battle of the Somme and could mount set-piece attacks against fortified field defences. The Arras sector then returned to the stalemate that typified most of the war on the Western Front.

Reginald Charles Bright is remembered at St George's, Holcombe where a small memorial tablet is mounted near the entrance.
He is remembered on Clayhidon's war memorial, his name besides his twin's, reunited.
Neither of the twins are listed in the Devon Roll of Honour for Dawlish, nor on the Dawlish Boys' School Roll of Honour or the Dawlish War memorial.
CWGC entry: Corporal HUBERT JOHN BRIGHT,   Service Number: 25800
Machine Gun Corps (Infantry), 17th Coy.   Died 17 April 1917, Age 20
Buried or commemorated at ARRAS MEMORIAL , Bay 10. France
Son of Frederick and Charlotte Bright, of Egypt Cottage, Hemyock, Devon.

The Arras Memorial is in the Faubourg-d'Amiens Cemetery, approximately 2 kms due west of the railway station.

Last known address: Queen Street, Honiton
Next of kin: Father, Frederick Bright

References: Free Birth Marriage Death records   Clayhydon tribute
Holcombe Village records   The Long, Long trail website history of Machine Gun Corps
Battle of Arras http://ww1centenary.oucs.ox.ac.uk/battle-of-arras/the-battle-of-arras-an-overview/
Machine gun corps archive group maguncor@bt.internet.com
Via subscription website, Ancestry.co.uk:
UK, Army Register of Soldiers' Effects   Census data
Medal Rolls Index Cards   Roberts Family Tree

Charles Maurice Sewell PETERS

Born Dawlish Q4, 1888   Died France 22 April 1917, aged 28

Private 9403   Honourable Artillery Company, 1st Battalion (Infantry)

Charles James Phillip Peters was a Grocer in Dawlish and married to Margaret Sewell. They lived at Piermont Place in 1891 with five of their six children; Mabel Mary S, 14, Maggie Sewell, 12, Gertrude Bessie, 10, Hilda A, 7, and Charles Maurice Sewell, 2. The children had all been born in Dawlish.

They moved to Portland Terrace and in 1901 Charles J.P. Peters was a Lodging house keeper. They had one more child, Philip Claud (1894-1967).

By 1911 they had left Dawlish for Essex and the parents were living at 3 Natal Road, Ilford with Charles Maurice Sewell Peters, aged 22, a Stockbroker's Clerk, as was his younger brother Philip Claud Peters, 17. Also at home was the third daughter Gertrude Bessie, 30, a warehousewoman (drapery). One of their children had died by this date.

A Short Service attestation survives which shows that Charles Peters took the loyal oath before a magistrate on 6th December 1915. At that date he was living at 3 Hampton Road, Ilford.

Charles married Ruth Mary Reed at Launceston Wesleyan Chapel on the 8th July 1916, following which event his 'next of Kin' is shown as Ruth Mary Peters of 3 Henley Road, Ilford.

It appears that he was enlisted at the Warley Depot of the Essex Regiment on 14th November 1916. On the following day he is entered on the Honourable Artillery Company (HAC) vellum membership books with attestation dated 15 November 1916, which is entered in his own hand and giving his address as 233 Henley Road, Ilford.

Two HAC infantry battalions and five artillery batteries were mobilised for active service overseas during the First World War. After the outbreak of war on 4 August 1914, the existing half Infantry Battalion was brought up to full strength and became the 1st Battalion, serving in France and Flanders from 18 September 1914.

All units formed by this regiment were of the Territorial Force

1/1st Battalion

August 1914: in Finsbury, London. Attached as Army Troops to 1st London Division.

12 September 1914: moved to Belhus Park.

20 September 1914: landed at St. Nazaire and placed onto Lines of Communication.

10 November 1914: transferred to 8th Brigade in 3rd Division.

9 December 1914: transferred to 7th Brigade in same Division.

14 October 1915: transferred to GHQ Troops.

9 July 1916: transferred to 190th Brigade in 63rd (Royal Naval) Division

> The 63rd (Royal Naval) Division was a United Kingdom infantry division of the First World War. It was originally formed as the Royal Naval Division at the outbreak of the war, from Royal Navy and Royal Marine reservists and volunteers, who were not needed for service at sea. The division fought at Antwerp in 1914 and at Gallipoli in 1915. In 1916, following many losses among the original naval volunteers, the division was transferred to the British Army as the 63rd (Royal Naval) Division, re-using the number from the disbanded second-line 63rd (2nd Northumbrian) Division Territorial Force.

As an Army formation, it fought on the Western Front for the remainder of the war.

During fighting on the Somme, the Germans constructed a formidable new defensive system some miles in their rear. From February 1917 they began to withdraw into it, giving up ground but in carrying out *Operation Alberich* they made the ground as uninhabitable and difficult as possible. British detected the withdrawal and cautiously followed up and advanced, but were brought to a standstill at the outer defences of the system.

http://ww1centenary.oucs.ox.ac.uk/battle-of-arras/the-battle-of-arras-an-overview/

HAC records show that Charles Maurice Sewell Peters embarked for France on the 1 March 1917 and was in the 27th Draft which joined the 1st Battalion on 29 March. He was wounded at the Battle of Arras on the 16 April and sent to hospital where he died on the 22nd April. He was buried in the Etaples cemetery.

The Dawlish Gazette of 5th May 1917 reported the death: More familiarly known to many in Dawlish as "Maurice" Peters, the eldest son of the late "Jim" Peters, formerly a grocer in Dawlish. His youthful days were spent in this town. He was aged 28, a keen man, who was connected with the Stock Exchange, and doing well.

Commonwealth War Graves entry: PETERS, CHARLES MAURICE SEWELL   Private   9403
22/04/1917   Age: 29   Honourable Artillery Company, 1st Bn.
Grave Ref: XIX. F. 13A.   Etaples Military Cemetery, Pas De Calais, France
Eldest son of Charles and Margaret Peters; husband of R. M. Peters, of "Hillside," 2, Berkeley Avenue, Reading, Berks. Native of Dawlish, Devon.

He is shown on the Devon Roll of Honour but no date or place of death is shown (22/4/1917, France).
Dawlish War memorial inscription: PETERS M.   GNR.   H.A.C.

He was awarded the British War Medal and the Victory Medal.
His widow, Ruth Mary Peters received a Death Grant of £2. 6s. 2d and a War Gratuity of £3 when she was living at 2 Berkeley Avenue, Reading, Berks.

Last known address: 233 Henley Road, Ilford, Essex
Next of kin: Widow, Ruth Mary Peters

References:
hac.org the website of the Honourable Artillery Company
wikipedia for 63rd Division
Birth Marriage Death refs
Refs via subscription websites:
Ancestry.co.uk and Find-my-past
UK, Soldiers Died in the Great War
UK, Army Registers of Soldiers' Effects
Census records
HAC registers

May 1917

In many ways George Knapman was a typical soldier from Dawlish on that Western front. The son of a farmer from South Tawton (which is about 5 miles east of Oakhampton, just south of today's A30). It is likely that George's father always looked back to South Tawton where he died in 1945 at the age of 80. George was the youngest son of John Knapman and his wife Amy and he had one sister and two older brothers."

George KNAPMAN

Born Kenn, 1896	Died France, 24 April 1917, aged 20
Private 40392	Royal Dublin Fusiliers, 1st Battalion

George was the third son of John William Edward Arthur Knapman (1865-1945) and Amy Endacott (1866 -).

John W E A Knapman was born in South Tawton and was the son of a farmer. He married Amy Endacott (born in Throwleigh) in 1892 and was the manager of a cider store, which the census record has altered to "Pub". In 1901 the family was living at Houndspool, West Dawlish, but they moved to be at 46 High Street in 1911.

They had four children, Maurice (1893-), John (1895-), Dora A (1896-) and George[56]. After leaving school George worked in Mr Shapter's ironmongery business in Dawlish.

The eldest son, Maurice, enlisted soon after the start of hostilities. John (Jack) was invalided our of the Wessex R.A.M.C. as a result of wounds to one of his eyes.

George's military record suggests that he may first have joined the Devonshire Regiment (quoted in UK, Soldiers Died in the Great War) and then the Suffolk Regiment, 2nd Battalion as a Private no 50483. Later he transferred to the Royal Dublin Fusiliers, 1st Battalion, as Private 40392. His Medal Roll Index Card only refers to the two latter regiments.

The report in the *Dawlish Gazette of 5th May 1917* refers to him being in the Home Force for twelve months before being passed for active service.

Headed,   THE GREAT SACRIFICE,

"It is with deep regret that we have to chronicle the deaths, while gallantly fighting for the country and the cause of the Allies.......George Knapman, Private, – Fusiliers (transferred from the 1th (*sic*) Devons. The keenest sympathy will be felt with Mr and Mrs W Knapman, of 47 High Street, much-respected residents, in the loss of their youngest son, who was aged 20. For 12 months he was in the Home Force. He was then passed for active service, and was home quite recently on draft leave. He was only a few weeks in France, and went into action on the 23rd April and was killed the following day........Before joining up deceased was in the ironmongery trade, and learnt the rudiments of the business at Mr J Shapter's. He was an unassuming young man liked by everyone.

Mr and Mrs Knapman have had an anxious time during this war. Their eldest son has been at the front since the early days of hostilities, and their second son, Jack, has been invalided out of the Wessex R.A.M.C. as a result of wounds, chiefly an injury to one of his eyes."

The regiment was involved in the Battle of Arras in April 1917 and the Arras Memorial contains his name among others.

---

56   GRO ref birth St Thomas district, 1896, Oct-Dec, Vol 5b, page 70

A Death Grant of £4. 11s. 8d was paid to his father, as was a War Gratuity of £7. 0s. 0d. He was then living at 14 Priory Terrace, Dawlish which is the address given for him in 1945. He died on 19 August, 1945 at Mill House, Zeal, South Tawton.

Commonwealth War Graves entry: KNAPMAN, GEORGE   Private   40392   24/04/1917
Age: 20   Royal Dublin Fusiliers, 1st Bn.   Panel Ref: Bay 9. Arras Memorial
Son of John William Edward Arthur and Amy Knapman, of 14, Priory Terrace, Dawlish, Devon.

George Knapman is included in the Devon Roll of Honour for Dawlish and on the Dawlish Boys' School Roll of Honour.

Dawlish War memorial inscription: KNAPMAN G.   PTE.   RL DUBN FUS.

Last known address: 46 High Street, Dawlish
Next of kin: Father, John William Edward Arthur Knapman

References: *Dawlish Gazette* report dated 5th May 1917
Text provided by Sheila Ralls   Birth Marriage Death records
Refs via subscription site Ancestry.co.uk: Census records
Medal Rolls Index Card   UK, Soldiers Died in the Great War
UK, Army Registers of Soldiers' Effects
Ireland, Casualties of the Great War

The Arras War Memorial - photograph from the Commonwealth War Graves Commission

The Stars and stripes

The United States of America joined the war in April 1917, at a point where the Allies were low on credit to pay for munitions being shipped across the Atlantic, and these were subject to U-Boat attack following the German declaration of unrestricted submarine warfare.

American public opinion had favoured neutrality and President Woodrow Wilson supported the view that America should stay out of a European war. There were many immigrant voices in the USA which supported the German cause, while others were resistant to the Tsarist Russian alliance which had been heavily involved in bringing the war to a head with their initial mobilisation of the army, supporting Serbia.

Attitudes changed after accounts of German atrocities in Belgium reached the press, and the sinking of the liner R.M.S. LUISITANIA in 1915 led to many seeing Germany as the agressor.

Britain and its allies were heavily dependent on food and raw materials being shipped across the Atlantic. In the early stages of the war they were vulnerable to surface raiders and small groups of German war ships were hunted across the oceans by the Royal Navy. The raiders' targets were primarily merchant shipping registered in Britain and flying the Red Ensign, but later German war ships sank neutral shipping if they thought that it was carrying supplies to Britain or allied ports, such as France.

As the U-Boat construction programme developed, longer ranging submarines began to have a greater impact on the security of shipping. It was their approach to American coastal waters that brought a threat to American-flagged ships and the point at which the United States declared war on Germany.

There was not an immediate change in military fortunes on land, for troops had to be trained and equipped, and then shipped to Europe. It was not until the latter part of 1917 that US troops began to appear on the Western Front, and then in small numbers under the command of General John Pershing. Insisting that his troops were not used to fill gaps in allied ranks, it was not until 1918 that individual units of US troops made an impact in battle.

May 1917

Henry MAY

Born: Thorverton, Q1, 1886   Died 22nd May 1917, France, aged 31
Private, 16549   Hampshire Regt, 2nd Battalion
Previously Private 53432   Royal Garrison Artillery

Henry May was from a family long established in Thorverton, part of the Tiverton registration district. His father, William, was born there ca.1832 and died in the district in 1905, aged 73. William May was a Master Mason and married Emma Western (1838-1902) ca 1858. They had nine children, all born in Thorverton:

Emily Mary May (1859-)	Louisa Western May (1861-)	Henry May (1864-)
William (1866-1915)	Tom (1870-)	Walter (1872-)
Eva (1878-)	Alice (1882-)	**Henry (1886-1917)[57]junior**

In 1871, the family was living at Silver Street, Thorverton and William was a Mason Master and employer, while his wife Emma is shown as a grocer. At that point Tom was their youngest child. They had settled in Brooke Terrace, Thorverton in 1881, and were still providing a home for Louisa, Henry (now also a mason), Tom, Walter and Eva.

In 1891 they were still at Brooke Terrace and William, 59, is shown as a builder/innkeeper and Walter, 19, has become a wheelwright, with Eva, 13, Alice, 9, and Henry, 5, still at school. Emma May was about 48 when her last child was born.

In 1901, at Buller Street, Thorverton, William (Senior), 69, is shown as retired, Tom, 32, is a stonemason, Walter, 29, is a wheelwright and Henry/Harry, 16, is a carpenter's apprentice. Next door, William (Junior)(1866-) is a stonemason and is married to Elisabeth from Torrington with four children, Isaac, son, 9, Gertrude, dau, 7, Walter C, son, 5, and Florence, dau, 2.

Henry junior's mother, Emma, died in 1902[58] and his father, Henry, in 1905[59].

Henry junior and Florence Sweet married in 1908 in Exeter[60]. Florence (b.Cullompton ca.1886) was a daughter of Julia Sweet (b. Port Isaac, N Cornwall, ca 1842), a widow in 1891 and 1911. The 1911 census shows Henry May, 24, and Florence living with Henry's mother-in-law Julia Sweet, 69 at No 4 Crown Court, Pancras Lane, Exeter. They had two children Albert, 3 and Beatrice, 1[61], both recorded as being born in Exeter and grandchildren of Julia Sweet. Henry is at this time a bricklayer.

At some time after April 1911, when the census took place, Henry and Florence moved to Dawlish and they had two more children. The notice of his death in the *Dawlish Gazette* records their home as being in Chapel Street. Chapel Street was so named because of the Congregational Chapel there, and it is now known as Albert Street, being a continuation of the Strand westwards.

---

57   GRO ref birth 1886, Jan-Mar, Tiverton, vol 5b, p 121

58   Emma's death record GRO ref Tiverton Sept 1902, vol 5b, p 243

59   Henry's death record GRO ref Tiverton 1905 Jan-Mar Vol 5b, p 314

60   Marriage record GRO ref Q4, 1908, Vol 5b, p 214

61   Beatrice birth record GRO ref Q4, 1908, Vol 5b, p 214

It is possible that Henry and Florence moved their family to Dawlish because of his work as a bricklayer, and possibly to set up home on their own.

The entry of his name on the town War Memorial suggests that his widow remained in the town after his death.

Henry enlisted at Exeter from his residence in Dawlish. One record shows that he was first with the Royal Garrison Artillery, Private 53432. He was transferred to the Hampshire Regiment. The 2nd Battn is shown as being engaged during 1917 in the First, Second and Third Battles of the Scarpe, The Battle of Langemarck, The Battle of Broodseinde, The Battle of Poelcapelle, The Battle of Cambrai. The fact that Henry is shown on the Arras Memorial suggests that he died during the Battle of Arras in the April – May actions, and this appears to be the case from the letter quoted by the *Dawlish Gazette.*

Henry May appears on the Devon Roll of Honour as Herbert May, Pte, Hants Regt – no date of death or location shown. (*The Christian name Herbert appears to be an error as the Commonwealth War Graves entry shows him to be Henry -ed*)

Dawlish War memorial inscription: MAY H.   PTE.   HANTS.REGT.

Devon Heritage site info:

16549 Private Henry May of the 2nd Battalion, the Hampshire Regiment. Son of William and Emma May. Born in Thorverton in the March Quarter of 1887. Died 27 August 1918 aged 31. (*Dates of birth and death incorrect-ed*)

From Thorverton War Memorial, his brother William

W. MAY	21429 Private William May of the 8th Coy, the 2nd/5th Battalion, the Devonshire Regiment. Born in 1866. Died 20 December 1915 aged 49. Buried in the churchyard of St.Thomas.

Commonwealth War Graves entry: MAY, HENRY   Private   16549   22/05/1917 Hampshire Regiment, 2nd Bn. Panel Ref: Bay 6.   Arras Memorial, France

UK Soldiers died in the Great War, 1914-1919:   Henry May,,   born Thorverton, Devon, Residence Dawlish, Devon.   Died: 22 May 1917   France & Flanders   Killed in action Enlisted: Exeter.   Private   16549 Hampshire Regiment, 2nd Battalion,   Formerly 53432, Royal Garrison Artillery.

Last known address: Chapel Street, Dawlish

Next of kin: Florence May, wife. His widow received the Death Grant of £7. 5s. 8d. And a War Gratuity of £11. 10s. 0d.

References:

Free Birth Marriage Death records   Dawlish Gazette, 2 June 1917

Refs via subscription sites: Census records

Forces War Records – Killed in Action, France

UK, Soldiers died in the Great War, 1914-1919

UK, Service Medal and Award Rolls, awarded British War Medal and Victory Medal, and 1914-15 Star

UK, Army Registers of Soldiers' Effects   Matthews Family Tree (ancestry.co.uk)

Walter Henry SCOTT

Born in St Thomas District Q2, 1890   Killed in action, Flanders, 28 May 1917, aged 27
Lance Corporal, R/15920   King's Royal Rifle Corps (KRRC)

Walter Henry Scott appears at 11 months old on the 1891 census as the youngest child of Henry William Scott (1852 – 1917) and Susan Gidley (1849 – 1935) at Rectory Cottage, Mamhead where Walter was born.

Henry had been born in Tedburn St Mary and became a gardener. He married Susan Gidley[62] in St Thomas District, which includes Mamhead, in 1874.

They had ten children. Two had died by the 1911 census. They were Alice Maud (1876-), Harriett Susan (1877-1958), Charles Eli (1880 -), all born in Clyst St Mary, Ada (1882-), Annie (1884-), Ethel (1885-), Hilda (1888-), Walter Henry (1890-1917), and Harry Reginald (1892-1918) – also a casualty of WW1.

The family were still living at Rectory Cottage in 1901. By 1911 the family had moved to Park Cottage, High Street/Strand Hill, Dawlish and Walter Henry Scott was 20 and the only child living at home, working as a gardener(market). At that time there were eight children of the marriage alive.

Walter received a Notice of conscription and enlisted with 'B' Corps of the 17th Division, King's Royal Rifle Corps on the 25th October 1915 at Coventry. His address was given as Forest Grange, Nr Kirby Muxloe, Leicestershire. He gave his home address as Park Cottage, High Street, Dawlish.

Walter married Lilian Annie Hinch (1892-) on 1st January 1916 at St Mark's Church, Swindon. She was one of three servants to Thomas Dawson, a boot factor in 1911, and was a nursemaid at Forest Grange, Hinkley Road, Kirby Muxloe (Hinkley Road runs west from Leicester, now the A47).

Lilian Annie Hinch was living with her grandparents at Coleshill, Faringdon, Berks, when she was 9 years old in 1901. It has not been possible to trace her parentage but her mother may have been a daughter of William and Mary Hinch and died after the birth of Lilian. The family were born in parts of Berkshire, Oxfordshire and Lincolnshire.

Walter and Lilian set up home at 22 Gloucester Street, Swindon. Walter's possessions of a watch(broken) and a cigarette case were sent to his widow at that address. She received a widow's pension of 13s. 9d. , a death grant of £3. 4s. 4d. and a War Gratuity of £7. 0s. 0d.

Walter is recorded as Killed in Action on the 28th May. His father had died a few weeks earlier on 14th April 1917 and it may be assumed that the news had recently reached Walter.

In World War I the KRRC was expanded to twenty-two battalions and saw much action on the Western Front, Macedonia and Italy.(Wikipedia) The 117th Brigade was a formation of the British Army during the First World War. It was raised as part of the new army and assigned to the 39th Division of the British Army

---

62   Marriage GRO ref St Thomas, 1874, Q2, vol 5b, p 94

117th Brigade Formation
- 16th Battalion, Sherwood Foresters (Chatsworth Rifles)
- 17th Battalion, Sherwood Foresters (Welbeck Rangers)
- **17th Battalion, King's Royal Rifle Corps (British Empire League)**
- 16th Battalion, Rifle Brigade (St Pancras)
- 117th Machine Gun Company
- **117th Trench Mortar Battery**

The division was composed primarily of recruits from the Midlands, London, and the south of England. Several of its battalions had been raised by local communities, and were named for their towns or industries. After training and home service, it deployed to the Western Front in early 1916, and fought in the Battle of the Somme. The following year, it saw action at the Third Battle of Ypres, and in **Battle of Arras 9- 30 May 1917.**

The Dawlish Gazette of 9th June 1917 reported the death of L/Cpl Walter Scott that with :"Captain H K Stevens, commanding a trench mortar battery, wrote to deceased's wife stating that it was his painful duty to convey the sad news, and expressing heartfelt sympathy. He pays a very fine tribute to the late gallant soldier, saying that the Battery mourns the loss of one of our best men; a man who was always cheerful and beloved by officers and men alike; a man in whom he (Capt Stevens) could place his utmost confidence. His noble example, his clean life, and his courage are all in our minds, and makes one ask why the men to go first seem always to be the best. . . . It seems wicked to say that it is God's will. . . . . If it is any consolation I can truthfully say that he died instantly. He was at his post during an enemy raid firing his gun, as was his duty, when a shell came over the emplacement killing him instantly."

(This report in the *Dawlish Gazette*, implies that he was serving in support of a trench mortar battery, but that he was attached as a rifleman from the KRRC)

Commonwealth War Graves entry: SCOTT, W H,   Lance Corporal   R/15920   28/05/1917
Age: 28   King's Royal Rifle Corps, 17th Bn.
Husband of Lilian A. Scott, of 22, Gloucester St., Swindon.
Grave Reference II. D. 10.   Cemetery: New Irish Farm Cemetery. This cemetery is north-west of Ypres/ Ieper in Flanders.

Walter Henry Scott is recorded on the Devon Roll of Honour but death recorded as 25th May, France

Dawlish War memorial inscription: SCOTT W.H.   L/CORPL   MORTAR BTY

Last known address: 22 Gloucester Street, Swindon
Next of kin: Mrs Lilian A Scott, 22 Gloucester Street, Swindon, Wilts

References:
Free birth, marriage, death refs   Wikipedia
Dawlish Gazette 9 June 1917
Refs via subscription websites;   Census records
British Army WW1 Service Records   UK, Army Registers of Soldiers' Effects
Ancestry.co.uk − Hellyer family tree (photo of the casualty)

Harry Norman John GIBSON

Born Wolborough, Newton, 3 November 1897   Died Greece, 27 May 1917, aged 19
Aircraftsman, 2nd Cl   F 14744   Royal Naval Air Service

Harry N J Gibson was the younger son of Harry Jennings Gibson (1867-1940), born in Kenwyn, Truro, and who became a railway clerk working for the Great Western Railway. He married Edith Mary Wills (1867-1933) in Truro in 1888.

In 1891 they lived at 11 Dominic Street, Kenwyn, Truro with their first child, Hilda Mary (1889-1896) who died aged 7.

They were in Plymouth in 1901, living at 23 Oxford Avenue, St Pancras by which time they had two sons, Frederick James (1891-) and **Harry Norman John** (1897-1917. They were both to enlist and serve in WW1.

By 1911, Harry Jennings Gibson had moved to become Station Master, Great Western Railway, Dawlish.

He and his wife Edith Mary were living at 3 San Remo Terrace, Dawlish with Harry Norman John Gibson, 13, a scholar, and mother-in-law and widow Mary Toms Wills, 73. It appears that Frederick James Gibson may have already started working for the Great Western Railway as a railway clerk.

> Frederick James Gibson enlisted in November 1915 and was discharged from hospital in 1919. He gave his address as 49 Cowper Road, Hanwell, Middx. He was beneficiary on his father's death in 1940.

Harry Norman John Gibson joined the Royal Naval Air Service (R.N.A.S.) on the 20th May 1916 "for service in land operations". He was on the books of H.M.S.PRESIDENT II in Yarmouth from May until 17th November, when he was based at Crystal Palace for a month before transferring to the Eastern Mediterranean until his death on 27 May 1917. H.M.S.PRESIDENT II was a Naval Accounting base for servicemen deployed in various places around the country.

In 1908, the British government recognized that the use of aircraft for military and naval purposes should be pursued. By 1912 the Royal Flying Corps had been formed and a number of its assets were transferred to support the Royal Navy.

The Royal Naval Air Service was officially formed on 1 July 1914, just a month before the outbreak of the War. Its tasks were fleet reconnaissance, patrolling coasts for enemy ships and submarines; attacking enemy coastal territory and later, attacking enemy targets much further inland. The new service was completely separate from the Royal Flying Corps except for the Central Flying School, which was still used, and became in effect a rival air force.

At the outbreak of the First World War in August 1914, the RNAS had 93 aircraft, six airships, two balloons and 727 personnel. The aircraft were a variety of Sopwith Pups, Camels, 1½ Strutters, Triplanes, Short S.184s and others, all being developed by different companies; some modified as sea planes with floats, but none yet ship launched. The weapons consisted mainly of hand held or sometimes lightly mounted and synchronized machine guns, and hand dropped 20lb bombs – these probably being fairly volatile. For Harry Gibson the role of an aircraftsman was of a semi-skilled nature, but he would have been instructed in many different tasks including moving, servicing, refuelling, and loading the aircraft for action. Bomb loading was most likely one of those tasks. In today's Navy his official title would have been Air Craft Handler.

Harry Gibson joined the RNAS during exciting times – 1916 was only 13 years after the Wright Brothers first powered flight, which lasted a total distance of 120 feet, and hence the speed of development of the aeroplane into something useful to support the war effort on many fronts was nothing short of meteoric. Of course the construction of the aircraft was rudimentary by today's standards and depended on the lightweight materials available, wood and fabric, held together with wire and string.

R.N.A.S. 'Sweetheart' badge.

The somewhat basic design of the propellers, made of wood, and depicted on the RNAS badge is in contrast to the refined four-bladed propellers on Spitfires in WW2.

In late 1916, Harry was transferred to RNAS MUDROS in the North Aegean Sea off Greece where he was part of No 2 Wing.

Mudros was a small Greek port on the Mediterranean island of Lemnos. It gained wartime significance with the determination of the Allies, in the early part of 1915, to attempt to seize control of the Dardanelles Straits, some 50km away. Once the Gallipoli campaign was called off, in evident failure at the close of 1915, Mudros' importance receded, although it remained the Allied base for the blockade of the Dardanelles for the duration of the war and was a principal base during the Salonika campaign in Greece. Operations were conducted to drive back attacks on Thessaloniki (Salonika).

Harry was based at R.N.A.S. MUDROS, Greece. "2 Wing were established at Imbros (Kephalo Point) on 31/8/15. The Wing was evacuated from Imbros on 18/1/16, absorbing 3 Wing on the same date. The Wing was based at Mudros by May 1916, remaining there until disbanded on 1/4/18, and becoming 62 Wing and 63 Wing RAF." *(invisionzone.com)*

On April 1, 1918 the RNAS was merged with the RFC to form the RAF. At the time of the merger, the Navy's air service had 67,000 officers and men, 2,949 aircraft, 103 airships and 126 coastal stations.

Harry's Naval Service Record shows that his death was caused by "accidental bomb explosion". Nowadays this would be described as a "Weapon Accident". The report in the *Dawlish Gazette* (See below) says that his death occurred 'on Whit-Sunday by the accidental explosion of bombs.'

The Dawlish Gazette of 2nd June 1917 carried this report. "One of the most grievous aspects of the war is the terrible toll it is taking of the flower of youth of the country. We regret to have to add yet another to the already long Dawlish list. Mr H.J.Gibson, stationmaster, has been officially informed that his youngest son, Harry Norman John ("Jack") aged 19, of the Royal Naval Air Service, was killed on Whit-Sunday by the accidental explosion of bombs. Deceased was on the island of Imbros and had been detailed for dangerous duty; it was understood at Salonika. Before enlisting about twelve months ago he had made a promising start in the scholastic profession. He was a pupil-teacher at the Dawlish C. School."

A family announcement of grateful thanks for expressions of sympathy appeared in the following week's newspaper.

Commonwealth War Graves entry:
GIBSON, HARRY NORMAN JOHN   Air Mechanic 2nd Class   F/14744   27/05/1917
Age: 19   Royal Naval Air Service, "F" Sqdn. 2nd Wing. H.M.S. "President II."
Grave Ref: II. H. 5. Struma Military Cemetery, Kalokostron, Greece.
Son of Harry Jennings Gibson and Edith Mary Gibson, of 3, San Remo Terrace, Dawlish, Devon.

> *(The Struma River flows through Bulgaria southward to the Greek frontier, then south-east into the Aegean Sea. From the Allied base at Salonika, a road ran north-east across the river to Seres, and it was this road that the right wing of the Allied army used for the movements of troops and supplies to the Struma front during the Salonika Campaign.*

H.N.J.GIBSON is shown on the Devon Roll of Honour but date & place of death are empty.

Dawlish War memorial inscription: GIBSON H.N.J.   AIRCRT   R.A.F. *(By the time that the War Memorial was in place the RNAS had become part of the RAF -ed)*

Last known address: 3 San Remo Terrace, Dawlish.
Next of kin: Harry Jennings Gibson, father
References: naval-history.net   First World War.com
Tribute note by Tom Elliott   CWGC website
Refs via subscription site, Ancestry.co.uk   UK RN & RM Graves Roll
Census data   Find a grave index

The Machine Gun Corps was formed on 14.10.1915 with the 23rd Machine Gun Company being formed on 15.1.1916 from the Machine Gun Companies of the 23rd Brigade, 8th Division.
The Machine Gun Corps were at the forefront of all major attacks, often in advance of the troops and at other times, remained to cover any withdrawals. Knowing their effectiveness they were targeted by enemy gunfire causing a very high casualty rate. The Corps became known as "The Suicide Club." The next casualty is remembered on these memorials.

MENIN GATE MEMORIAL,   M.G.C. WAR MEMORIAL
YPRES, BELGIUM.   HYDE PARK, LONDON.

June 1917

William Henry PITTS

Born St Thomas District, Q4, 1887   Ki.a., Flanders, 22 June 1917, aged 29

Private 7882   Devonshire Regiment

Lance Sergeant, 17565   Machine Gun Corps (Infantry)

William Henry Pitts was the son of Edward Elston Pitts and Mary Ann Fawdon.

The Pitts surname derived from Flemish immigrants who arrived in the Middle Ages. They settled in Pett, Kent and Pitt in Hampshire. The Old English word "pytt" meant pit.

Edward Elston Pitts (1858-1934)[63] started life in the Union Workhouse in Crediton where, at the age of two, he was described as a 'scholar'. He is listed in the 1861 census with others of the same surname including his mother Charlotte:

William Pitts, unmarried,	63,	Mason's labourer	born Crediton
Maria Pitts, marr,	81,	Weaver, wool	"
Charlotte Pitts, unmarried	21,	Shoebinder	"
Edward Pitts,	2,	Scholar	"

William Pitts (1798-1867) was the only child from the marriage of Joseph Pitts (1776-1852) to Elizabeth Stone (1776-1803). Joseph then married again, on 26 February 1804, to Maria Croot (1777-1864) and they had five children. It is Maria (Croot), now a widow, who is in the workhouse with her step-son.

The evidence from other family trees (Ancestry.co.uk) suggests that William did not marry, and earlier census returns show him in St Thomas Union Workhouse, Wonford (Exeter) in 1841 and Cheriton Road Union Workhouse, Crediton in 1851.

The census of 1851 gives a possible clue to Charlotte's parents: (viz FIP family tree)

Park Street, Crediton

Joseph Pitts, Head, marr	78,	Parish pay, Carpenter	born Crediton	
Maria Pitts, wife,	73,	" , Weaver	"	
Charlotte, grand daughter	12,	Scholar	"	
John, son,**	30,	Shoemaker	"	
Ann, grand daughter	10,	Scholar	"	
Harry, grandson	8,	"	born Weston-Super-Mare	
John, grandson	6,	"	"	

**John Pitts (1814-1885) married Sarah Hookway (1810-1847) in Exeter in 1833 when he was 19. They moved to Weston-Super-Mare and he was a shoemaker in 1841 (census record). They had seven children before her early death in Weston-Super-Mare at the age of 36. They were :

Henry (1835-1837), Ann Elizabeth (1836-), Henry William (1837-1837), Charlotte (1839- 1919), Ann (1839-), Henry "Harry" (1842-1880), John (1846-1852).

John Pitts, a widower, came home to live with his parents and the four youngest children as are shown in the 1851 census, above.

William's ancestors were Devonian, living in Newton St.Cyres in the early 1700s and by the early 1800s were living in Crediton. His ancestry shows lives of struggle, poverty and desertion. His great grandmother and grandmother had both been deserted by their partners before later marriages.

---

63   Birth record GRO ref 1858, Oct-Dec vol 5b, page 378

His great great grandparents, grandmother and father had all been, at various times, on Parish support, with his father being brought up in Crediton Union Workhouse until the age of 14.

The workhouse was the last resort for many poor single mothers, whose families could not support them. It did however offer some medical facilities for the newborn at a time when people had to pay for a doctor's services. Those who ended up in the workhouse were the very poor, aged, infirm, mentally disturbed, single mothers and children. Adults were separated; all wore workhouse uniforms and were recorded as inmates.

The Poor Law Handbook stated:-

"The care and training of children are matters which should receive the anxious attention of Guardians. Pauperism is in the blood and there is no more effectual means of checking its hereditary nature than by doing all in our power to bring up our pauper children in such a manner as to make them God-fearing, useful and healthy members of society."

Despite this terrible start to life, William Pitts' father, Edward Elston Pitts, became a farm labourer and married Mary Ann Fawdon (1855-1930) in 1878 in Crediton[64] and they had 7 children. She was a general domestic servant for Richard Ellis, a farmer in Chagford. Like most agricultural labourers he had to find work each year, moving from Crediton to Drewsteignton, Marldon, Kenton, Dawlish and Cofton. They were both buried here at the Church of St.Mary, Cofton.

In 1881 Edward and Mary Pitts were living at No 3 Stanton Cottage, Marldon, where Edward was a farm labourer. They had two children:

Hannah Fawdon Pitts, (1878-)	born in Crediton
Edward Samuel Pitts, (1879-)	born in Drewsteignton.

At the next census (1891) they were at Cofford Mill Cottage, Kenton with four more children:

Emily Jessie Pitts, (1882-1969-)	born in Kenton
Rosalina Alice Pitts, (1885-)	"
William Henry Pitts, (1887 -)[65]	"
Leah Louisa Pitts, 4 months old (1891-1931)	"

In 1901 The parents had moved to Duckaller Cottage, Port Road, Dawlish and William Henry, 13, and Leah L, 11 had been joined by Albany John (1893-1931), 7, born in Dawlish.

The other children had moved away by 1911 and one of their number had died, as recorded in the census. The parents were living at Westwood, Cofton, Starcross, with Albany John Pitts, 17, joined also by Albert Edward Pitts, 11, a grandson. By this time Edward's occupation is shown as a gardener, as is his son Albany.

On an unknown date William Henry Pitts joined the Devonshire Regiment, Service No. 7882. In 1911 he was recorded as being stationed in Malta with the 2nd.Battalion. It is likely that he then returned to Devon before being stationed on Jersey with the 1st Battalion.

Early In 1914 William married[66] Ethel Beatrice Westcott [67] in Exeter.

64	Marriage record GRO ref Crediton, 1878, Apr-June, vol 5b, p 685
65	Birth record GRO ref born, St Thomas district, Oct-Dec 1887, Vol 5b, p 7
66	Marriage record GRO ref Exeter, 1914, Jan-Mar, vol 5b, p 172
67	Birth record GRO ref Born Lambeth Jan-Mar, 1890, vol 1d, pa 565

The Westcott family had moved to Middlewood, Dawlish and Ethel's father, George H P Westcott was a pensioner of the Metropolitan Water Board. In the 1911 census he records that he was a widower and a gardener. His first wife, Mary Ann Westcott died in Apr-June 1898, aged 45, and he married again to Elizabeth Holborrow who died in Lambeth in early 1905. It appears that George Henry Palmer Westcott then moved to Devon, where he died at the R.D.& E. Hospital on the 12th September 1918.

On 21st August 1914 the 1st Battalion, Devonshires, landed at Le Havre, where they were reinforced by nearly 500 reservists from Exeter. This accords with the Medal Roll Index Card for William H Pitts that shows his "date of entry" (France) as 22-8-14 which entitled him to the award of the 1914 Star.

In September, during their first spell in the line, they suffered 100 casualties from shelling. In October on the La Bassee Canal they supported the badly mauled 1st Dorsets and helped capture Givenchy Ridge. The Devons performed well during a bitter three-week battle but lost two thirds of their officers and a third of their men. From November they occupied Messines Ridge in rain and sleet, often knee- or waist-deep in mud and icy water.
On 21st April 1915 they occupied Hill 60, which had been captured on 17th April. Counter-attacks and heavy shelling cost them more than 200 casualties.
On 31st July 1915 they moved to the Somme. When the offensive began on 1st July 1916 the Devons were at Arras but returned to the Somme, to consolidate the line around Longueval. Shellfire and German counter-attacks cost them 265 casualties. In September they made two very successful advances near Guillemont at a cost of 376 casualties.

There are no surviving records which show when William Henry Pitts transferred to the Machine Gun Corps. The Medal Roll Index Card hints that he was no more than a Private with the 1st Devons, and this suggests that he may have transferred to the Machine Gun Corps (Infantry) soon after its formation in October 1914. During 1916-17 the Machine Gun Corps took part in the Battle of the Somme. From 14th March to 5th April 1917 he would have fought during the German retreat to the Hindenburg Line and later that month he probably fought at the attacks on Heudecourt and Villers Guislands. In June 1917 he was moved to Ypres to prepare for a new offensive.

The Army Registers of Soldiers' Effects show that William was serving with the 23rd Company of the Machine Gun Corps at the time of his death on 22nd June 1917. All of the Corps records were lost in 1922, when a "mysterious" fire completely destroyed their HQ and archives.

By 1917 he was a Lance Serjeant. This was not a formal rank. His appointment was made by his Commanding Officer and unlike the regulations for formal ranks, could be taken away for disciplinary reasons, without a court martial. Previously he would have been a Corporal and this appointment gave him extra pay and the right to wear three chevrons on his sleeve.

He was killed in action on 22nd June,1917,a few weeks before the 3rd Battle of Ypres. His body was not recovered. He was awarded the 1914 Star, the Victory Medal and the British War Medal.

After William's death, Ethel Pitts married Alfred Bowles in Oct-Dec 1920 (Dartford, Vol 2a, p1571) and the CWGC website records her address as 8 Battle Road, Erith, Kent.

CWGC reference: Lance Serjeant WILLIAM PITTS   Service Number: 17565
Machine Gun Corps (Infantry)   23rd Coy. Died 22 June 1917   Age 37 years old
Buried or commemorated at Ypres (Menin Gate) Memorial   Panel 56.

A Death grant of £ 5. 12s. 9d. Was paid to his widow and sole legatee Ethel, and a War Gratuity pof £17. 10s. 0d. To his widow Ethel B in September 1919.

Cofton memorial inscription: William Pitts. Mach.Gun Corps.   June 22nd 1917
Last known address: Duckaller Cottage, Port Road, Dawlish
Next of kin: Ethel Beatrice Pitts, widow

References:
Birth, Marriage Death records
wartimememoriesproject.com/greatwar
The 1st Battalion of the Devonshire Regiment
http://www.keepmilitarymuseum.org/history/first+world+war/the+devonshire+regiment/the+first+battalion
Refs via subscription website: Census records
UK, Army registers of Soldiers' Effects   UK, Soldiers died in the Great War
Family trees – Ancestry.co.uk   DEVON Newton ST Cyres B Pitts
Hookway Surname Study   FIP tree   Webb

Devonshire Regt   Machine Gun Corps   1914 Star   British War Medal   Victory Meda

The Third Battle of Ypres

On July 31, 1917, the Allies launch a renewed assault on German lines in the much-contested region near Ypres. The attack begins more than three months of brutal fighting, known as the Third Battle of Ypres, often referred to as Passchendaele and lasting until November 6th.

The third Battle of Ypres was intended by Sir Douglas Haig to destroy German submarine bases located on the north coast of Belgium, but was in fact driven by Haig's (mistaken) belief that the German army was on the verge of collapse, and would be broken completely by a major Allied victory.

Wilfred Claude WILLIAMS

Born Dawlish, Q1, 1897   Died 31 July 1917, Flanders, aged 20

Private 40149   Royal Tank Corps

Wilfred Claude Williams was the son of John and Bessie Williams. Wilfred was born in Dawlish, his mother's home town, early in 1897[68]. The common name of Williams makes a certain identity difficult but the marriage of John Williams (1868-1898) to Bessie Slocombe (1870 -) is linked to the Baptism of Wilfred Claude Williams in St Mark's Church (since demolished) on 4th March 1897. The father, John, is described in the register as a grocer and the mother is Bessie.

Bessie Williams, nee Slocombe, was born late in 1870[69] and Baptised in St Gregory the Great on 7th December 1870. In the 1871, census the Slocombe family are shown living at No 3 Brunswick Place, Dawlish, where the father, John Slocombe, 38, is a Plasterer and Rose, his wife, 38, is a housekeeper. There were six children with them, Louisa, 15, Mary J, 13, Annie Maria, 11, John, 9, William, 5 and Bessie, 5 months.

> Annie Maria Slocombe (1861-) married a hairdresser, Alfred William Lane (1857-) in 1884[70].
> By 1891 they had moved to Dawlish, No 2 Vaughan Terrace, with two children, born in Bexley, Kent; Rose D, 3 and William H, 0. They were next door to her parents John and Rose Slocombe, who had moved to 1 Vaughan Terrace, West Cliff.
> Also in 1891, John Slocombe (1862-) is married and has followed in his father's trade of plastering. His wife, Marie, 32, and their daughter Mary, 5, are living at No 3 Vaughan Terrace with his sister Bessie, 20, who is unmarried.

Bessie Slocombe was 25 when she married John Williams, 28, in St Gregory the Great, Dawlish on 21 March 1896.

The marriage register of Bessie Slocombe and John Williams shows that John's father was Thomas Williams, and a cross reference to the 1881 census shows a John Williams in Beach Cottage, Dawlish, as a Grocer's Assistant born in Bodmin, Cornwall. Thomas Williams (1829-1905) and Belinda Varcoe (1830-1910) brought up eight children in Bodmin over 19 years, and John Williams is among them.

It appears that John Williams died in 1898, aged 28, and this can be confirmed by obtaining a death certificate [71].

After the death of John Williams, Bessie can be found in 1901 with her son at the home of her sister Annie Maria and brother-in-law, Alfred W Lane, at 39 Fest Road, Kingston-upon-Thames. Hairdressing is a mobile occupation and they may have moved back to an area that he knew well from childhood, and where they had married. They had four children and Bessie was there with **Wilfred Williams,** 4, nephew to the Lane family.

In 1905, the widow Bessie Williams married once more to Charles Christopher Pound, another hairdresser, conducting his business at 17, the Strand, Dawlish. It would appear that Pound had been married previously.

---

68   Birth record GRO ref 1897, Jan-March, Newton Abbot district, vol 5b, p 98

69   Bessie birth GRO ref 1870, Q4, N.A.district, vol 5b, p 111

70   Bessie marriage GRO ref 1884, Q2, Croydon, Surrey Vol 2A, p 327

71   Death cert GRO ref 1898, June , N.A., vol 5b, p 89

In 1911 the census shows the household:

Charles Pound, 48, hairdresser (born in Torquay), Bessie Pound, 38, Wilfred C Williams, 14, step-son and apprentice hairdresser and Cyril W Pound, 4, son, born in Teignmouth.

Bessie Pound died on 9th August 1944, aged 73[72], at 2 Selborne Road, New Malden Surrey and left her effects to her son, Cyril Williams Pound, dental practitioner.

There are no surviving records to show when Wilfred C Williams enlisted at Exeter. From the following account of the formation of the Royal Tank Corps he may have first joined the Machine Gun Corps.

"Through mud and blood to the green fields beyond". - Tank Corps motto.

Tanks were used for the first time in action on the battlefield of the Somme on 15 September 1916. 36 Mark 1 tanks of C and D Companies arrived on the start line for the renewal of the Somme offensive: this action was later designated as the Battle of Flers-Courcelette. Arguments continue as to whether it would have been better to wait until much larger numbers of tanks were available before they were used in battle. The Heavy Section Machine Gun Corps was re-designated as the Heavy Branch MGC in November 1916.

The Tank Corps was formed from the Heavy Branch MGC on 27 July 1917 and the Battalions adopted numbering rather than letter designations (although tank names followed the same lettering: for example, 7th Battalion tanks were all named with a letter G, like Grouse, Grumble, etc.) Each Tank Battalion had a complement of 32 officers and 374 men.

By summer 1917 tank numbers had increased and the better Mark IV's were available. Sadly, the tanks deployment in the Third Battle of Ypres (July-November 1917), known as the battle of Passchendaele, proved to be another slog through deep mud. The area became a tank graveyard as machine after machine ditched in deep trenches and shell holes, sank, stuck and was shelled. Morale in the Tank Corps was low and confidence of the rest of the army destroyed. Although there was a bright incident when tanks did well at St Julien, the tanks needed to be given a fighting chance.

Private Wilfred Claude Williams lost his life on the opening day of the assault on Ypres. He is recorded among those on the Menin Gate memorial.

A death grant of £3. 14s. 3d. was paid to Bessie Pound, as was the War Gratuity of £4. 10s. 0d. Awards of the Victory medal and the British War medal were made later.

Wilfred C Williams is recorded on the Devon Roll of Honour

Dawlish War memorial inscription: WILLIAMS W.C.   GNR.   TANK CORPS

Commonwealth War Graves entry: WILLIAMS, WILFRED CLAUDE   Private   40149
31/07/1917   Tank Corps, "G" Bn.   Panel Ref: Panel 56.   Ypres (Menin Gate) Memorial
Last known address: 17 The Strand, Dawlish
Next of kin: Bessie Pound, mother
References: BMD records
The Long, Long Trail - http://www.1914-1918.net/tanks.htm
Refs via subscription sites: Census records   UK, Soldiers Died in the Great War
UK, Army Registers of Soldiers' Effects   Baptism and Marriage records
Ancestry.co.uk - Barbour family tree

---

72   Death cert GRO ref 1944, Sept, Surrey North Eastern district, vol 2a, p 81

William Joseph MARKS

Born 16 March 1890, Clyst St Lawrence (St Thomas) Died 2 August 1917, aged 27
Gunner, 216145   Royal Field Artillery, 'D' Battery, 150th Brigade

William was the second son of John and Eliza Marks and was born in Clyst St Lawrence where his father was an agricultural labourer (1891 census). The family was, like so many in rural areas, dependent on work on the land.

Grandfather Joseph Marks (1830-1894) married Maria Moxey (1832-1905) at Woodbury Salterton in East Devon on 14 July 1885. Their son, John Marks, was born at Rockbeare in Spring 1865 and later gained work as a groom and gardener. He married Eliza Flay (1868-1946) from Talaton in the Spring of 1887 and they had five children, including William Joseph Marks who may have been the twin of a daughter, Emily.

John and Eliza's five children were Sidney (1889-), Emily(1890-), William (1890-1917), Rosina (1893-), and John Marks (1895-). Their father was working as a gardener/groom in 1901 and they lived at Strete Ralegh in 1911 where he was a "Gardener domestic". At this time William was the only child living at home and was a "farm labourer". According to newspaper reports, John Marks took employment at Luscombe Castle, Dawlish subsequently. He died in the winter of 1943.

William Joseph Marks married Elizabeth Jane Pile (Q4, 1881-) in St Mary's Church, Rockbeare on 24 April 1912. Elizabeth, was 30 and eight years his senior when she married William Joseph Marks. A daughter, Ruby N M Marks, was born and registered in September 1912 in St Thomas. (Ruby N M Marks married Ernest H Hayman in Sept 1933)

Elizabeth Jane Pile was the eldest of nine children of Philip and Mary Ann Pile (1858-). Philip Pile (b. Otterton,1855-) was a "labourer" at Otterton (1891), a "waggoner on farm" at Otterton (1901), and a "farmer" at Palmers' Farm, Rockbeare in 1911.

It is recorded that William Joseph Marks enlisted at Exeter, but no further detail survives of his service record.

The *Western Times of 31 August, 1917* reported, under MARSH GREEN heading, "Much sympathy is extended to Mrs W. Marks, whose husband, Gunner William Marks., R.F.A., was killed in action on August 2nd. The deceased, who leaves a widow and one little girl, was greatly respected by all who knew him. He was competent and skilled in all kinds of agricultural work, and was also a sidesman of the church at Marsh Green. He had only been at the front about a month. He was the second son of Mr and Mrs J Marks, late gardener at Strete Raleigh."

Similarly, in the *Western Times of 25 August,1917* it reports among Dawlish casualties "Gunner Marks, RGA., son of Mr Marks, gardener, Luscombe Castle."

From the Passchendaele Archive:

> Gunner William Joseph Marks served in "D" Battery of the 150th Army Brigade of the Royal Field Artillery. The Army Brigade participated in the Third Battle of Ypres. On the 20th of July 1917 it took up positions near the Dead End of the Yser Canal in Ypres. Its headquarters were based on the Ypres ramparts. From here the Batteries of the Brigade shelled German positions in wake of the offensive. On the 31st of July, the first day of the offensive, the Batteries of the Brigade limbered up and vacated their positions at the Dead End.

They took up new positions near the hamlet of Wieltje, possibly along the Oxford Road. The HQ of the Brigade was located at the Cart Dugouts. At 08.30 a.m. the Brigade was in position and started supporting the British advance. Throughout the next couple of days there was much artillery activity on both sides. During the month of August the Potijze road, Bellewaerde and the area of Wieltje were regularly shelled by the German artillery. Gunner William Joseph Marks was killed in action near Wieltje on the 2nd of August 1917. Although artillery activity had been less frequent than on the previous days, it's highly possible that Gunner William Joseph Marks fell due to German shelling. He was buried in Vlamertinghe New Military Cemetery.

Vlamertinghe New Military Cemetery (*below*) is located 5 Kms west of Ieper/Ypres town centre and to the south of the village of Vlamertinge (Vlamertinge is the modern spelling of Vlamertinghe). Vlamertinge is located along the Poperingseweg.

Gunner W J Marks is shown in CWGC records as "Marks W J, Gunner, 216145 RFA 'D' Battery, 150th Brigade, died 2/8/1917 age 27. Husband of Elizabeth J Marks of Marsh Green, Rockbeare, Exeter."

Dawlish War memorial inscription:
MARKS W GNR RGA
It may be assumed that his father asked for his name on Dawlish War Memorial, despite his widow living in Rockbeare.
W Marks is not recorded on the Devon Roll of Honour for Dawlish, nor on the Dawlish Boys' School Roll of Honour.

Devon Heritage site info: 82992 Gunner Walter Robert Marks of 163 Brigade, the Royal Field Artillery. Son of Frederick and Alice Marks. Born in Walthamstow in 1898. Died 14 July 1916 aged 18. (*believed to be an error – ed*)

Last known address: Strete Ralegh, Whimple
Next of kin: Elizabeth Jane Marks, widow
UK, Army Registers of Soldiers' Effects 1901-1925
Marks, William Joseph, D/ 150 Brigade, RFA
Death Grant £3/1s/11d to Widow, Elizabeth Jane (15/12/17)
War Gratuity £3 " " " (10/11/19)

References:
https://archives.passchendaele.be/en/soldier/1540
Free BMD birth and marriage data CWGC record
refs via subscription sites: UK, Soldiers died in the Great War 1914-1919
"William Joseph Marks, residence Rock Bear, Devon, death- France & Flanders"
UK, Service Medal and Award Rolls Bond family tree (Ancestry.co.uk)
216145 Gnr, Marks, William Joseph (dead 2/8/17) Victory Medal and British War Medal
Census data

Thomas Norman LEWIS

Born Courtown, Wexford, 2 December 1890   died 8 August 1917, aged 26

Act/Corporal 56682   Royal Garrison Artillery, 321st Siege Battery

Thomas Norman Lewis came from a North Devon family although he and his siblings were born in Ireland. His grandparents were Thomas Lewis (1829-1913), an agricultural labourer and Elizabeth Staddon (1828-), both born in Ilfracombe. Their son, Thomas born in Ilfracombe on 1st February 1855 was one of five children at the time of the 1861 census. Young Thomas joined the Royal Navy on 1st January 1873, and one month later at age 18 he started a 10 year engagement. He became an Able Seaman in April 1875 and transferred to the Coastguard Service as a Boatman in March 1881. Up to that point his character was shown as 'exemplary'.

Thomas Lewis (1855-) married Mary Bray (1853-1924) in Q1 1881 and in that year's census she is living with her parents, William and Ann Bray at Berry Village, Berrynarbor where she was born. She is listed as a Coastguard's wife.

Mary followed Thomas to Ireland and was at Crosshaven when the first three children were born:

> Lucy (1882-)
> Annie Elizabeth (1885-) and
> Constance Mary (1887-1974).

Thomas was moved to Courtown, Wexford, on 19th January 1887, in command of boats. It was while he was there that they had:

> Emily Francis (1888-1946)
> **Thomas Norman (1890-1917)**
> William Bray (1892-1976) and
> Rosina May (1896-1984).

Thomas was promoted to Chief Boatman at Rosslare on 31 May 1897 and to Chief Boatman in Charge in August 1900. In 1901 the family were at Mossyglen, Greencastle, Donegal.

From 7th July 1903 until retirement on 3rd February 1910 he was based at Dawlish.

The seven Lewis children were still living at home in 1911 when the family were at Iddesleigh Terrace, Exeter Road, Dawlish and most were employed: Lucy was a dressmaker, Annie Elizabeth did housework, Constance Mary was a dressmaker, Emily Francis was a shop assistant in a drapery, Thomas Norman was an assistant clerk in Dawlish Brewery, William Bray was an assistant golf professional at Warren Links and Rosina Mary was at home.

Thomas Lewis was shown as a Naval Pensioner in the rank of Chief Petty Officer and lodging house keeper. They had one lodger, Charles Frank Chitty, 33, who was a golf professional at Warren Links.

Thomas Norman Lewis, aged 24, was medically examined on 16th January 1915 and measured at 5' 8 3/4" and weighing 143 lbs (fraction under 10 stone), having fair complexion and blue eyes. He enlisted in the Royal Garrison Artillery at Shepherd's Bush, Middlesex on 19th January 1915. He is unusual in being documented in a service record that survived the fires in the blitz of WW2.

He joined the RGA at Newhaven on the 20th January and was posted as a Gunner for training on the 27th. He was rated 3rd class at Dover on 1st May 1915 and served as a Gunner at Malta from 18th June 1915. He became a Qualified Gun Layer on 1st August 1916.

He returned to Britain and joined the 321st Siege Battery on 31st December 1916 and was promoted to Acting Bombardier on 6th April 1917. He embarked at Southampton on 11th May for Le Havre, arriving next day. He was promoted to Bombardier on 29th May 1917 and was promoted to 'Acting Corporal vice 337638 Hardy, performing duties from 17th June 1917.'

General Haig ordered General Herbert Plumer, the commander of the British Second Army which occupied the Ypres Salient, to produce a plan in late 1916. Plumer believed that a force of 35 divisions and 5,000 guns would be necessary, which was far beyond the amount of artillery in the British Expeditionary Force.

Haig informed his Army commanders that his objectives were to wear down the German army, secure the Belgian coast and connect with the Dutch frontier by capturing Passchendaele Ridge and advancing on Roulers and Thourout, to cut the railway supplying the German garrisons holding the Western Front north of Ypres and the Belgian coast. An attack by the 4th Army would then begin on the coast, combined with an amphibious landing in support of the main advance to the Dutch frontier.

Thomas Norman Lewis was killed in action on 8th August 1917.

Great War Forum- Robert Dunlop posted: "The war diary for 321 Sge Bty survives at Kew under their reference WO95/217.

321st Siege Battery:- Here is the actual entry in the War Diary for August 8th.

"Battery and billets heavily shelled. 6 NCOs and men killed in battery position.. Men still continued on the operation targets. Fire 400 rounds."

From another respondent - "321 having joined 84 HAG (Heavy Artillery Garrison) on 16 June and recorded as in action on the 17th (66 HAG diary)."

The other men killed that day from 321 Sge Bty were: Gnr 76393 BALLS, George

A/Bdr HUGHES, David 46867,   **Cpl LEWIS, Thomas Norman 56682**

Gnr TAYLOR,George Edward 177935   Gnr ROUTLEY, Edmund J S   92982

"This appears to be a direct hit on a gun of which the 6in Howitzers were manned by 10 men. One common factor is that the buried bodies were later dug up and reburied at Voormezeele. It does appear to be in connection with German retaliation for II Corps V Army counter battery work in the days following the attack on Westhoek Ridge."

He was buried, as so often, on the field of battle and was exhumed and reburied in Voormezeele Enclosure No 3 extension ' 2 miles south of Ypres'.

His possessions were returned to his father later in the year.

His British War and Victory Medals were received by his mother on 12th August 1921.

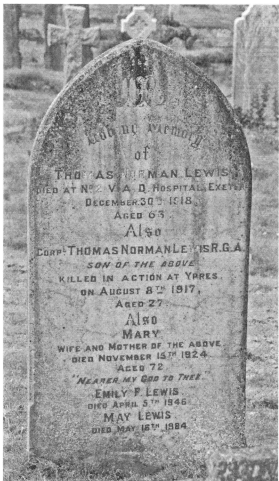

His father had died on 30th December 1918 at No 2 War Hospital, Exeter and the effects of £245.3s.8d passed to his widow. On her death at the Cottage Hospital, Dawlish on 15th November 1925, her effects of £50.1s.3d passed to Annie Elizabeth Lewis, spinster.

Commonwealth War Graves entry: LEWIS T N Corporal 56682 8/8/17 R.G.A. 321st Siege Battery

Cemetery: VOORMEZEELE Enclosure NO 3 – 4 km south-west of Ypres/Ieper

Headstone in Dawlish cemetery

After his death a payment of £9.3s.10d was made to his father. Following the death of his father in 1918 the War Gratuity of £12.10s.0d was paid to his mother in 1919.

His brother William was shown as serving with the 5th Battalion, Devonshire Regiment.

Thomas Norman Lewis is recorded on the Devon Roll of Honour and the Dawlish Boys' School Roll of Honour.

References: Free BMD index   Great War Forum

Refs via subscription websites: R N Service records

Probate records   Census data,   Army Service records

UK, Army Registers of Soldiers' Effects.   Ireland, Casualties of WW1

Albert MAYNE

Born Dawlish, 16 June 1896   Died France, 9 August 1917, aged 21

Private 18321   Coldstream Guards, 1st Battalion

Albert Mayne was the grandson of James Mayne (1822-1891) and Sarah Brook (1818-1895). They had married in the summer of 1847[73].

James was a farm labourer, born in Dawlish, and Sarah was a laundress, born in Honiton/Kenton (Census records differ) and they lived in 3 Church Cottages, Dawlish. Their children were George (1845-), John (1848-), Mary Ann (1851-), James (1853-), and Henry (1856-1919) all born in Dawlish.

Henry Mayne married Sarah Ann Cox (1855-1916) in the summer of 1875[74]. Henry was also an agricultural labourer and his wife a laundress. They had nine children between 1876 and 1896, who were:

      Jessie   (1876-)

      Henry Charles   (1878-)

      William J   (1879-)

      Emily J   (1883-)

      Ernest J   (1885-)

      Alice Mary   (1888-)

      Alfred Samuel   (1890-1906)

      Frederick T   (1893-)

      Albert   (1896-1917)

By 1911 Henry and Sarah Ann were living at 11 Old Town Street with the two youngest children, Fred, 18, a labourer for the railway company, and Albert, 14, an errand boy for a draper. The Census record also shows that eight of the nine children survived to that date, Alfred Samuel having died in 1906 at age 16.

Albert married Alice Edith Hills in the summer of 1915[75] when he was 19, and they had one child, Derrick Mayne, who was born[76] on 15 July 1916. There is a record of a marriage[77] of a Derrick W Mayne to Margaret E Kitto in Exeter in the July-Sept quarter of 1959, and sight of a marriage certificate will show if he was Albert and Alice's son. Derrick died[78] on 25 August 1996 in Hertfordshire.

Of **Albert's** military record there is little to tell us of when he enlisted. The Medal Roll shows that he was entitled to the Victory Medal and the British War Medal, and the Register of Soldiers' Effects shows that the Death Grant and War Gratuity were paid to his widow Alice E Mayne.

It is possible that Albert may have been a conscript and have trained on Salisbury Plain. He had joined the Coldstream Guards, 1st Battalion.

---

73   Marriage ref GRO 1847, July-Sept, Newton Abbot district vol 10, p 202

74   Marriage ref GRO 1875, April-June, N.A. vol 5b, p 280

75   Marriage ref GRO 1915, July-Sept, N.A. vol 5b, p 381

76   Birth ref GRO 1916, 15 July, N.A. vol 5b, p 127

77   Marriage ref GRO 1959, July-Sept, Exeter, vol 7a, p 878

78   Death ref GRO 1996, 25 August, Hitchin & Stevenage 1c, District 5341C, entry 269

General Haig ordered General Herbert Plumer, the commander of the British Second Army which occupied the Ypres Salient, to produce a plan in late 1916. Plumer believed that a force of 35 divisions and 5,000 guns would be necessary, which was far beyond the amount of artillery in the British Expeditionary Force.

Haig informed his Army commanders that his objectives were to wear down the German army, secure the Belgian coast and connect with the Dutch frontier by capturing Passchendaele Ridge and advancing on Roulers and Thourout, to cut the railway supplying the German garrisons holding the Western Front north of Ypres and the Belgian coast. An attack by the 4th Army would then begin on the coast, combined with an amphibious landing in support of the main advance to the Dutch frontier.

Private Albert Mayne was most likely a member of a scouting party sent out in the week 23-28 July to ascertain the strength and depth of enemy defences. Night patrols attempted to bring back prisoners for interrogation prior to the major assault. Philip Gibbs, official war correspondent, reported that there was not much fighting except "quick raids for body-snatching and machine-gun grabbing."

It is quite likely that a Coldstream Guards patrol had been surprised and the Germans would have criss-crossed the area with machine-gun and rifle fire.

The Dawlish Gazettte of 4th August 1917 carried a report that "the end of last week a Holcombe Soldier, Pte Reginald Honour of the Coldstream Guards, wrote home saying that a comrade of his, **Pte Bert Mayne**, of Dawlish, had been very seriously wounded in the legs and stomach."

His pals would have dragged Albert back to a trench for immediate bandaging of wounds. From there medical orderlies carried him to a Casualty Clearing Station for treatment and assessment. Those who stood a chance of recovery were then loaded on ambulances for bumpy and painful rides away from the battle area to hospital. Albert was taken to a General Hospital at Le Treport, near Dieppe.

Albert died of his wounds on August 9th 1917 and is buried in Mont Huon Military Cemetery at Le Treport. He was 21 years old.

Casualties

The British Official History recorded Fifth Army casualties for 31 July – 3 August as 27,001, of whom 3,697 were killed.

Commonwealth War Graves entry: **Albert Mayne**, Private 18321 Coldstream Guards, 1st Bn.
  Date of Death: 09/08/1917 Age: 20 (*actually 21-ed*)
  Cemetery: <u>MONT HUON MILITARY CEMETERY, LE TREPORT</u>

Location Information
  Le Treport is a small seaport 25 kilometres north-east of Dieppe. The Cemetery is 1.5 kilometres south of the town. The Cemetery stands on the D940.

Historical Information
  During the First World War, Le Treport was an important hospital centre and by July 1916, the town contained three general hospitals (the 3rd, 16th and 2nd Canadian), No.3 Convalescent Depot and Lady Murray's B.R.C.S. Hospital. The 7th Canadian, 47th and 16th USA General Hospitals arrived later, but all of the hospitals had closed by March 1919.

As the original military cemetery at Le Treport filled, it became necessary to use the new site at Mont Huon. There are now 2,128 Commonwealth burials of the First World War in the cemetery. The cemetery also contains more than 200 German war graves.

Additional Information:
Son of Henry and Sarah Mayne, of Dawlish, Devonshire; husband of A. E. Mayne, of Stevenage, Herts. The CWGC reference shows that Alice had moved to Stevenage, perhaps to live with her son Derrick. She is elsewhere shown to have died in Letchworth on 28 August 1967.
Albert Mayne is recorded on the Devon Roll of Honour with the Christian name "Bert" and without date or location of death. He is also listed on the Dawlish Boys' School Roll of Honour.

Dawlish War memorial inscription: MAYNE. B.   PTE.   COLDM GDS

Devon Heritage site info: 775210 Gunner Bertie Mayne of "B" Battery, the 245th West Riding Brigade of the Royal Field Artillery. Born in Leeds in 1895. Died 1 November 1918 aged 23. (*This information does not correspond with the CWGC entry, nor the regiment shown on Dawlish War Memorial. - ed*)

Last known address: 11 Old Town Street, Dawlish (1911 census)
Next of kin: Alice Edith Mayne, widow

References:
Free BMD (Birth Marriage Death records
Commonwealth War Graves Commission website
Subscription sites for :
Census and family tree information.
Medal Rolls and Register of Soldiers' Effects.

Coldstream Guards badge

Charles Henry BLACKMORE

Born: Dawlish, 22 July 1890   Died 29 August, 1917, aged 27

Private 827055   47th Battalion, Canadian Infantry

Charles Henry Blackmore was the great grandson of John and Elizabeth Blackmore.

John Blackmore (1791-1864?) was born in Barnstaple and married Elizabeth Perkins (1796-1875?) on 28 June 1818 at Chudleigh. She was born in Kingsteignton. They had two sons, James Blackmore and John Perkins Blackmore (1821-1901), both born in Chudleigh.

James Blackmore (1819-1905) married Elizabeth Leare (1819-1886) in Chudleigh Parish Church on 25th June 1843 and they lived at 75 Clifford Street, Chudleigh. James was a sawyer and carpenter. They had a large family:

Mary Jane	1843-	
James	1844-1849	
John	1846-1849	
Walter **	1847-1918	married Emma Quantick and they were parents to Reginald Charles Blackmore 1890- 22.9.1917 (q.v.)
Clara Ann	1849- 1944	
Joseph	1851- 1915	married Mary Jane Pike (1859-1927)
		His occupation was woodman and the family lived in Mamhead. They had a son, Andrew Blackmore(1886-1918), and in 1911 he was living in Ashcombe and was an Asylum Attendant at the Devon County Lunatic Asylum, Exminster. His name is engraved on the Ashcombe memorial, as this would have been his residence at the time of his enlistment. His name is also inscribed on the Mamhead memorial inside St Thomas Church, a memorial plaque inside Exminster Hospital, and another inside Exminster Church. He was killed in Syria on 21 November 1918.
James Henry	1852-1853	
John Albert	1854-	
Charles H	1856-1939	
Alice	1858-	
Thomas Leare	1860-1932	
Elizabeth Ellen	1862-	
Andrew **	1864-1946	married Clara Kate Dawe (1863-1932) who was born in Dawlish.

** The sons Walter and Andrew Blackmore were both carpenters. Each married and had a son who is remembered on Dawlish War Memorial. These were the cousins **Charles Henry Blackmore** and Reginald Charles Blackmore (k.i.a. 22/9/17) who died only days apart.

Andrew Blackmore married Clara Kate Dawe[79] in 1888. Clara K Dawe was the sister of Bessie Dawe, the wife of Henry John Hill (1867-1921).

Bessie Dawe and Henry John Hill were the parents of James Henry Hill (q.v.) who was killed on April 10th, 1917 and of Russell Hill (q.v.) who died in 1920, also remembered on Dawlish

---

79   Marriage ref GRO 1888, September, N.A., vol 5b, p 194

War Memorial. A further son, Frances Edward Hill (1894-1970) served in the War and survived.

In 1891, Andrew and Clara Blackmore were living at 1 Helena Place, Dawlish with Elsie Minnie (1888-), and **Charles Henry Blackmore**, 8 months.

In 1901 they were at 2 Hatcher Street, with two more children, Gwendoline Rose, (1892-1967) and Gladys M (1896-1927).

In 1911, Andrew and Clara had moved to the School House, Old Town Street, with their daughters Elsie Minnie, a domestic housemaid, and Gwendoline Rose a milliner's apprentice. Andrew was then a carpenter and joiner, and Clara was Caretaker of C C Schools.

It appears that he trained as a teacher at St Luke's College, Exeter, which had been a teacher training college since 1839. Charles Henry Blackmore was boarding at 3 Exeter Road, Crediton in 1911 and he is shown as an Assistant Schoolmaster, employed by Devon County Council. He was 20. His Canadian military record shows previous military experience as "St Lukes College, Company 4th Devons". This indicates that he joined the 4th Devons when he was undergoing teacher training.

He sailed from Bristol aboard the Royal George on 14th June 1911 and emigrated to Canada and was followed by his sister Gladys in 1913. *(Family information has been supplied by the granddaughter of Gladys in Canada -ed)*

On the outbreak of War men enlisted to join new regiments from Canada, Australia, New Zealand, India and other parts of the British Empire. Charles was deemed to be too short at 5' and ¾" for the initial enlistments in Canada. He had been working as a book-keeper and "Teacher Public School".

Charles was living at 410 Sherbrook Street, New Westminster when he was able to enlist with the Canadian Over-seas Expeditionary Force in Vancouver on October 27th, 1916, following the formation of 'Bantam Regiments' for which he was then deemed eligible.

New Westminster is a historically important city in the Lower Mainland region of British Columbia, and is a member municipality of the Greater Vancouver Regional District.

As the oldest city in western Canada, New Westminster has a long and rich history. In 1859, the Royal Engineers arrived from England to establish the first capital of the new colony of British

Columbia.

The chosen site was selected both for its beauty and strategic location on the Fraser River.

Charles H Blackmore   47th Battalion badge   War Memorial, New Westminster

Enlistment papers show that Charles joined the 143rd (British Columbia Bantams) Battalion. This battalion went overseas but was broken up and the men sent to either of two Reserve Battalions or the Canadian Railway Troops.

The 47th Battalion recruited in New Westminster, Vancouver and Victoria.

The **Battle of Hill 70** was a battle between the Canadian Corps and five divisions of the German 6th Army. The battle took place along the Western Front on the outskirts of Lens in the Nord-Pas-de-Calais region of France between 15th and 25th August 1917.

The objectives of the assault were to inflict casualties and to draw German troops away from the 3rd Battle of Ypres, rather than to capture territory. The Canadian Corps executed an operation designed to first occupy the high ground at Hill 70 quickly, and then establish defensive positions, from which combined small-arms and artillery fire, some of which used the technique of predicted fire for the first time, could be used to repel German counter-attacks and inflict as many casualties as possible. A later attempt by the Canadian Corps to extend its position into the city of Lens itself failed. Both sides suffered high casualties and Lens remained under German control. In both the German and the Canadian assessments of the battle it succeeded in its attrition objective.

The battle consisted of extensive use of poison gas by both sides, including the newly introduced German Yellow Cross shell containing the blistering agent sulphur mustard. Ultimately, the goals of the Canadian Corps were only partially accomplished. The Canadians were successful in preventing German formations from transferring local men and equipment to aid in defensive operations in the Ypres Salient but failed to draw in troops from other areas.

(ex-Wikipedia)

Charles Henry Blackmore is listed as having died of wounds and it is reasonable to assume that he was involved in some manner in the Battle of Hill 70 and died soon afterwards.

The Dawlish Gazette of 1st September 1917 carried, under the heading "PRO PATRIA",

"Mr and Mrs A Blackmore of Lytton House, Dawlish, were notified yesterday afternoon of the death of their only son, Pte. Charles Blackmore, of the Canadian Expeditionary Force. Deceased was only welcomed home from Canada, where he had done well, about two months ago. The Homeland's need proved an irresistible call to his patriotism. He left a sister behind in the Dominion. He was a teacher by profession – certificated and college-trained – but very soon discarded it in Canada for more profitable employment. His prospects overseas were bright and he had looked forward to "making good" still better after the war."

In the following week's paper there appeared mention of letters from his unit.

"Respecting the lamented death at the front of Pte. C H Blackmore, of the Canadian Infantry, briefly reported in our last issue, his parents Mr and Mrs A Blackmore of Lytton House, have received two letters from France. One from a chum, Pte Archie B Russell, who, in tendering his deepest sympathy, says: "Deceased was on duty with me in "No Man's Land" when he was sniped in the head and never regained consciousness. His body was taken out and properly buried a short distance behind, from which it will eventually be removed and placed in the Canadian Cemetery for our own brave fallen lads. Your son was liked by all the platoon, and his loss will be greatly felt, especially by myself, as he was in my section, and I knew several of his personal friends in Western Canada." The other letter was from Capt Harold McCausland, Chaplain, who gives particulars of Pte. Blackmore's death and the exact location of the grave, which he says is carefully marked. He adds. "Please accept the very deep and sincere sympathy of the Officer Commanding and all ranks. Your boy died a very manly and gallant death, doing his duty to King and country in the face of great danger. Surely such a death must merit final reward.""

The Vimy memorial to Canadian dead in the Pas de Calais is about 8km NE of Arras. 4 Divisions of the Canadian Corps captured Vimy Ridge on the 9th April 1917.

Commonwealth War Graves entry: BLACKMORE, CHARLES HENRY   Private   827055

29/08/1917   Canadian Infantry, 47th Bn.   **Vimy Memorial**, *above*

He is shown on the Devon Roll of Honour and the Dawlish Boys' School Roll of Honour.
Dawlish War memorial inscription: BLACKMORE C.H.   PTE.   47TH CAN.
Devon Heritage site info:

827055 Charles Henry Blackmore of the 47th Battalion (Quebec Regiment), the Canadian Infantry. Son of Andrew and Kate Blackmore of Dawlish. Born in Dawlish 22nd July 1890. Died 29 August 1917 aged 27.

The Vimy Memorial overlooks the Douai Plain from the highest point of Vimy Ridge, about eight kilometres northeast of Arras on the N17 towards Lens. (CWGC website)

Last known address: 410 Sherbrooke Street, New Westminster, British Columbia, Canada
Chas Blackmore is listed on the New Westminster War Memorial, British Columbia.

Next of kin: Clara Blackmore, mother, Lytton House, Regent Street, Dawlish
References:
> Free Birth, Marriage, death refs
> CWGC
> Attestation paper, Canada
> https://www.newwestcity.ca/
> http://1914-1918.invisionzone.com – Great War forum
> Battle of Hill 70 – Wikipedia
> Private correspondence with descendant
> Refs via subscription websites:
>> Census data
>> Family trees – Ancestry.co.uk
>>> Gregson/Blackmore (compiled by a great neice)
>>> Blackmore - Bond

It will be clear from reading of the family marriages that Dawlish was a busy small town with many personal connections being made. Some times a difficult circumstance will place members of a family in need of support. One such arises with the next casualty when reading the detail of the 1901 census.

Helen Annie Ashby married an army officer, Gerald Townley-Parker in Hinkley, Leicestershire in the summer of 1890. He should have been "a good prospect", being the son of a wealthy retired army officer whose household in 1881 in Brownsover, Warwickshire comprised two sons, a butler, footman, usher, two grooms, six helpers, a Housekeeper, housemaid, kitchen maid, scullery maid and an under house maid.

Unhappily Gerald Townley-Parker died aged 33 at Dawlish 2nd February 1892, a few weeks after the birth of his only child, Violet Caroline Townley-Parker, on 11th December 1891. It was said that they were living at Bridge House, Dawlish. Earlier in 1891 the census found them at Hill House, Melford, Suffolk.

Some confusion can be avoided in reading census results when recognising Helen Annie Ashby as the daughter of her widowed mother Helen Ashby, who was a visitor to The Rectory, Swindon, Glos in 1891 and a widow living on her own means. In 1901, she is described as "Grandma" below the entry for 9 year old Violet Townley-Parker when **in the household of John and Matilda Hockaday** in Dawlish. At that time Helen Townley-Parker was being treated in a private nursing home in 22 George Street off Hanover Square, London, and that may have caused her to place her daughter in the care of her mother in the home of the local cab proprietor, John Hockaday. His family were living at Hope Cottage, Plantation Terrace, a pretty neo-Gothic cottage of some size.

In Part One of this story of Dawlish, there is mention of the women who helped form the Dawlish Red Cross Voluntary Aid Detachment (VAD) and the role taken by Mrs Townley Parker as Commandant until she handed over to Maude Hildyard. Violet Townley-Parker supported her mother in VAD work.

In 1915 Violet Caroline Townley Parker was married to Lt. Col.Guy de Hoghton, Bt and gave her address as Bridge House, Dawlish on the wedding register at All Saints, Margaret Street, Marylebone, London on 11th February 1915. Sadly, the marriage failed in 1919. Violet next appears on record, aged 48, in the 1939 England and Wales Register, living at Alton, Hampshire with Adrienne Crom, daughter of a Belgian refugee family who came to Dawlish, and is shown as aged 28, with "unpaid domestic duties". A note shows Adrienne as a Member of the Belgian Red Cross, Ambulancier et Auxiliare de la Sante Publique. She also had a brief career in opera.

Percy John HOCKADAY

Born Q2, 1884, in Dawlish   Died 31st August 1917, Sudan, aged 33

Sergeant, 15361   Royal Engineers, 'K' Telegraph Company

Percy John Hockaday was the second son of John Hockaday and Matilda Hayes Bevan.

John Hockaday was the eldest son of William Hockaday (1823-) who had been born in Lewtrenchard and married Martha (1826-) from Bridestowe, West Devon.

By 1871 William was set up as a 'Fly Proprietor' and living at 3 Westcliff Hill, Dawlish with his children, all born in Dawlish, who were:

Mary A Hockaday	(1852-)	assisting her mother, a Lodging House keeper
John Hockaday	(1854-1922)	a Fly driver **
Emma "	(1862-)	a scholar
Frederick "	(1864-)	"
Richard "	(1866-)	"
Elizabeth "	(1868-)	
Thomas "	(1870-)	

** A fly is a fast carriage with two wheels and usually drawn by one horse, also known as a handsom cab.

John Hockaday and Matilda Hayes Bevan (1855-1945) married in 1879. Matilda was from Chudleigh. They had four children of which the eldest had died young:

Percy John Hockaday	(1880-1882)
Winifred Hockaday	(1882-1929),
Percy John Hockaday	(1884-1917),
Alfred Hayes Hockaday	(1886-1965).

In 1881 John Hockaday is listed in the census at 16 Brunswick Place, Dawlish but his wife and her first son Percy, 8 months old, were staying at the time with her mother, Mary Bevan, in Fore Street, Chudleigh. Her mother was a milliner and dress maker.

Percy John Hockaday was baptised in St Gregory's on 5th March 1884, and the birth was registered in the April-June quarter of 1884 (Newton Abbot district, vol 5b, page 118). He was given the same names as their first child, by that time deceased.

Photo, Percy dressed as a groom at Hope Cottage

John Hockaday ran a carriage hire business and was located at Brunswick Place in 1891, and at Hope Cottage, Plantation Terrace in 1901.

By this time there were twelve in the household at census time. As well as he and his wife, Percy was working as a coach painter, and Alfred was at home; there were two boarders, both bank clerks; Helen Ashby, a widow aged 64 and living on her own means was there with her daughter Violet Caroline Townley-Parker, aged 9; there were also a cook, a nurse, parlourmaid and an housemaid.

By 1911 John and Matilda Hockaday had moved to Exeter where he was a stableman, possibly indicating a failure of business in Dawlish or the impact of the new motor cars. They were living at 16 Eaton Place, Exeter with their daughter Winifred who had married Henry Thomas Simmonds (1880-) in 1905 and their child, John Henry L Simmonds (1910-). John and Matilda had adopted a son, Ernest John Gilman Hill (1901-) and there were three boarders.

Photo, Alfred and Percy with a sister (?) at Hope Cottage

Alfred Hayes Hockaday, married Dorothy Lucy Farleigh in 1909 and was working as a labourer for a railway contractor. They had a son, Jack Mervyn Hockaday (1910-1995).

From the news report in the Western Times of 7th September 1917 it appears that **Percy Hockaday** joined the Royal Engineers ca 1904 when he was twenty and specialised in wireless telegraphy. He may have been serving abroad at the time of the 1911 census, but in 1912 he was at home and **Percy** married Gertrude Gummer (1891-) in Exeter. It is not known if they had children or if she married again after his death. A War Gratuity of £18. 10s. 0d. was paid to his widow Gertrude in 1919.

The Royal Engineers had established a 'C' Troop in the late 19th century for communications. A major step forward in military communications was the invention by Alexander Graham Bell, in 1876, of the telephone and its subsequent introduction into military service.

In 1884 'C' Troop amalgamated with the 22nd and 34th Companies, Royal Engineers, to form the Telegraph Battalion Royal Engineers. The Battalion took part in the Nile Campaign and later played a prominent part in the 4th Ashanti War 1895 – 1896. Members of the detachment hacked a 72 mile path through the jungle from the Cape coast to Prahsu for an overhead line. They reached the enemy's capital and later their Commander was presented with the Ashanti King's chair to commemorate the detachments excellent service.

Percy John Hockaday was appointed Inspector of Telegraphs for the Egyptian Government in 1912 and although granted leave in 1914 he remained in Egypt and the Sudan on the outbreak of war.

Percy John Hockaday was entitled to the 1915 Star as well as the British War Medal, the Victory Medal and the Sultan's Sudan (1910) Medal with the 'Darfur 16' clasp (see below). This last was given by the Khedive of Egypt in respect of a punitive expedition carried out in response to a rebel leader obtaining guns and ammunition that threatened to join forces with the Turks against the Allies. (See a full account in http://www.kaiserscross.com/188001/224322.html)

A Medal Roll Index Card gives his rank as Sergeant and this is adopted here.

His death was given as sunstroke.

Further information about the Royal Engineers' role in developing and inspecting telegraph services may be found in the extensive Sudan Archive in Durham University Library. There are papers relating, inter alia, to the Sudan Government Railways 1911-1932, Posts and Telegraphs 1914-1932 (Boscott A.J.) and Egyptian Army 1909-1935 (Butler S.S.).

He is remembered on the Devon Roll of Honour as 'Hockaday, Percy John, Divn Insp, R.E., 31 Aug 1917, Egypt' and on the Dawlish Boys' School Roll of Honour as 'Hockaday.P.J. Divn Ins, Tel'.
http://www.angelfire.com/realm3/ruvignyplus/004.html

Dawlish War memorial inscription: HOCKADAY.P.J. Divn Ins, Tel R.E.

Commonwealth War Graves entry: HOCKADAY, PERCY JOHN   2nd Corporal   15361 31/08/1917   Royal Engineers, K. Telegraph Coy.

Grave Ref: 6. C. 16. Khartoum War Cemetery, Sudan.

http://www.kaiserscross.com/188001/224322.html

Last known address: 16 Eaton Place, Exeter

Next of kin: Gertude Hockaday, widow
References:
Birth marriage death refs
profile by Sheila Ralls
Royal Signals website
Darfur campaign 1916
Census data
UK, Army Registers of Soldiers' Effects
British Army WW1 Medal Rolls   Index   Cards

Holroyd Edward HAMLYN

Born Q1 1895, Teignmouth   Died 16 September 1917, aged 22

L/Cpl, service no 28018   Somerset Light Infantry, 7th Battalion

The Hamlyn family were from Teignmouth. The Hamlyn surname was introduced into England around 1066. It derived from the personal name Hamon, meaning home and was first recorded in Devon in 1121. Holroyd Edward Hamlyn is remembered on Teignmouth seafront memorial and St James' memorial window, Teignmouth, as well as at St Mary's Church, Cofton.

Holroyd Edward Hamlyn was the fourth child of Thomas William Hamlyn (1866-1945) and Emma Full (1866-1940) of Teignmouth. Thomas W Hamlyn was a dock labourer. They married in 1889 and had ten children between 1890 and 1907:

Edith Harriet Hamlyn	1890-1977
Asenath Eveline Hamlyn	1891-1978
Henry Thomas Hamlyn[80]	1893-1916
Holroyd Edward Hamlyn	1895-1917
Gladys Victoria Hamlyn	1897-1997
Thomas William Hamlyn[81]	1899-1918
Sidney Hector Hamlyn	1901-1973
Frederick Albert Hamlyn	1902-1985
Eglon Ernest Hamlyn	1905-1985
Samuel Mervyn Hamlyn	1907-1991

They lived at 26 Bitton Hill, Teignmouth in 1901 and 1911. After leaving school **Holroyd Edward Hamlyn** became a mason's labourer.

He was sent to the front with the 12th Labour Battalion of the Devonshire Regiment as Private no. 17269. He was later promoted to Lance Corporal, where he was required to supervise a section, which is a small team of up to four soldiers. He would have worn one chevron on his sleeve.
He was later invalided home. On returning to the front he was attached to the 7th Battalion, Somerset Light Infantry, service no. 28018.

The connection with Dawlish is through his name appearing on the War Memorial in Cofton churchyard. In 1915 he married Caroline Crews (1887-1964) who lived at Cofton.
Caroline Crews was born ca 1887 to John Havill Crews (1861-1938) and Caroline Coggins (1859-1929). He was a general labourer and they were a mobile family as shown by the birth places of their children in the 1891 census:

Elizabeth	dau	(1883-)	born	Heavitree
Annie	dau	(1885-)		Topsham
Caroline	dau	(1887-1964)		Powderham
John H	son	(1888-)		Cofton

At this point they were living at Cockwood. Later, Caroline Crews took a position of servant cook to William Edgelow, physician of Braddon Villa, Torquay (1911 census).

---

80   Henry Thomas Hamlyn was a Private in the Devonshire Regiment, killed on the first day of the Battle of the Somme 1 July 1916.

81   Thomas William Hamlyn died in action in Flanders on 4 April 1918

After Holroyd Hamlyn's death Caroline married twice more. In the Oct-Dec quarter of 1919 she married[82] John Dodge (1876-1951). John Dodge was a gardener living at Westwood, Cofton and he was a first cousin to Arthur George Dodge (q.v.) who is also remembered at St Mary's, Cofton, for he died in Iraq on 28th December 1917.

John Dodge died on 30th June 1951 at Middlewood, Starcross and left proceeds to his widow Caroline Dodge and a son Harold John Dodge who is mentioned also in the Probate of Caroline Rawlings (Caroline Fowler), see below.

After the death of John Dodge, Caroline married[83] William G Fowler (1876-1958) in 1951. William Fowler died[84] in 1958 and Caroline Fowler (Caroline Rawlings) died at Newport, Isle of Wight on 3 January 1964, aged 77. There is no record of a marriage to a Rawlings. Probate was granted to a solicitor and to Harold John Dodge, Mill hand.

There is little information available about the activities of the 7th Battalion, Somerset Light Infantry apart from a reference to being involved in attacks in the Langemarck area during August and September 1917 in one of the stages of the Third battle of Ypres (Passchendaele). The Regimental History provides no specific information to prove an instance of storming German blockhouses with Canadian troops. There is no doubt that they were in the front line at this time, as shown by the report from his Commanding Officer, writing to his widow stating:-

> "It is with the greatest regret that I have to inform you of the death of your husband, who was killed in action on the 16th.inst. He was at the time occupying a small post in the front line and his death, which was instantaneous, was caused by a German shell. He was buried behind the post which he had held and a cross was erected to mark the grave. Although Lce.-Corpl. Hamlyn had been with us a short time, I always found him a brave soldier and his loss to the Company at this time will be felt both by the officers and men with whom he served."

Commonwealth War Graves entry:
> Lance Corporal,   Service No: 28018   Date of Death: 16/09/1917   Somerset Light Infantry, 7th Bn
Panels 41 to 42 and 163a, Tyne Cot Memorial, Zonnebeke, West Flanders

Holroyd is not recorded on the Devon Roll of Honour for Dawlish, nor on the Dawlish Boys' School Roll of Honour.
The Teignmouth War Memorial carries his name along with those of his two brothers.
Devon Heritage site shows "Lance Corporal Holroyd Edward Hamlyn of the 7th Battalion, the Somerset Light Infantry. Son of Thomas and Emma Hamlyn of Teignmouth and brother of Henry and Thomas (see above). Born in Teignmouth in the March Quarter of 1895. Died 16 September 1917 aged 22. "

A small Death Grant was paid to his widow, Caroline and a War Gratuity of £6.0s. 0d. Was also paid in 1919.

82   Marriage GRO ref 1919, Oct-Dec, Newton Abbot, vol 5b, page 418
83   Marriage GRO ref 1951, Oct-Dec, NewtonAbbot, vol 7a, p 1011
84   Death GRO ref 1958, Oct-Dec, Exeter, vol 7a, p 382

Last known address: 26 Bitton Hill, Teignmouth
Next of kin: Caroline Hamlyn, widow

References:
Teignmouth seafront memorial   Teignmouth St James's Memorial window
H Roche, Teign Heritage Centre   Cofton churchyard memorial
CWGC
refs via subscription websites:
         Census records   Beale family tree

Memorial at St Mary's Cofton, *below*   Tyne Cot Memorial, Zonnebeke, West Flanders

William Robert HOLLOWAY

Born Withington, Lancs, 2 November 1889   Died Flanders, 20 September 1917, aged 27

2nd Lieutenant   69th Company, Machine Gun Corps (infantry)

William Robert Holloway was the third successive William in his family tree. The first, his grandfather, was a licensed victualler. He and his wife were living in Old Alresford, Hants in 1871 with their son William George Holloway (1866-1925) who was born in Marnhull, a small village 3 miles north of Sturminster Newton, Dorset. He was baptised on 3 June 1866 in Lydlinch a few miles to the south-west. His father was then described as a "yeoman, born in Sedgehill, Wiltshire."

William George Holloway began a mobile career and married Lucy Downs (1866-1927) in St Mary's, Atherstone, Warwickshire on 27 December 1888.

The first of fourteen children (of which twelve survived by the 1911 census) was **William Robert Holloway** who was born at Ladybarn on 2 November 1889. Ladybarn is a small suburban area between Withington and Fallowfield on the edge of Manchester. A second child to appear in the 1891 census was Alice, a daughter of 2 Months. In 1891 they were living at 4 Mayfield Road, Levershulme, Lancashire and William George Holloway was a contractor's timekeeper.

William George Holloway's work for contractors, principally Sir John Jackson Ltd, can be traced in the places of birth of their children:

> from 1889-1891 in Levershulme, Lancashire;
>
> 1895 in Barry, Glamorgan;
>
> 1897-1902 in Keyham, Devonport;
>
> 1906 – 1909 in Kinlochleven, Argyllshire.

In the last position he was Master of Lodge Glencoe Freemasons and **WRH** was Senior Deacon.

William Robert Holloway is shown in 1901 at the age of 11 with his family at 74 Goshen Street, Devonport where his father was acting as a Contractor's Cashier. William G and Lucy had eight children at that point.

William R H attended Devonport Technical School in the years of the family residence there (He later received a reference from the Principal of DTS for his application to be considered for a Commission in 1916.).

In 1909 their father, William G Holloway, went with his son, Albert, to South America to build the railway over the Andes from La Paz, Bolivia, to Arica on the Chilean coast. **William** was to join them.

At the census in 1911 their mother, Lucy, was living as 'head' of household at 2 Ryburn Villas, Rowanfield Road, Cheltenham with ten children:

Alice Holloway, 20, single	born in	Levenshulme,Lancs
Caroline Louise Holloway, 15, single,		Barry, Glamorgan
Lucy May Holloway, 13,		Ford, Devonport
Thomas Neal Holloway, 12,		Ford, Devonport
Lilian Ellen Holloway, 11		Keyham, Devonport
Margaret Maud Elizabeth Holloway, 10		Keyham, Devonport
Doris Irene Holloway, 8		Keyham, Devonport
Mary Downs Holloway, 4		Kinlochleven, Argyll
Phyllis Sarah Holloway, 3		Kinlochleven, Argyll
George Ian Holloway, 1		Kinlochleven, Argyll

The report in the *Dawlish Gazette of 29th September 1917* says that William Robert Holloway "came home from South America to join the colours, after spending six years there with his brother, who is at present serving on the Western Front." That would be a reference to Albert Reginald Holloway. His father had meanwhile been engaged in constructing the Al Hindaya barrage across the Euphrates, south west of Bagdad, when he was interned by the Ottomans for the duration of the Great War. He died in a boating accident in Newfoundland in 1925, with his son Albert, and they are commemorated on their grave in Corner Brook, Newfoundland. Their monument also commemorates WRH and his mother, Lucy.

William Robert Holloway signed his attestation for Short Service (For the Duration of the War) and swore an Oath of Allegiance in Stoke-on-Trent on 12th May 1915 for service in the Motor Machine Gun Corps. He was not married. The form shows that he was a Machinist and Electrician and living at 19 Cornford Grove, Balham, London SW. This address is that given in Elsie Holloway's statement of 1918 for Lucy Holloway and eight children, most probably where they had lived while W G Holloway was interned by the Turks.
The descriptive report on enlistment show that his father was at the time in Damascus.

William was appointed (unpaid) Acting Bombardier on 2nd July 1915 and promoted to Corporal on 8th August and posted to the British Expeditionary Force (BEF). He disembarked at Le Havre on 6th February 1916.
William applied for a Temporary Commission on 6th August 1916 from the 19th Motor Machine Gun Battery, B.E.F, France. He had at that point reached the rank of Corporal with a regimental number 1158. His commanding officer gave a character reference for the 15 months in which he had been under his command and stated that "his moral character has been exemplary." Brigadier General Lecky personally interviewed WRH and recommended him for training at the Artillery Training School.
On 29th August he was accepted for admission to Cadet School in England and ordered to report to S.D.3 War Office, on return from leave granted from 29th September to 8th October 1916.

On 24th February 1917, WRH was granted a Temporary Commission as 2nd Lieutenant in the 19th Motor Machine Gun Corps.

Four days later, William Robert Holloway married Elsie Elizabeth Currey by licence at the Register Office, Aston, Birmingham on 28th February, 1917. He was 27 and she was 21 and they were living at 205 Bordesley Green. He was able to sign as a 2nd Lieutenant, M.G.C. (Electrical engineer); Elsie was a munition worker. Neither of the parents signed the register (her father was already serving in France, see below).
William made a Will in her favour dated 1st June 1917 which was witnessed by two 2nd Lieutenants in 69 Company, M.G.C.
Elsie Elizabeth Currey was the daughter of Thomas and Bessie Currey of Dawlish. Thomas Gibins Currey (1861-1921) of Dawlish married Bessie Shapter (1861-) of Ashcombe on Christmas Day 1882[85], and they went on to have ten children of which nine survived by 1911.

---

85   Marriage GRO ref St Thomas, Oct-Dec 1882, vol 5b, p 71

Thomas was a general labourer and builder's labourer, and was drafted into the Army Service Corps at the age of 45 on 15th September 1915. *(this is the age given on the Short Service Attestation, but his real age was 54. He may have been attracted to serve by the Army pay, to support his family.)* His military record survived the Blitz and it shows that he was a Private, no 304814 in No 2, Labour Corps of the A.S.C. and arrived at Rouen on 22nd September 1915. He remained in France until September 1918 when he was returned to Home Establishment (Over-age) and was discharged on 1st October 1918.

The Machine Gun Corps was established on 14 October 1914, with King George V as its Colonel-in-Chief. The best men from the Rifle Brigades were chosen and underwent additional training. They had to learn how to fill ammunition belts, strip down and re-assemble their machine guns, both Maxim and Vickers, rectify stoppages, map reading, tactics and most important of all, to learn how to work out firing angles. In addition, they learned semaphore signalling and Morse code.

By 1915 the Maxim Machine Gun was replaced by the more efficient Vickers Machine Gun, which became the Corps insignia. This gun had a tripod base, and a barrel encased with a jacket, which held water to keep the gun cool. Including 10lbs. of water it weighed 58.5lbs and had a six-man crew. Two men carried the equipment, two carried the ammunition and two helped to reload empty canvas ammunition belts. Each belt held 250 rounds and the gun could fire 500 rounds per minute.

It had an effective range of 2.5 miles and by the use of plunging fire was effective in attacking enemy held road junctions, supply lines, trench systems and areas of increased enemy troop build-up.

The Corps' duties included accompanying the first wave of every assault and to remain to cover every retirement. This often meant being well ahead of the infantry. Knowing the effectiveness of machine guns, each post became the target of every enemy gun within range. Casualties were very high and the Corps was nicknamed "The Suicide Club".

There are no surviving records for the Machine Gun Corps. They were all burnt when their H.Q. was burnt to the ground in a "mysterious" fire in 1922, shortly after the Corps was disbanded.

On 20th September 1917 the phase of the third battle of Ypres known as the Battle of Menin Road commenced.

On 28th September Mrs W R Holloway wrote to the War Office,

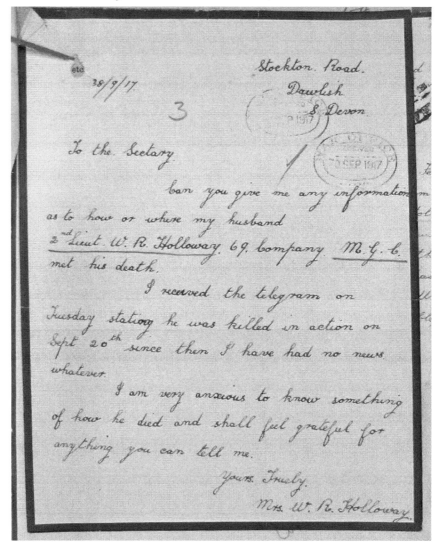

The Military Secretary replied on 1st October suggesting that she write to the Officer Commanding, 69th Company, Machine Gun Corps for particulars. On 9th February 1918 the *Dawlish Gazette* reported the receipt of a letter from the Captain, Commanding 69th Coy, MGC to say that "Your husband was killed in action leading his men over the parapet on 20th September. He was hit by a piece of shrapnel in the head and died almost immediately....Your husband was respected and like by all who knew him, both Officers and men, and we all feel his loss very much, and all unite in offering you our sincerest sympathy...."

In due course the effects of 2nd Lieut: W R Holloway were sent by registered post comprising 1 wrist watch with strap and guard, 1 identity disk and chain, 1 cigarette case and 1 photo.

Elsie Elizabeth Holloway was recognised as the next of kin and declared that a child, William Robert Holloway, was born on 5th February 1918.

Other relatives were "8 children of the deceased officer's mother, Lucy Holloway, residing at 19 Cornford Grove, Balham, S W London."

Elsie also stated that William Robert Holloway was born at 44 St George's Road, Burnage, Fallowfield, Withington. Her statement was given in the presence of the Vicar of Dawlish on 28th February, 1918.

Elsie Elizabeth Holloway married again, to George H Baker in late 1920[86]. There were two further children of this marriage.

William Robert Holloway is shown on the Devon Roll of Honour as "Holloway W.E.   Lieut M.G.C. " No date or place of death is indicated.
Dawlish War memorial inscription: HOLLOWAY W.E.   LIEUT   M.G.C.

Devon Heritage site info: W.HOLLOWAY - 2nd Lieutenant William Robert Holloway of the 69th Company, the Machine Gun Corps. Son of William George and Lucy Holloway; husband of Elsie Elizabeth Baker (formerly Holloway), of 7 King St, Dawlish; Born in Sculcoates, Yorkshire in the December Quarter of 1890. Died 20 September 1917. (*Date and Birth location incorrect, see above-ed*)

Commonwealth War Graves entry: HOLLOWAY, WILLIAM ROBERT   Second Lieutenant   20/09/1917 Age: 28   Machine Gun Corps (Infantry), 69th Coy.
Panel Ref: Panel 154 to 159 and 163A. Tyne Cot Memorial, Flanders
Son of William George and Lucy Holloway; husband of Elsie Elizabeth Baker (formerly Holloway), of 7, King St., Dawlish, Devon.

Last known address: Stockton Road, Dawlish
Next of kin: widow, Elsie Elizabeth Holloway

References:
Birth Marriage Death refs   Officer Records, National Archives, Kew
Correspondence with family members, including family history data.
Research by the late Campbell Brown re Corporal Hubert John Bright, MGC (died 17/04/1917)
Refs via subscription sites: Marriage refs
Census entries   Military record T G Currey
Clarke family tree – Ancestry.co.uk   Currey family tree

At the Service of Commemoration in St Agatha's R.C. Church on 20th September 2017 members of his family attended and gave the tribute.

86   Marriage GRO ref Newton Abbot, 1920 Oct-Dec, vol 5b, page 290a

Charles Frederick KING

Born Dawlish, 28 October 1882   Died Flanders, 20 September 1917, aged 34
2ⁿᵈ Lieutenant   Devonshire Regiment (attached to 1ˢᵗ/9th Battalion, King's Liverpool Regiment)

Charles Frederick King came from a family based in Gillingham, Dorset, until his father became a school master in Dawlish.

His grandparents, George and Elizabeth King, were born in Gillingham and George King (1830-) was a tailor employing one man and two boys in his business. They had five children by the 1871 census, being James Frederick (1855-), Ellen J (1857-), William C (1859-), Lucy A (1865-) and Kate Eliza (1867-).

James Frederick King was a pupil teacher after an education at Gillingham Grammar School.
He married Frances Mary Nicholls in 1881[87]. Frances was the daughter of Joseph Nicholls of White Hall, Handsworth, Birmingham.

Charles Frederick King was baptised at St Gregory the Great, Dawlish on 10ᵗʰ December 1882[88].
The 1891 census shows the family at 3 Longlands, and James F King is an 'Elementary School teacher'. The family comprised: James Frederick King, 35, Frances, his wife, 28,
Charles Frederick, 8, Winifred Mary, 6, Eileen Dorothy, 4, Muriel, 2, and Ethel M, 5 months.

In the 1901 census James F King described himself as schoolmaster & organist with three more children, Marjorie (1897-), Mervyn (1900-), Marion (1900-).
By 1911, James F King was a 'Head Schoolmaster of a Council School', most probably Dawlish Boys' School. His wife, Frances, was an assistant teacher.
In the *Western Times of 21 December 1914* it was reported that "Dawlish Parish Church choir carollers, under the direction of Mr. J. F. King, commence this evening. The proceeds to be given to the local Red Cross Society." He is frequently mentioned in newspaper reports as choir-master and organist and clearly was a focal point for musical activity in the town.

James Frederick King initiated the Boys' School Roll of Honour which hung in the lobby of the School and was recorded in the *Dawlish Gazette of December 19, 1914* as "containing the names of those Old Boys of the school who have either given their lives for their country or been wounded in battle. At present the number is eleven, five killed and six wounded."

Charles' mother, Frances, became a volunteer with the Dawlish Voluntary Aid Detachment (VAD) and worked as Head Cook from November 1914 to April 1915 and then as a needleworker until April 1919. Mildred King was a Nurse at Torquay V A Hospital during 1916.

Charles Frederick King was educated at Dawlish Boys' School and is recorded on their Roll of Honour.
After leaving school, Charles joined the Royal Navy in 1900 as an Assistant Clerk (Paymaster's Branch) and was promoted to Clerk in July 1901, and to Assistant Paymaster in October 1903, a rank that he held until completion of 12 years in 1913.

---

87   Marriage GRO ref Newton Abbot, 1881, Apr-Jun, Vol 5b, page 214
88   Birth ref GRO N.A., Q4, 1882, vol 5b, page 122

On the outbreak of war he joined the Gloucestershire Regiment, 13th Battalion, in August 1914 in the rank of Captain, but resigned in 1916 when he enlisted with the Coldstream Guards as a Private, no 17806. He served with the British Expeditionary Force in France from March 1916 and was promoted in the field "for courage in the trenches".

He was gazetted 2nd Lieutenant, Devonshire Regiment on 26 June 1917, and was then attached to the 6th (Territorial) Battalion the King's (Liverpool Regiment). The *Dawlish Gazette of Saturday, October 6th, 1917,* reported that " While he was home on leave in Dawlish he gave an instructive lecture to the Dawlish Volunteer platoon. He might have stayed behind as Lecturer and Instructor, but he chose to go to the Front, and was taken from the Devons and attached to the King's Liverpool Regiment."

Charles Frederick King was killed in action on the Menin Road on 20th September 1917. He had been reported as missing since 20th- 25th September. In the course of a letter he wrote to his parents he said," I am honoured by having to lead over the first rush... I'm lucky, but it's a hard nut to crack."

The plan prepared by General Plumer was to capture the Gheluvelt Plateau which gave commanding views of the German lines and there were to be a series of attacks at six-day intervals, supported by reinforcements of medium and heavy duty artillery. It was to start on the 20th September with the aim of destroying German strong points, pillboxes and fortified farms. A famous painting by the war artist Paul Nash shows the shattered trees, deep shell holes filled with water and heavy thunder clouds menacing two lone soldiers.

On 20th September 1917 the 9th Division attacked at 0540 with the 27th and South African Brigades. The front line was east of the village of Frezenburg and along the line of the Frezenburg Ridge and the attack was in the direction of Zonnebeke 2400 yards away, although the final objective that day included the capture of Zonnebeke and Bremen Redoubts some 800 yards from the start line. Hanebeek Wood was quickly taken and the 27th Brigades' final objective the Zonnebeke Redoubt. The enemy made no show of strength and 40 prisoners were taken.

The Dawlish Gazette of 13th October printed the content of a letter from G Tyson.

> "Dear Mrs King, - I felt it my duty to write and tell you how awfully sorry I was to hear of the sad news that your son was killed in action on the 20th ult. He went over with his platoon under the second in command of my Company. I was away on a course at the time and when I returned heard the news. I made numerous enquiries as to his death and now understand that he was killed by machine gun fire and death was instantaneous. This is just from information from one of the men in my Company... It is difficult to get authentic news. Your son's servant states that the last he saw of Mr King was up at a place called 'Galapoli'; after that he was never seen. And it is feared he was killed. It was a great blow to me. Although he had not long been with the Battalion I thought a great deal of him, and found what a good soldier and fine fellow he was. He did awfully good work and was very popular with the men and all officers. His loss is keenly felt in the Battalion. -Yours faithfully, G Tyson"

The Colonel wrote "He had not been with us long, but we all took to him at once, and I am certain he was a very fine soldier, and a great loss."

In the tribute given at his centenary Service of Commemoration, Michael Clayson said;

"Today we remember a man who died on the Western Front having made the choice to return to the field of battle despite having been offered the honourable alternative of remaining safe at home as an instructor. His fair share of the action as a combatant was already completed, but he chose to go back....

In 1913 he left the Navy and returned to civilian life. Little did he know that just one year later he would be enlisted as a soldier in the King's army.

Fought in large part to relieve pressure on the French further along the line, the Passchendale campaign was fought over horrendous terrain. A fellow officer described it - *"...Those who took part in it will never erase from their minds its many ghastly features, among which the mud and the multitude of dead will stand out pre-eminent. Of the former it must be said that the sodden condition of the ground, though it stopped our advance, certainly prevented many casualties from shell-fire, but at the same time many a wounded man was sucked down into the horrible quagmire and stretcher-bearers found their task in many cases beyond their powers"..*

Sadly this may well have been the fate of Charles King, for he is one of the multitude of soldiers with no known grave, memorialised at Tyne Cot.

He said he was honoured to be fulfilling his duty leading his men into battle,

Let his own words be his epitaph as we remember him today."

The grave to Percival King and plinth tribute to Charles Frederick King in Dawlish Cemetery

He is recorded on the Devon Roll of Honour,
Dawlish Boys' School Roll of Honour,
De Ruvigny's Roll of Honour.
Dawlish War memorial inscription:
KING C.F.   LIEUT.   DEVON REGT.

Commonwealth War Graves entry: KING, CHARLES FREDERICK   Second Lieutenant
20/09/1917   Age: 34   Devonshire Regiment, attd. 1st/9th Bn. The King's (Liverpool Regiment)   Panel Ref: Panel 38 to 40. Tyne Cot Memorial, Flanders
Son of James Frederick and Frances M. King, of 3, Longlands, Dawlish, Devon. Formerly Asst. Paymr. R.N., 13th Bn. Gloucestershire Regt. and Coldstream Guards.

Last known address: 3 Longlands Terrace, Dawlish
Next of kin: father, James Frederick King
References:
Free Birth Marriage Death refs   Red Cross VAD records for Dawlish
Refs via susbscription website, Ancestry: The Navy List
UK, De Ruvigny's Roll of Honour 1914-1919   Census records   UK, medal records

Reginald Charles BLACKMORE

Born Q4, 1890 Dawlish	Died 22 September 1917, Palestine, aged 27
Lance Corporal, 240413	Devonshire Regt, 5th (Prince of Wales) Battalion

Reginald Charles Blackmore was the great grandson of John and Elizabeth Blackmore.
John Blackmore (1791-1864?) was born in Barnstaple and Elizabeth Perkins (1796-1875?), born in Kingsteignton. They married on 28 June 1818 at Chudleigh. They had two sons, James Blackmore and John Perkins Blackmore (1821-1901), both born in Chudleigh.

James Blackmore (1819-1905) married Elizabeth Leare (1819-1886) in Chudleigh Parish Church on 25th June 1843 and they lived at 75 Clifford Street, Chudleigh. James was a sawyer and carpenter. They had a large family:

Mary Jane	1843-	
James	1844-1849	
John	1846-1849	
Walter	1847-1918	married Emma Quantick and they were parents to **Reginald Charles Blackmore**.
Clara Ann	1849- 1944	
Joseph 1851- 1915		
James Henry	1852-1853	
John Albert	1854-	
Charles H	1856-1939	
Alice	1858-	
Thomas Leare	1860-1932	
Elizabeth Ellen 1862-		
Andrew1864-1946		married Clara Kate Dawe (1863-1932) who was born in Dawlish. They were parents of Charles Henry Blackmore

The sons Walter and Andrew were both carpenters in turn. Each had a son who is remembered on Dawlish War Memorial and Reginald Charles Blackmore and Charles Henry Blackmore (1890-29/8/1917) q.v. were cousins who died only days apart.

Walter Blackmore was baptised in Chudleigh Anglican church on 17th October 1847. He went to Chudleigh Primary School and was first employed as a Plough Boy (1861) before he became a carpenter and lived in Chudleigh. He was living at home in 75 Clifford Street, Chudleigh in 1871.
Walter married Emma Quantick in the July-Sept quarter of 1875 and they moved to Dawlish (ca 1884) where the 1891 census shows at 20 Old Town Street, Dawlish:

Walter Blackmore	Head,	41	Carpenter	born	Chudleigh
Emma "	Wife,	36			Coryton, Devon
Alfred "	son,	12	Scholar		Mamhead
Frederick	son,	9	"		"
Nelly (Elizabeth Ellen) dau		6	"		"
Polly (Mary Ann)	dau	3	"		"
Reginald	son	5mths		born	Dawlish
James "	father widower 71		retired carpenter		Chudleigh

The 1901 census shows them at 29 Old Town Street with four children:

Fred	1882-	a carpenter
Ellen	1885-	dressmaker
Polly	1888-	also a dressmaker
Reggie	**1890 – 22/9/17**	a scholar

Reginald Charles Blackmore was born in the 4th quarter of 1890 in Dawlish[89]. After leaving school he worked as a compositor for a printer.

In 1911 aged 21 he lived with his parents at 2 Frederick Terrace with his sister Elizabeth /Ellen Cole, who was married and with her daughter Phyllis Ethel Cole (1908-) and son Charles Reginald Cole (1910-).

We do not know when Reginald joined the army, only that he enlisted at Plymouth. He is likely to have joined the Territorials before the war started. He was a fine athlete, and a member of Dawlish Football Club.

The Devonshire's 1/5th (Prince of Wales's) Battalion
(from http://www.keepmilitarymuseum.org)

In 1908, when the Volunteers became part of the newly formed Territorial Army, two longstanding Devon volunteer units merged to form the 5th (Territorial Force) Battalion of the Devonshire Regiment. Based on Plymouth, the 5th recruited from the south-west of the county. The outbreak of war found them at their annual camp on Woodbury Common, Exeter. They never returned.

The 1/5th were in Millbay, Plymouth, later in August 1914 as part of Devon & Cornwall Brigade, Wessex Division. They sailed for India on 9th October 1914, landing at Karachi 11 November 1914. They came under orders of 3rd (Lahore) Divisional Area at Multan. In December 1915 they moved to Lahore.

They spent two years at Multan, supplying drafts to units in operational theatres, including 50 men who in 1915 were sent to join the 2nd Dorsets at Kut el Amara. In March 1917 they left for Egypt and landed at Suez, Egypt on 4th April 1917. Early May found them at El Arish.

On 25th June 1917 they transferred to 232nd Brigade, 75th Division.

This formation was created during the war. On 16 March 1917 the War Office gave permission to the GOC Egyptian Expeditionary Force, Sir Edmund Allenby, to form a new Division from the units of the Territorial Force which were now arriving from India. On 21 May further instructions were given that the three infantry brigades should incorporate Indian battalions; this was augmented on 11 June by instructions that each brigade should have three Indian battalions and one British. It was, strictly, a Division of the Territorial Force but "indianised" to a great extent. Division HQ came into existence at El Arish on 25 June 1917. The complete Division was a long time in formation, the artillery not being full to establishment until October 1917.

In June 1917 they crossed into Palestine, where General Allenby was planning how to capture Jerusalem by Christmas. Their baptism of fire came on 8th July at Samson's Ridge, near Gaza, when they were heavily shelled. On the 20th they suffered 80 casualties from shelling at Umbrella Hill while supporting the Bedfordshire Regiment's attack.

After Beersheba was captured in late October the Battalion took part in the advance towards Jerusalem.

---

89   Birth GRO ref 1890, Q4, Newton Abbot district, vol 5b, page 92

The Western Times of Friday 28 September 1917 reported: 'Pte. Reg.Blackmore, Devons, son of Mr & Mrs Blackmore, Frederick Cottages, Dawlish, has been dangerously wounded in Egypt. His parents received official news on Tuesday. Pte. Blackmore went to India on the outbreak of war, being a Territorial Volunteer. He was a fine athlete, and a member of Dawlish Football Club. Previous to the war he was engaged as a printer with an Exeter firm.'

Reginald Charles Blackmore is recorded on the Devon Roll of Honour as 'Blackmore, Reginald Charles, L/Cpl, Devon Regt, 23rd Sept 1917, Egypt' and on the Dawlish Boys' School Roll of Honour as 'Blackmore, R.C. Lnce Corporal, Devon Regiment.' *below.*

Dawlish War memorial inscription: BLACKMORE R.C.   L/CORPL.   DEVON REGT.
Devon Heritage site info:
240413 Lance Corporal Reginald Charles Blackmore of the Devonshire Regiment, the 5th(Prince of Wales) Battalion (Territorials). Son of Walter and Emma Blackmore of Frederick Terrace, Dawlish. Born in Dawlish in the December quarter of 1890. Died 22 September 1917 aged 27.

Commonwealth War Graves entry: BLACKMORE, R C   Lance Corporal 240413
22/09/1917   Age: 25 Devonshire Regiment, 1st/5th Bn.
Grave Ref: D. 97. Deir El Belah War Cemetery, Palestine.
Son of Mrs. Emma Blackmore, of 2, Frederick Terrace, Dawlish, Devon.

Last known address: 2 Frederick Terrace, Dawlish
Next of kin: Walter Blackmore, father (died in 1918).
A Death Grant of £9. 4s. 4d. Was paid to his father in 1917 and a War Gratuity of £14. 0s.0d was paid to his mother in 1919.
An award of the British War Medal and the Victory Medal was made to his next of kin
References: Free Birth Marriage Death refs
http://www.1914-1918.net/devons.htm
http://www.keepmilitarymuseum.org
Refs via subscription websites: census records
UK soldiers who died in the Great War   UK, Army Registers of Soldiers' Effects
Gregson/Blackmore family tree – Ancestry.co.uk

An empty chair

As time passed the realisation must have crept into the Jackson household in the Manor House that the last male heir, Wilfred George Jackson, was not going to come home. His death is recorded in Part One of this series, but it was not confirmed by the War Office for two years.

The first telegram to Miss Jackson, in April 1915 simply reported that he had been "reported wounded and a prisoner". A series of visits to the survivors of his section in hospital produced confusing accounts of the action, but many suggested that he may have been wounded and taken prisoner. An example, below, suggests that he may also have been wounded on the previous day.

2nd East Kent,

JACKSON, 2nd Lieut. W.G.

Informant was wounded in a trench at St. Jean on April 24th, and when he left the trench at dark Lieut. Jackson was still there with the rest of the company and he was slightly wounded. The next day that company was surrounded and captured, but a Sergt. Beech escaped, rejoined the regiment, and told informant all about it. That sergeant informant says is now with the regiment.

Reference: L/Cpl. King, 8925,
2nd East Kent.
Teignmouth Hospital.
Home address: 43 New Road, Chatham.

London
June 21st.
Dr. F.N. Morton Palmer.

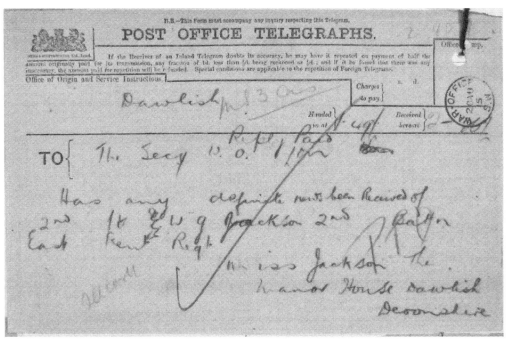

Wilfred Jackson's sister kept up the pressure on the War Office, as can be seen in this telegram of 20th August 1915, four months after his disappearance.

Nov. 15. 1915.

THE MANOR HOUSE,
DAWLISH.

Miss Jackson's compliments
She will feel greatly obliged
if you will send her a form
to fill in - for making enquiries
respecting her nephew.
2nd Lieut W.G. Jackson
2nd Battn The Buffs.
reported wounded & taken prisoner
on April 23rd and of whom
nothing definite has since
been heard.
Kindly address as above.
The Secretary. The War Office.

Later that autumn one of the spinster Jackson's wrote in a firm hand, seeking definite news of Wilfred.

The War Office scanned reports from German prisoner-of-war lists provided by the Red Cross and could occasionally confirm the situation of an individual but the task must have been massive.

Eventually a view was taken by the War Office and a letter written to his sister.

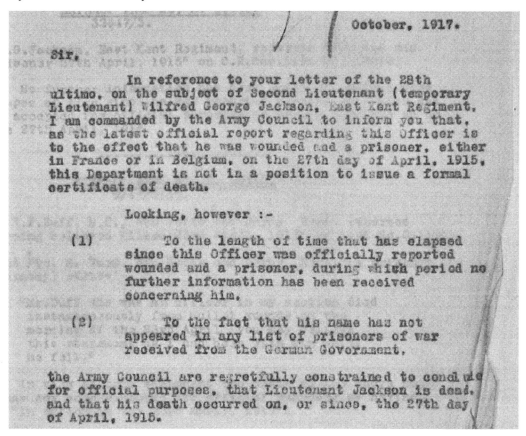

October, 1917.

Sir,

In reference to your letter of the 28th ultimo, on the subject of Second Lieutenant (temporary Lieutenant) Wilfred George Jackson, East Kent Regiment, I am commanded by the Army Council to inform you that, as the latest official report regarding this Officer is to the effect that he was wounded and a prisoner, either in France or in Belgium, on the 27th day of April, 1915, this Department is not in a position to issue a formal certificate of death.

Looking, however :-

(1)   To the length of time that has elapsed since this Officer was officially reported wounded and a prisoner, during which period no further information has been received concerning him.

(2)   To the fact that his name has not appeared in any list of prisoners of war received from the German Government,

the Army Council are regretfully constrained to conclude for official purposes, that Lieutenant Jackson is dead, and that his death occurred on, or since, the 27th day of April, 1915.

The Jackson family put the matter of his death and administration of his Will into the hands of Francis Cole, a solicitor in Dawlish.

The National Archive at Kew still retains a file on the army career of Wilfred George Jackson from which these documents have been copied.

William Frank TAPLEY

Born   Dawlish, Apr-Jun 1884   Killed in action, France, 4 October 1917, aged 33
Private, no 21368   Devonshire Regiment, 1st Battalion

The Tapley family had lived around Exeter for many generations. Daniel and Ann Tapley were in Pinhoe with three children when James Tapley (1819-1892) was born. His nine siblings were born either in Pinhoe or in parts of rural Devon.
James married Sarah Greenslade (1817-1917) in 1848 and they had four children, the youngest being William John Tapley (1857-1931) who was born in Ashcombe and Baptised in Starcross on 1 March 1857.
The 1871 census places James and Sarah in Dawlish Road Cottage, Wick, Kenton. James was an agricultural labourer and his daughter Sarah Jane, aged 16, was a Dressmaker. William John was still at school, aged 14.

In 1878 William John Tapley married[90] Harriet Joanna Davey (1853-1927) who was born in Islington, Middlesex.
In 1881, William was a gardener and they had their first child, Jane Pinkham, aged one, and William's mother-in-law, Harriet P Davey, living with them at Wick, Kenton, as well as the parents James and Sarah Tapley and their eldest daughter Sarah Jane. William and Harriet went on to have four children:

Jane Pinkham Tapley (1880-)   Baptised at St Gregory the Great 22 February 1880
Emily Eliza Tapley (1881-1932)   "   "   22 June 1881
William Frank Tapley (1884-1917)[91]
Arthur John Tapley (1889-1969) born 5/9/1889[92] Died 1969[93]. Baptised at Cofton Chapelry 27 October 1889 with his older brother William Frank Tapley.

In 1891 the census shows the family at Week in Dawlish parish with the four children at school apart from the youngest, Arthur John, aged one. The grandparents were living in the adjoining property, aged 72 (James) and 75 (Sarah).
In 1901 they had moved to Rise Lodge, Dawlish, and William, aged 16, was a gardener like his father.
In 1911 they had moved into Dawlish itself and were living at No 1 Court, High Street and William was the only child still living at home and working as a gardener.

William Frank Tapley may have been conscripted during 1916 to join the Devonshire Regiment. He died during the third battle of Ypres, known also as Passchendaele. The record shows only "presumed dead" and this implies that his body was not recovered.
The *Western Times of Tuesday 20 November 1917* reported, "Private F Tapley .... is officially reported missing since October 4. He belongs to the Devon Regiment and is a marksman and sniper."

90   Marriage GRO ref 1878 Apr-Jun, Newton Abbot, vol 5b, page 205
91   Birth GRO Ref 1884 Apr-Jun, St Thomas, Vol 5b, p 82
92   Birth GRO ref 1889 Dec, Newton Abbot, vol 5b, page 106
93   Death GRO ref 1969 Dec, Newton Abbot, vol 7a, p 1428

The 1st Battalion had moved up to an assault position on the evening of the 3rd October 1917.
(Extract from The Devonshire Regiment history)

"At 6 a.m. the assaulting troops went over in splendid order and with great determination. The Devons having to keep touch with the 13th Brigade, whose goal was Polderhoek Chateau. *(Polderhoek was a small hamlet north of the Menin Road close to the village of Gheluvelt and not far from Polygon Wood. It saw fighting during the First Battle of Ypres in 1914 and then remained in German hands until after the end of Third Ypres in 1917; by that time the whole area was a lunar landscape.)*

Dash was out of the question over such ground, but despite swamps, mud and the German shells, the battalion kept well up to the barrage. They had hard fighting, for the Germans were in strength and resisted stoutly. Indeed, No Man's Land was full of them for, as prisoners explained later, the Germans had been lining up for an attack in which three divisions would have been used against the Fifth Division alone. A bog, too, at the Southern end of Cameron Covert proved impassable. Later on, German counter-attacks drove both them and the D.C.L.I. back a little, but reinforced from the supports by two companies of the East Surreys, they made good a line just West of and through the Covert, though only about twenty men and one officer of No. IV were left to hold it.

The mud delayed movement, but, as some compensation, it was so soft and deep that it smothered the shell bursts and the casualties came almost entirely from machine-guns. These were numerous and well served. The leading wave had to swing to the right to avoid one particularly bad swamp. Others, keeping their direction better, penetrated further and dug in N.W. of the chateau. A few apparently even reached the final objective about North of the chateau, but all in vain. It was a nasty position. The chateau, or rather the strong point constructed from its ruins, was on a crest. The woods N of it had been almost completely cut down, and its machine-guns swept the surrounding area, commanding the only possible passage over the Reutelbeck. There were several pill-boxes level with the chateau, and these proved to be held in considerable force by the enemy, who soon disposed of the handful which had reached the final objective, hardly any of whom got back. However, the bulk of the attackers managed to dig in just West of the Polderhoek woods, and there they held on all day, though under considerable artillery fire and repeatedly counter-attacked. More than once Germans were seen advancing in several waves and caught by the barrage and heavily punished."

Dawlish War memorial inscription: TAPLEY W.F. PTE   DEVON REGT.

Devon Heritage site info: 21368 Private William Frank Tapley of the 1st Battalion, the Devonshire Regiment. Son of William and Harriet Tapley. Born in Dawlish in 1884. Died 4 October 1917, aged 33.

Devon Roll of Honour records his death, without date, and that he was "missing".
He was awarded the British War Medal and the Victory Medal.

Commonwealth War Graves entry: TAPLEY, WILLIAM FRANK   Private   21368
04/10/1917   Devonshire Regiment, 1st Bn.
Panel Ref: Panel 38 to 40. Tyne Cot Memorial, Flanders
Last known address: 1 Court, High Street, Dawlish

Next of kin: Father, William John Tapley
References:
Free Birth Marriage Death refs
Refs via subscription websites:
UK, Army Registers of Soldiers' Effects
Ancestry family histories;
    Lieutenant Richard Tapley tree
    Harrison-Hewitt tree
https://greatwarphotos.com/2012/03/06/flanders-polderhoek-chateau/

Census records
UK, Soldiers Died in the Great War.

Tyne Cot Memorial - CWGC website

The Hooge Crater

Another Dawlish casualty was to die on the same day and is also remembered among the many names at Tyne Cot.

Albert Henry WEST

Born Dawlish July-Sept 1889   Died France, 4th October 1917, aged 28
Private 26971   8th (Service) Battalion, Devonshire Regiment

Albert Henry West was a cousin of George Carter West (q.v.) who died on 15th April 1917 fighting with the Australian Forces.

Their joint grandparents were Edward and Fanny West. Edward West (1813-1874) was born in Kenton and was a gardener. He married Fanny Pike (1817-1892), who was born in Exeter, on 30th August 1835.

In 1861 Edward and Fanny lived at 9 Regent Street, Dawlish with six children, including Thomas Pike West who later became the father of Albert Henry.:

William Charles West	(1841-1921)	
Mary Ann West	(1846-1924)	
Frederick Pike West	(1849-1923)	father of George Carter West
<u>Thomas Pike West</u>	<u>(1851-1931)</u>	<u>father of Albert Henry West</u>
George Edward West	(1854-1902)	worked for the Post Office, Dawlish,1911
Robert John West	(1856-1919)	

Their eldest daughter, Frances West (1839-1893) was living away as a servant, a position she held in various households over the following thirty years.

Thomas Pike West married[94] Mary Ann Maria Warren (1851-1923) in 1879. He was a builder's labourer and they lived at 9 Badlake Hill. They were to have five children, all of whom were living at the time of the 1911 census:

Frank West	(1880-)
Ernest West	(1881-)
Caroline Lydia West	(1884-)
Edward I West	(1886-)
Albert Henry West	**(1889-1917)**[95]

Albert Henry West is shown on the Dawlish Boys' School Roll of Honour. By 1911 he was 21 and a servant and baker to Rupert Charles Curtis, a confectioner shopkeeper in the High Street, Dawlish. The *Dawlish Gazette of October 20, 1917* records that he was a baker by trade and an esteemed employee of R C Curtis.

It is recorded that Albert enlisted at Newton Abbot. He may be the West in a photograph on page 181.

He married Lizzie Dorcas Arnold in Lady St Mary's Church, Wareham, Dorset, on 14th October 1916. Lizzie was born[96] in Kingston, Surrey in 1892 and had been living in Dawlish. Albert gave Wareham as his address, being a Private in the 44th Training Reserve Battalion. This unit was originally the 11th Devonshires Reserve Battalion which had formed in Exeter in November 1914. It

---

94   Death of Mary West ref GRO Newton Abbot, 1923, Sept, vol 5b, p 104

95   Birth record GRO ref, July-Sept 1889, Newton Abbot district, vol 5b, p 104

96   Birth record GRO ref Mar 1892, Kingston, vol 2a, p 321

moved to Wareham in May 1915 and became the 44th Training Reserve in the 10th (Reserve) Brigade on 1st September 1916.

At some point Albert was transferred to the 8th (Service) Battalion which was sent to France in 1915. He would have joined it some time after his wedding. In April 1917, during the Battle of Arras, both 8th and 9th (Service) Battalions attacked Ecoust with great success and light casualties but, a month later, capturing part of Bullecourt cost them 382 killed and wounded. Early October found both Battalions near Passchendaele enduring the worst of the Third Battle of Ypres. It is here that Albert lost his life.

The 8th's move to the front had been a most unpleasant experience. Leaving their bivouacs at Chateau Sigard an hour before sunset on October 2nd, they had threaded their way to Hooge Crater, first along pave roads and then by corduroy tracks. After passing Hooge (Mines were laid under Gerrman defensive positions, using the explosive ammonal, as well as gunpowder and guncotton. The largest mine of the war so far was blown on the 19th of July at 7 p.m. The crater made was estimated at 120 feet wide and 20 feet deep. The crater was captured by men from the 1/Gordon Highlanders and 4/Middlesex. Ten of the latter were killed by debris from the mine as they waited in advanced positions.)

It was, as one account says, " a question of sticking to the corduroy or duck-board tracks, or sticking in the pools of mud and water which otherwise monopolized the scene."

The whole place was an ocean of mud, in which every other feature seemed to have been obliterated except the pill-boxes and the Butte in Polygon Wood, at which battalion headquarters were eventually established. As the battalion neared the Butte it had to go right through a German barrage which there was no avoiding. Luckily, the mud did at least minimize the effect of the shells, and the 8th reached their positions with about 25 casualties.

> To these there were several additions during the 3rd, partly among the ration-parties, who had to negotiate the barrage on their way up, partly from the shelling and sniping to which the troops in front were subjected.

The work of the ration-parties was not, as a rule, easy and here it was particularly difficult, but the 8th had a splendid Transport Officer in Lieut. Imbert Terry, and his determination and resourcefulness rose superior even to the most formidable obstacles and difficulties; he never failed to get his rations up or keep his horses fit, and his untiring and assiduous labours meant much to the 8th throughout the war. But worse than any shelling or sniping was the fact that the rain, of which there had already been a superabundance, started again.

Early on October 4th, A and C Companies lined up on a tape corresponding approximately to Jubilee Trench. When they were ready B and D fell back through them from the outpost line and took station, B in readiness to mop up behind A and C, D in reserve. The battalion's frontage was about 400 yards. the two waves were 70 yards apart, the reserve the same distance in rear; the Borders and Gordons followed 200 yards further back.

The enemy were holding no well-defined position, but were scattered about in pill-boxes and small posts on slightly rising ground. Shortly before" Zero" a German barrage came down. Then, at 6 o'clock, the British guns opened fire, the barrage moving forward 100 yards every four minutes, and the attack started. A Company, under Captain Frood, encountered a pill-box whose garrison also manned a dug-out covered by a machine-gun in rear. However, a Lewis gun engaged and neutralized the machine-gun, while bombers rushed and took the position. A little further on a grenade-thrower gave some trouble, but Captain Frood worked round its flank with a section and rushed it, taking 20 prisoners, though he himself was wounded. Twenty minutes after" Zero" A was on its objective, just West of Jay Barn, and had got touch with the 91st Brigade. (Albert West was among the caualties on that day)

The Germans, though in great force, had not put up as good a fight as usual. This was also Cs experience: it met little serious opposition, the Germans surrendering quite freely, though when the company reached its objective snipers about 150 yards to the front gave some trouble, as our protective barrage prevented men going forward to deal with them. Meanwhile B, under Captain Roper, following hard behind A and C, had "mopped up" most effectively: a strong point just behind Captain Frood's first pillbox was dealt with by a Lewis gun, 20 Germans being killed here; some hutments further to the left yielded 50 prisoners and a machine-gun just in rear which A opened fire was put promptly out of action. Effective work was also done by the reserve company, which accounted for two pill-boxes which previous lines had missed. D, however, had the heaviest casualties, mainly through having caught the enemy's barrage before "Zero." Altogether the attack had been a brilliant success, especially as the smoke and the total absence of landmarks made keeping direction most difficult. The British barrage had been excellent, and the first line had kept right up to it and had lost very few men. Indeed, casualties had been extremely light, far fewer than the prisoners, who numbered nearly 250 (a dozen machine-guns and trench mortars were also taken), drawn from half-a-dozen different regiments. It came out from them that our barrage had caught the Germans forming up to attack, the overhead machine-gun fire which had supported our advance had been particularly deadly, and in consequence the defenders were found half demoralized and ready to surrender.

At 8.10 a.m. the Borders and Gordons came through the 8th, to be equally successful in attaining their objective. It was now that the 8th's worst trials were to come. As the day wore on the German shell fire, observed and directed by aeroplanes, increased in intensity. "No sooner had we dug a fresh trench in what seemed a quiet spot," writes one officer, "than a hostile aeroplane would fly only a few yards over our heads, and we soon learnt what that foreboded."
The almost incessant rain complicated matters, not merely by reason of the discomfort and additional fatigue, but because it interfered greatly with trench digging. Directly men got down a couple of feet the trenches filled with water. Mud clogged rifles and Lewis guns, had the battalion been counter-attacked in force half its rifles would have been out of action and casualties mounted up. Moreover, instead of being relieved, the 8th had to remain in the captured position until about midnight on October 7th-8th.

All through October 7th and 8th the shelling persisted, and the casualty list rose steadily. When at last the 22nd Brigade relieved the 20th there was no relief for the 9th Devons. The 8th, exhausted with a long turn in the line, and" almost finished for want of sleep," got back to Chateau Sigard early on October 8th. They had in the end quite a heavy casualty list, six officers and 57 men killed, 11 men missing, eight officers and 198 men wounded, 280 of all ranks, nearly half those who had gone into action. Still, the battalion had achieved all that had been set before it, had taken almost as many prisoners as it had had casualties, apart from other losses inflicted on the enemy, and this despite adverse conditions of ground and weather.

(Extracted from "The Devonshire Regiment 1914-1919" by C Atkinson, 1926)

Albert Henry West is recorded on the Devon Roll of Honour, and on the Dawlish Boys' School Roll of Honour.

Dawlish War memorial inscription: WEST A.H.   PTE DEVON REGT
Devon Heritage site info: 26971 Private Albert Henry West of the 8th Battalion, the Devonshire Regiment. *Parents not yet identified*. (My italics -ed) Born in Dawlish in the September Quarter of 1889. Died 4 October 1917 aged 28.

Commonwealth War Graves entry: WEST, ALBERT HENRY   Private   26971
04/10/1917
Devonshire Regiment, 8th Bn. Panel Ref: Panel 38 to 40.   Tyne Cot Memorial, Flanders

Last known address: High Street, Dawlish
Next of kin: widow, Lizzie Dorcas West. Lizzie married[97] again in Exeter in 1919 to Harry J Cross.

References:
Free Birth, marriage, Death refs   Great War Forum.
ww1battlefields.co.uk
refs via subscription website Ancestry: Census records
UK, Army Registers of Soldiers' Effects   Probate record
Family trees on Ancestry.co.uk:
        Hearne
        Gary & Gail
        Chambers

In September 2014, 30 members of the Dawlish Royal British Legion went on a WW1 Battle Fields and Cemetery Tour. We also visited Tyne Cot Cemetery and paraded at the Menin Gate. Given our Chairman's and others previous service, and links with the Devon and Dorset Regiment, a short Act of Remembrance was conducted at Panels 38 – 40 at Tyne Cot and wreaths were laid particularly in memory of William Frank TAPLEY and Albert Henry WEST. Photographs were taken of the ceremonies.

---

97   Marriage GRO ref Exeter, March 1919, vol 5b, p 165

Herbert Arthur GARRETT,

Born Q3, 1897 in Penge, Kent   Died 7th October, 1917, aged 20

Private   M/334051   Army Service Corps, MT

Herbert A Garrett was the only child of John Thomas Herbert Garrett (1871-1933) and Edith Annie Johnson (1875-1959) and the grandson of Luke and Elizabeth Garrett.

Luke Garrett (1834-1885), was born in Bradford Abbas, Dorset, and his wife Elizabeth born in West Camel, Somerset. Luke Garrett appears in the 1871 census as an Inn Keeper at The King's House Inn, Chilthorne Domer, Somerset. He also became a cattle dealer (1881 census) and the family moved to Preston Street, Preston Plunknett, Yeovil. They had two children by a previous marriage, Rose Gaul (1856-) and Ellen Gaul (1858-), and three boys of their own, George Ernest Garrett (1869-), John Thomas Herbert Garrett (1871-) and Edgar J Garrett (1874-).

J T H Garrett[98] had been born in Chilthorne, near Yeovil in 1871.

After the death of Luke in 1885, the widow Elizabeth moved to 70 Maple Road, Penge, Lewisham where she was with J T Herbert Garrett, 20, single and a "Copyist at the Treasury, Whitehall", and Edgar, 17, single, a "CC clerk" (census return 1891).

John Thomas Herbert Garrett married Edith Annie Johnson in Croydon District in July-Sept, 1895. She had been born in Herne Hill, Surrey.

By 1901 their son, Herbert Garrett[99], had been born and they were living at 1 Taplow Villas, Adams Hill Road, Lewisham, and J T H G was a retail silversmith's assistant.

A change of career took place for they moved to 'Homeleigh', Holcombe by 1911 when the census records Herbert Garrett as a "fruit farmer and small farming shopkeeper". Their only child is shown as Herbert Arthur Garrett.

There is a surviving partial Service Record for **Herbert Arthur Garrett** which shows that he had been a market gardener, working for Robert Garret of Bank Street, Teignmouth. It is likely that this was a misprint as there exists a partial memo from Herbert Garrett of Bank Street, Teignmouth to the Recruiting Officer and dated February 26th, 1917. The memo heading refers to the farm being Ash Farm, Holcombe. The content of the memo is faint and indecipherable, unfortunately.

With the introduction of conscription into the Army in 1916, his father appealed to the Dawlish Urban Tribunal, applying for exemption for the second time in late August 1916.

Mr H W Sparkes, solicitor and military representative on the Tribunal "indignantly resisted the appeal. Sparkes was also guardian and uncle to Etienne Geoffrey Milward (k.i.a. 02/09/1916 q.v.). "They were sending poor miserable married men to fight and trying to keep home strong, able-bodied, single men." (*The Western Times 29 August 1916).*

The Tribunal sat again in March 1917 to hear a case for a re-hearing of an appeal following a medical report. "The Tribunal decided not to grant a re-hearing, but they sent forward a strong recommendation that a substitute should be found. This, however, would not prevent Garrett going at once." (*The Western Times 13 March 1917).*

---

98   Birth GRO ref Yeovil, 1871 Jan-Mar, vol 5c, p524

99   Birth GRO ref Croydon 1897 Sept , vol 2a, p 289

Herbert Arthur Garrett was enlisted at Grove Park, Newton Abbot in the Mechanical Transport section of the Army Service Corps on May 28th 1917, at the age of 19 and 9 months. It was noted that he was a Wesleyan and was described as an agriculturist and market gardener.

In a short service career he embarked on "Corinthia" at Devonport on 28th July, trans-shipped to "Princess" at Durban, South Africa, on 11th September and disembarked in East Africa at Kilwa Kiwimji on 19th September.

He was admitted to the military hospital at Kilwa on 4th October with dysentery and died three days later.

A telegram was sent to his father dated 10th October saying that his son had been dangerously ill and he died on 8th October. A second telegram was sent to correct this to state that he died on 7th October 1917 at No 19 Stationary Hospital, Kilwa Kiwimji. *(Modern Kilwa Kivinje, on the coast, about 200 km south of Dar-es-salaam, Tanzania.)*

His death was recorded by the Adjutant General's office, Dar-es-salaam, on 16th October 1917 as the cause being Dysentery (due to Field operations).

Commonwealth War Graves entry: GARRETT, HERBERT ARTHUR   Private   M/334051
Army Service Corps, M.T. Reinforcements
Grave Ref: 2. D. 1   07/10/1917   Age: 203. DAR ES SALAAM WAR CEMETERY, Tanzania.
Only son of Herbert and Edith Annie Garrett, of Queen's Building, Teignmouth, Devon, England. Born at Penge, Surrey, England.

H A Garrett appears on Teignmouth seafront War memorial, north face. He is listed on the Holcombe War Memorial panel mounted on the west face of St George's, Holcombe.
The Medal record shows that he was awarded the Victory Medal and the British War Medal.

Last known address: 'Homeleigh', Holcombe
Next of kin: John Thomas Herbert Garrett, father. It appears, from the CWGC entry that the parents moved away from Holcombe to Teignmouth soon after WW1. A death grant of £1. 11s. 8d. Was paid to his father. The Probate record at the death of his father in 1933 shows that he left £5,960 – 10s – 5d and their address as Queen's Buildings, Wellington Street, Teignmouth.

References:
Free birth, marriage, death refs   Holcombe Church War Memorial panel
Notes from Teign Heritage Centre, Teignmouth
The Army Service Corps in the First World War - http://www.longlongtrail.co.uk/army/regiments-and-corps/the-army-service-corps-in-the-first-world-war/

Other refs via subscription websites: census data
UK, Soldiers died in the Great War 1914-1919   Army Service Record (partial)
Bardon family tree (Ancestry.co.uk)   UK, Army Registers of Soldiers' Effects
Probate Record (JTHG)

Philip Gladstone POPE

Born, Wellington, Somerset, 11 August 1887   Died Flanders, 16 October 1917, aged 30
Lieutenant   Royal Field Artillery

Philip Gladstone Pope was the son of Sydney Philip Pope (1859-1937) and Jessie Gladstone (1863-1958) and the grandson of John Pope. The Pope family had been solicitors in the 19th century.

John Pope was in practice in Exeter in 1861 when the census showed, living at Langam Villa, Pennsylvania Road, Exeter:

John Pope,	Head,	38,	Solicitor,	born Wellington, Somerset	(1823-1903)
Jane Pope,	wife,	28		born Rewe, Devon	(1833-)
John Pope,	son,	5		" Exeter	
William W Pope, son,		3 ½		" "	
Sydney P Pope	son	1		" "	

Ten years later John and Jane Pope were living at Hills Court, St David's, Exeter with Sydney, 11, Jessie E, 9 and Reginald H, 7. The later children were also born in Exeter.

> John Pope the younger went on to study law and became a solicitor himself, being named in the Will of Philip Gladstone Pope.
> Reginald Henry Pope (1864-1945) was ordained in the Church and was also, as an uncle, named in the Will of Philip Gladstone Pope, see below.

In 1881 Sydney Pope was a lodger at 11 Duchess Road, Edgbaston, Birmingham where he was shown as a solicitor's clerk.
Sydney P Pope married[100] Jessie Gladstone in Birmingham in 1886.

By 1891 Sydney and Jessie Pope had moved to Exeter, and were living at 43 Manston Terrace, Heavitree with their first child, Philip Gladstone Pope who was born in Wellington, Somerset in 1887. He was baptised in St John's Church, Wellington on 14th September, 1887. They went on to have another child but it had died by the census of 1911, by which time they had moved to Howden, Tiverton.

Philip Pope was sent to boarding schools, first to Looker's Park in Hemel Hemstead (1901 census) and then to Rugby School. He left school ca 1905 and studied law, as an articled clerk to a solicitor, most probably Hesketh W Jelp, 12 Norfolk Street, Strand, London.
P G Pope was boarding at New Hampton Court Club, East Molesey, Surrey in 1911 at the age of 23. From here a journey by Southern Railway would take him to work.
Also in 1911, the census shows that Madeleine Roissier was a visitor from Jersey at Sydney and Jessie Pope's home at Tiverton.

Philip Gladstone Pope married Madeleine Roissier in St Helier, Jersey on 17 April 1912. Madeleine's father also was a solicitor. Philip Alfred Roissier (1957-1926) and Florence Jessie Valentine Ouless (1860-) had one son and a daughter, Madeleine (1890-1964).

---

100   Marriage GRO ref 1886 Oct- Dec, Birmingham, vol 6d, p 315

Philip and Madeleine had a son Philip William Gladstone Pope[101](1913-2002) who was born to them in Exeter on 25 April 1913. See later material on his life. They appear to then live in Oak Park, Dawlish. His name was included on Dawlish War Memorial.

Philip G Pope applied for a 'Temporary Commission in the Regular Army for the Period of the War' on 26th November 1915 and he was gazetted and placed in the Special Reserve on 3rd December. He gave as his address c/o Messrs J & S P Pope, 25 & 26 Gandy Street, Exeter and his father and uncle were in practice at Gandy Street. His address for correspondence was 'Ashley', Oak Park, Dawlish. The form also shows that he 'was a Lance Corporal in the Rugby School Cadet Corps in 1901' in response to the question about previous service. Hesketh W Jelp certified to his 'good moral character for the last four years and upwards'.

Philip Pope expressed a preference for serving in the Field Artillery and he was serving with the Royal Field Artillery when he was killed in action.
He made a Will on 12th February 1916, and Probate was granted to Madeleine Pope (his widow) and as executors his uncles, John Pope and Reginald Henry Pope, Clerk in Holy Orders. The gross value was £2,803. 15s. 4d.

A telegram announcing his death was sent from the War Office to his widow on 19th October 1917 and a formal letter from the War Office on 6th November 1917 gave details of his grave in the Huts Military Cemetery, Dickebusch, South West of Ypres. It stated that it was marked 'by a durable wooden cross with an inscription bearing full particulars'.

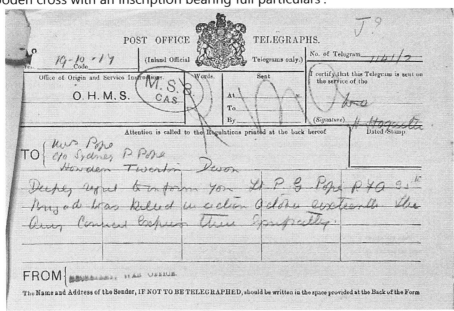

Madeleine Pope returned to live in Exeter, at 7 St Leonard's Road and died at Poltimore Nursing Home on 18 December 1964.
Probate was granted to Philip William Gladstone Pope, Brigadier H.M.Army, her son.

He died at Warminster, Wiltshire on 30th July 2002, see obituary below.

    An obituary in the Daily Telegraph reveals a courageous career of P W G Pope as a soldier. He won a Military Cross in the Syrian Campaign in 1941 and a Distinguished Service Order

101   Birth GRO ref Apr-Jun 1913, Exeter, vol 5b, p 122

in North Africa in 1942 while serving with the 1ˢᵗ and 25ᵗʰ Field Regiments Royal Artillery. After WW2 he reached the rank of Brigadier, serving in a number of training roles before retirement in 1968. He married in 1942 Christine Hartshorne and they had a son and two daughters.

P G Pope is listed on the Devon Roll of Honour but without the date or place of death shown.

Dawlish War memorial inscription: POPE P.G.   LIEUT.   R.F.A.
Devon Heritage site information echoes that on the CWGC entry, below
Commonwealth War Graves entry: POPE, PHILIP GLADSTONE   Lieutenant   16/10/1917
Age: 30 Royal Field Artillery, 31st Bde.
Grave Ref: XIII. B. 13. The Huts Cemetery, West Flanders
Son of Sydney Philip and Jessie Gladstone Pope, of Howden, Tiverton; husband of Madeleine Pope, of Ashley, Dawlish, Devon.

The Huts Cemetery, Belgium about 6 km south west of Ypres. (CWGC)

Last known address: 'Ashley', Oak Park, Dawlish

Next of kin: Madeleine Pope, wife
References: The National Archive, Kew for Officers' records
Free Birth Marriage Death refs to GRO   The Daily Telegraph – obituary of Brigadier Philip Pope
records via subscription website: Census records UK and Jersey
Probate records

Leonard Reggie STEPHENS

Born Q1, 1897 Dawlish
Private, 202040

Died 26 October 1917, aged 20
15th Battn, Royal Warwickshire Regt

Leonard Reggie Stephens was the second son of William Stephens (1863-1909) and Emily Gunningham (1860-1936). William was a gardener and had been born at Elworthy, Somerset and he married Emily (born in Ash Priors, Somerset) in Q1, 1891 in the Newton Abbot district.
In 1901 they were living at a cottage (near Rock Cottage) Cockwood with William Edwin Stephens (1893-1982) aged 7 and Leonard Reggie Stephens aged 4.

The boys were at school in Cockwood and appear in a school photo.

Left, Leonard Reggie Stephens and William Edwin Stephens.

William Stephens died on 28th September 1909 at the young age of 46 and Emily was working in 1911 as a Housekeeper to Edward Wollacott, a retired fur merchant, at Faleide, Southbrook, Starcross, with her two sons. William Edwin was 16 and working as a Grocer's apprentice.
Later, Emily moved to 11 Parson Street, Teignmouth according to the CWGC site record and she died on the 21 January 1936 at 6 Higher Brook Street, Teignmouth. She left her effects to her son William Edwin Stephens, a labourer. William Edwin Stephens was reported wounded in the *Western Times of 20 November 1917.*

Both boys served in the same regiment, the 15th Battalion of the Royal Warwickshire Regiment.
In this photo Leonard Reggie is standing at left and his older brother is sitting. The third soldier is not known.

Leonard Reggie Stephens

The daughter of William Edwin Stephens has written that her father was wounded in the war while her uncle was killed in action. There are no surviving Service Records but it is shown that Leonard enlisted at Newton Abbot and he was 'killed in action'. His personal items were returned to his mother.

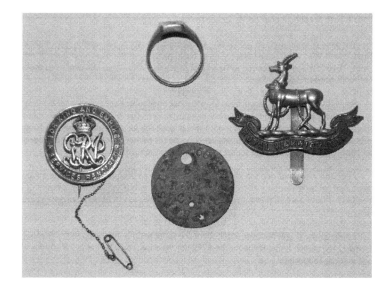

The King commands me to assure you of the true sympathy of His Majesty and The Queen in your sorrow.

He whose loss you mourn died in the noblest of causes. His Country will be ever grateful to him for the sacrifice he has made for Freedom and Justice.

Milner

Secretary of State for War.

15th (Service) Battalion (2nd Birmingham) Royal Warwickshire Regiment

15th (2nd Birmingham Pals) Battalion, Royal Warwickshire Regiment was raised in Birmingham in September 1914 by the Lord Mayor and a local committee.

After training, they joined 95th Brigade, 32nd Division on the 26 June 1915. They proceeded to France, landing at Boulogne on the 21st of November 1915. On the 28 December 1915 they transferred to 14th Brigade, 5th Division, one of many units exchanged to stiffen the inexperienced 32nd Division with regular army troops.

On the 14th of January 1916 they transferred to 13th Brigade, still with 5th Division.

In March 1916 5th Division took over a section of front line between St Laurent Blangy and the southern edge of Vimy Ridge, near Arras. They moved south in July to reinforce The Somme and were in action at, High Wood, The Battle of Guillemont, The Battle of Flers-Courcelette, The Battle of Morval and The Battle of Le Transloy. In October 1916 they moved to Festubertand remained there until March 1917 when they moved in preparation for the Battles of Arras. On 7 September 1917 the 5th Division moved out of the line for a period of rest before, being sent to Flanders where they were in action during the Third Battle of Ypres.

The Third Battle of Ypres (also known as Passchendaele) commenced on 26 October 1917, the date of Leonard's death.

In the Third Battle of Ypres an offensive was mounted by Commonwealth forces to divert German attention from a weakened French front further south. The initial attempt in June to dislodge the Germans from the Messines Ridge was a complete success, but the main assault north-eastward, which began at the end of July, quickly became a dogged struggle against determined opposition and the rapidly deteriorating weather. The campaign finally came to a close in November with the capture of Passchendaele.

At the end of the day, 26th October, five strong points had been established and the line advanced 300-400 yards. General Gough, the Army Commander, sent a message:" Please convey to all ranks engaged in to-day's operations my very great appreciation of their gallant efforts; they have my sincere sympathy, as no troops could have had to face worse conditions of mud than they had to face owing to the sudden downfall of rain this morning. No troops could have done more than our men did to-day, and given a fair chance, I have every confidence in their complete success every time."

Later, the 5th Division was sent to Italy and took up positions in the line along the River Piave in late January 1918. This was a strategic and political move agreed by the British Government at the request of the Allied Supreme War Council, as an effort to stiffen Italian resistance to enemy attack after a recent disaster at Caporetto. Many diaries at this time, by men who had witnessed slaughter in the floods of Passchendaele, talk of the move and Italy as being "like another world".

They were recalled to France to assist with the German Advance in late March 1918 and were in action during the Battles of the Lys. On the 14th of August 1918 the 5th Division was withdrawn for two weeks rest. They then moved to the Somme where they were more or less in continuous action over the old battlegrounds until October and saw action in the Battles of the Hindenburg Line and the Final Advance in Picardy. On the 6th of October 1918 the 2nd Birmingham Pals were disbanded with troops transferring to the 1st and 3rd Birmingham Pals Battalions.

Leonard Reggie Stephens is commemorated on the War Memorial in Cofton Churchyard.
He and his brother went to school in Starcross. He is not listed on the Dawlish Boys' School Roll of Honour, nor on the Devon Roll of Honour for Dawlish.

Commonwealth War Graves entry:
Private   Service No: 202040   Date of Death: 26/10/1917 Age: 21
Royal Warwickshire Regiment,   15th Bn.
Grave Reference: LXVI. G. 3. Tyne Cot Cemetery, Zonnebeke, West Flanders
Additional Information:
Son of William and Emily Stephens, of 11, Parson St., Teignmouth, Devon. Native of Cofton, Starcross, Devon.

Last known address: Faleide, Starcross

Next of kin: Emily Stephens (mother) of 11 Parson Street, Teignmouth.

References: Private letters   CWGC website entry
Cofton churchyard memorial
refs via subscription website, Ancestry: Census records
Stephens family tree (ancestry.co.uk)   UK, Army Registers of Soldiers' Effects
UK, Soldiers Died in the Great War

William BLATCHFORD

Born Ipplepen, 26 May 1891   Missing in action, assumed dead, 26 October 1917, aged 26
Private PLY /1971 (S)   Royal Marine Light Infantry, 2nd Battalion, Royal Naval Division

William Blatchford was the son of a farmer, John Blatchford*, and had been working as a shepherd until he enrolled in the Royal Marines at Exeter on 12th February 1917. William's grandfather, James Blatchford, had been farming for some years at Whitchurch, near Tavistock. James Blatchford (1812-1904) was married to Grace Oxenham (1817-1909) and in 1871 they were farming at Moortown, Whitchurch and the census record shows:

James Blatchford , Head, 60,		farmer of 150 acres employing 2 men,	born Sampford-Spring	
Grace Blatchford, wife, 53			born Whitchurch	
Elizabeth	dau, 26	(1845-)		"
John Blatchford *	son, 20	(1850-1930)		"
Emma	dau, 18	(1853-)		"
Martha M	dau, 15	(1856-)		"
Frederick	son, 10	(1861-)		"
Alfred	son, 8	(1863-)		"

John Blatchford (1850-1930) married Ann Creber(1849-1901) on 1 May 1875. She was also from a farming family, at Sheepstor, and the daughter of John and Elizabeth Creber.
In 1881 they were established at North Huish, Totnes district, with three children:

John Blatchford,	Head, 30	farmer		born Whitchurch
Ann "	wife, 30			born Sheepstor
Frederick William,	son, 5	(1876-)		born Meavy
Thomas	son, 3	(1878-1916)**		"
Ida Mary	dau, 1	(1880-)		born North Huish

In 1891 they had moved to Lylesford, Ipplepen where they had four more children:

Alfred Henry	son, 9	(1882-)		born North Huish
John	son, 6	(1885-)		"
James	son, 4	(1887-)		born Ipplepen
Emmaline	dau, 2	(1889-)		"

In 1901 they were established at Hensford Farm House, Dawlish, with two more children:

William,	**son, 9**	**(1891-1917)**		**born Ipplepen**
Grace,	dau, 6	(1895-)		"

Ann had died early in 1901 leaving John Blatchford a widower and working his farm as an employer in his own account. There were six sons and three daughters, the eldest, Ida Mary being shown as carrying out "Housekeeper duties". The five oldest boys are shown as farm workers, at home.

Ten years later, in 1911, still at Hensford Farm, the three oldest children had left home and John Blatchford is employer of the four younger sons with Emmaline taking over the role of housekeeper. Ida Mary is shown as beneficiary in the Will of John Blatchford at his death on 28 September 1930, when he lived at Creedy Barton, Shobooke, Crediton.

** Thomas H Blatchford was a Private in the Royal Marines, No. 15599 (Ply) lost in the sinking of H.M.S. DEFENCE at the Battle of Jutland on 31 May 1916 – ref naval-history.net and Ipplepen St Andrew's War memorial

William Blatchford may have been conscripted or he could have been an RMLI recruit when he enlisted at Exeter on 12th February 1917 for three years. His papers show that he was a shepherd, and baptised in the Church of England.

He was 5' 10" tall with fresh complexion and blue eyes, and he was sent for training to the Royal Marine Depot, Deal, Kent until 27th May when he was transferred to the strength of the Plymouth Division.

It is likely that he went straight to one of the RND reserve battalions training at Blandford Camp. The reinforcement draft in July 1917 was formed up at Blandford.

He embarked at Folkestone for Boulogne on the 30th June and arrived on 1st July. From 10th to 31st July he was at the Royal Naval Division Base Depot near Calais. On 2nd August he was drafted to the 2nd Royal Marine Battalion and he was one of a party of 28 other ranks who joined the 2nd Royal Marine Battalion in the field on 2nd September. The battalion then moved forward into support trenches between Gavrelle and Oppy.

The badge of the Royal Marine Light Infantry

William Blatchford was reported "Missing" and later "assumed dead" as a result of enemy action" on 26th October 1917.

The record shows that on the 24th: "Operation Order No. 90 issued. Bn. Proceeded by route march to IRISH FARM."

Oct 25 Operation Order No. 91 issued. Bn. Proceeded into line pm & took up position for attack.

Oct 26 Front Line 5.40 am. Bn. Attacked enemy's position opposite its front in conjunction with other Bns. of the 188th Inf. Bde. Objectives gained and consolidated. Casualties 7 Officers and 301 Other Ranks.

The difficulties faced in this landscape are described in the 188 Brigade Report of Operations noting:

> "The concrete building shown as Varlet Farm did not exist in reality and, except for a few scattered bricks, all the farm buildings had completely disappeared ... owing to the flooded shell holes in the neighbourhood, the farm moat could scarcely be recognised."

At the end of the day five strong points had been established and the line advanced 300-400 yards. General Gough, the Army Commander, sent a message: "Please convey to all ranks engaged in to-day's operations my very great appreciation of their gallant efforts; they have my sincere sympathy, as no troops could have had to face worse conditions of mud than they had to face owing to the sudden downfall of rain this morning. No troops could have done more than our men did to-day, and given a fair chance, I have every confidence in their complete success every time."

William is recorded on the Devon Roll of Honour for Dawlish.
Probate was granted to his father, John Blatchford, retired farmer, in 1918.

Dawlish War memorial inscription: BLATCHFORD W.   PTE.   R.M.L.I.

Commonwealth War Graves entry:
Private   Service No: PLY/1971(S)   Date of Death: 26/10/1917   Age: 26
Regiment/Service: Royal Marine Light Infantry   2nd R.M. Bn. R.N. Div.
Memorial: TYNE COT MEMORIAL Panel Reference: Panel 1 and 162A.
Additional Information: Son of John Blatchford, of Creedy Barton, Newton St. Cyres, Exeter.

> Tyne Cot is now the largest Commonwealth war cemetery in the world in terms of burials. At the suggestion of King George V, who visited the cemetery in 1922, the Cross of Sacrifice was placed on the original large pill-box. There are three other pill-boxes in the cemetery.
> There are now 11,961 Commonwealth servicemen of the First World War buried or commemorated in Tyne Cot Cemetery. 8,373 of the burials are unidentified but there are special memorials to more than 80 casualties known or believed to be buried among them. Other special memorials commemorate 20 casualties whose graves were destroyed by shell fire. There are also 4 German burials, 3 of which are unidentified.

Last known address: Hensford Farm House, Dawlish
Next of kin: John Blatchford, father

References:
Free Birth Marriage Death records   National Archive, Kew for R.M. service record
Fleet Air Arm Museum for personnel records
Extracts from "Royal Marines in the War 1914-1919"
Refs via susbcription websites: Census data   Probate records
Devon Heritage site for Dawlish War Memorial
UK, RN & RM War Graves Roll   Ware family tree (ancestry.co.uk)

In the Third Battle of Ypres an offensive was mounted by Commonwealth forces to divert German attention from a weakened French front further south. The initial attempt in June to dislodge the Germans from the Messines Ridge was a complete success, but the main assault north-eastward, which began at the end of July, quickly became a dogged struggle against determined opposition and the rapidly deteriorating weather. The campaign finally came to a close in November with the capture of Passchendaele. Many of the dead from the campaign are in Tyne Cot Cemetery.

Tom POOK

Born, Tedburn St Mary, 1880   Died 26 October 1917, aged 37
Private, No 26714   Devonshire Regiment, 8th (Reserve) Battalion

Tom Pook was the son of George and Mary Ann Pook and was born[102] in Tedburn St Mary in the last quarter of 1880. George Pook (1844-1923) and Mary Ann (nee Soper, 1846-1931) were from families rooted in Tedburn.

They were living at that time in Towns End Cottage and George was a gamekeeper. Both parents and the first five children had been born in Tedburn St Mary, and appear in the 1881 census as:

George Pook	(1844-)	Head	Gamekeeper	
Mary Ann "	(1844-)	wife	Gamekeeper's wife	
Elizabeth "	(1868-)	dau	Scholar	
Harry "	(1870-)	son	"	
Harriett Hela "	(1872-)	dau	"	
Mary "	(1874-)	dau	"	
Lilly "	(1876-)	dau	"	
Sidney "	(1878-)	son	born Whitestone	
Tom "	**(1880-1917)**	**son**	born Tedburn St Mary	

In 1891 they had moved within Tedburn to Downs Cottage and there were three more children:

Frederick "	(1883-)	son	{
Mabel "	(1886-)	dau	{ born Tedburn St Mary
William "	(1888-)	son	{

In 1901 there had moved again to 'Little Heaven' and the oldest child still at home was Lilly, then 23. The 1911 census reveals that 10 children were born and still living, as were the parents.

Tom appears again in the 1911 census, aged 30, living as a single man and gardener/caretaker at Eastdon House, Starcross. At that time Eastdon House was the home of John George Denman Partridge who bought it from the family of Charles Eales. While he was there Tom helped plant fruit trees and his employer, John G Partridge, took him to Exeter in 1912 to choose trees to plant. It was recorded that they still produced fruit in 1984 when the family sold the house.

In all of the references Tom is shown as 'Tom' and not Thomas.
Tom married Emily Philpot at Dawlish Parish Church on 5th October, 1912.
They both gave their address as 10, The Strand, Dawlish.

Emily was the daughter of Henry Philpot, a labourer shown as deceased, although her mother had died but her father lived until 1916. The Philpot family came from Kent. Henry Philpot[103] (1845-1916) was born in Hunton, between Tonbridge and Maidstone and his wife, Mary Ann Chilton (1845-1882) was born nearby in Peckham, Kent. They went to live in Barming, also close by, where Henry was an agricultural labourer and they had most of their nine children, although four had died by 1911 when Henry was living with a widow and her son in Maidstone.

---

102   Birth GRO ref St Thomas, 1880, Oct-Dec, vol 5b, page 65
103   Death GRO death ref Maidstone Dec 1916, vol 2a, p 1148

Emily is recorded as a servant in various households in Hastings (1901), and Cheltenham (1911), when she was a nurse in the Geidt household. Bernard George Geidt was a member of the Indian Civil Service working in Bengal when he married Agnes Ellen Woolaston in Christchurch, Hampshire in October 1890. They returned to India where they had three sons, the youngest of which was Charles Uppleby Geidt (q.v.) who is remembered on St Mary's, Cofton war memorial. Agnes Ellen Geidt died in India in 1894 and Bernard Geidt married for the third time, to Violet Louisa Waterfield in St Mary's Cofton in October 1902.

Violet Waterfield's parents, William and Louisa Waterfield, were tenants and living at Eastdon House, Cockwood, in 1902 (Kelly's Directory). William Waterfield died in 1907 and his widow continued to live there with Captain Waterfield until 1910.
Bernard and Violet Geidt had a son in 1904 (at Eastdon?) who died in infancy and they then moved to Bengal where they had another son in 1907. When Bernard Geidt retired in May 1908 from the Indian Civil Service, where he had been a High Court Judge, it seems likely the Geidt family retired to Cheltenham and acquired a nurse, Emily Philpot, for their son who was one year old.
It is not clear if Emily Philpot had been employed while they were living in the Newton Abbot district 1902-1904.

Tom Pook enlisted at Newton Abbot and was given the Service Number 26714 in the 8th (Service) Battalion of the Devonshire Regiment. The 8th Devons was the first service battalion formed by the Regiment in the First World War. Raised in August 1914 from a nucleus of officers and NCOs from the 1st Battalion, they quickly spawned a second battalion – the 9th – who became their twin and with whom they would serve very closely until 1918.
In early August 1915 the 8th, and then the 9th, joined 20 Brigade in the 7th Division in France.

After the briefest experience in the line, both Battalions were hurled into the Battle of Loos on 25th September 1915. In this single battle the 8th suffered 639 casualties and the 9th 476, including eight men from Dawlish who were lost on this day (see Part one of this series for accounts of their lives). The survivors of the two Battalions held the position until the evening of 26th September, when they were withdrawn.

After a spell near Givenchy both Battalions moved to the Somme area. The Somme remained a relatively quiet sector until the offensive began on 1st July 1916. On the 4th July the Padre of the 8th Devons, Capt Crosse, buried 160 officers and men of both Battalions at Mansel Copse, erecting a plaque: "The Devonshires held this trench. The Devonshires hold it still."

In April 1917 during the Battle of Arras both Battalions attacked Ecoust with great success and light casualties but, a month later, capturing part of Bullecourt cost them 382 killed and wounded. It seems likely that Tom Pook was injured at this time for he wrote a letter from Endell Street Military Hospital, London, on 24th May referring to a bad ankle injury. This was a celebrated military hospital set up and run by women doctors and nurses. In due course he rejoined his regiment in France.

The hospital where Tom was recovering in London is the subject of a new book by Wendy Moore, "**Endell Street** The Trailblazing Women Who Ran World War One's Most Remarkable Military Hospital". The story is built on the role of two women doctors, former suffragettes, Louisa Garret

Anderson and Flora Murray who took over the St Giles and St George Workhouse just north of Covent Garden. At a time when men headed most medical facilities the staff of doctors and nurses were all women. Male supremacy in the training of doctors returned after the war and the hospital was closed in 1919.

At a time when hospitals are at the forefront of our minds comes a letter from a notable hospital just over a century ago. Few examples of letters written by casualties have survived the passage of time.

From his hospital bed, Private T Pook 26714, 8th Devons E Ward, Endell Street Military Hospital wrote on 24th May 1917 to Mr Partridge; "Dear Sir, I've no doubt you will be surprised to see that I have got back to England again. I have been here about a fortnight sent me from a hospital in France. I have put my ankle out it has been very bad but it is getting better now. I am very pleased to get back and must think myself lucky to have pulled through it as I have done up to now without a scratch. It has been terrible hardships this winter and we have been in really the thick of it chasing up the Germans on their retreat of which they have been driven back several miles from where they were last November when I went up the line.

The place I came now from was close to where the hard fighting has been going on Bullecourt. The 8th Devons took the village adjoining a few weeks ago. We took them rather by surprise."

"I hope the garden is going on alright and the rain that we had a few nights ago I believe was needed badly in Devon. Shall be pleased to be able to look at Eastdon again when I get my leave. All the villages around where I was in France were all destroyed, fruit trees and all gardens laid to waste."

Early October 1917 found both Battalions near Passchendaele enduring the worst of the Third Battle of Ypres. On the 26th in an unsuccessful attack on Gheluvelt both lost heavily – especially among their officers, only three of whom from the two Battalions emerged unscathed.

The battalions had moved forward on the evening of the 25th October and dug in to prepared positions for the assault. There was little shell fire overnight but the boggy ground necessitated some changes of position.

At 5.40am an attack was launched with the intention of capturing the Gheluvelt and Zandvoorde spur and securing a hold on the Tower Hamlets ridge (in the vicinity of Zonnebeke and Becelaere, Flanders) . Aerial reconnaissance had shown German positions in strongly defended pill boxes and consolidated shell holes. The War Diary records land features, "the ground slopes upwards nearly to the first objective then, dipped and rose again up to the church in Gheluvelt, which was in a comparatively commanding position. From there it fell away rapidly to the final objective and from there, dropped down into low ground. The only prominent landmarks were the MENIN road, which was clearly marked by stumps of trees, the Polderhoek chateau and the church and mill in Gheluvelt."

It is clear from the detailed report that the advance of the 9th Battalion was met with heavy rifle and machine-gun fire from strongly defended positions and pill boxes. The 8th Battalion was intended to move up from the rear and take over the advance and in doing so also lost many men. In the course of the attack "all Lewis guns and Vickers machine guns were out of action from shell-fire and mud, and rifles had become unworkable owing to the mud." Further, the enemy counter-attack at 10am was mounted by "lightly-equipped troops and many of them were armed with revolvers. This gave them the advantage over our men, many of them stuck in mud, and most of whose rifles had become unserviceable."

The report by the Lieutenant Colonel in command ends with the statistic that 2 Officers were killed and 4 were missing, 20 other ranks were killed and 105 were missing ("there must be a certain number of prisoners but there must also be a large number killed and lying in German territory").

Cofton War memorial inscription: Thomas Pook,   8th Devon Regt   October 26th 1917

Commonwealth War Graves entry: Pook T,
Rank: Private   Service No:26714   Devonshire Regiment 8th Bn.
Date of Death: 26/10/1917   Age:37
Cemetery: HOOGE CRATER CEMETERY   Grave Reference: VIII. A. 8.
Additional Information:Son of George and Mary Ann Pook, of Tedburn St. Mary, Devon; husband of Emily Pook, of Flat 3, 167, Victoria St., Westminster, London.

Hooge Crater Cemetery -CWGC

Last known address: 10 The Strand, Dawlish.
Next of kin: Emily Pook, wife. It is not known if there were children of the marriage.
References:
Free Birth, marriage, death refs   Marriage certificate (GRO)
http://www.keepmilitarymuseum.org/history/first+world+war/the+devonshire+regiment/ the+eighth+and+ninth+battalions
Kelly's Directory, Devon 1902
Refs via subscription website (ancestry.co.uk)
Census data   Army enlistment forms for William Pook
Devonshire Regiment war diaries
Family trees: Ancestry.co.uk   Davies   Scott
Buttery   Charles Herbert Philpot   Kingman Ford & Wilson
Partridge family records

BREAD AND PEACE

Russia had taken a leading part in the outbreak of WW1 by placing its armed forces on full mobilisation ahead of other nations. Russia was in alliance with Serbia, which was being blamed by Austria for protecting the terrorist group responsible for assassinating Archduke Ferdinand and his wife in Sarajevo. A demand by Austria to pursue the terrorists was met by silence and it led to a declaration of war on Serbia by Austria. This limited central European conflict could not be contained once Russia placed its forces against its western boundary, not only of Serbia and Austria but also of Germany. In consequence, Germany declared war on Russia on 1st August 1914.

There was an expectation that Germany would also take the opportunity to attack France which had an alliance with Russia. To move on France, German forces may have skirted the main part of Belgium, but the assault instead was a push across Belgium to secure the Channel ports including Antwerp for use by Germany as submarine bases. At this point Britain was drawn in to support France (Entente Cordiale of 1904) and Belgium (treaty of London 1839).

By 1917 the war was resembling a bloody stalemate on all fronts. But in Russia the Revolution that began with the Bolsheviks taking power after the strikes and riots for food (bread and peace) of February 1917 and the removal of Tsar Nicholas II led to Vladimir Lenin and the Petrograd Government coming to power.

In October 1917 the Marxist Government led by Lenin turned to ending the war with Germany by negotiating a ceasefire. The cost of the war in Russian lives was enormous, as it was in WW2. A local ceasefire was brought into force on 4th December 1917 on the Eastern Front and this was followed by the Treaty of Brest-Litovsk, signed on March 3rd 1918. It was signed between the Russians and the Central Powers (The German Empire, the Austro-Hungarian Empire, Kingdom of Bulgaria, and the Ottoman Empire).

The impact of the Treaty of Brest-Litovsk was to release large numbers of German forces from their Eastern front to reinforce those on the Western Front. Meanwhile White Russian forces loyal to the Tsarist regime were still fighting a civil war with the Bolsheviks, and Britain sent some troops to Russia in support of the White Russians, to little avail.

The arrival of American troops on the Western Front in late 1917 was a blessing and has been used by some to suggest that the American support won the war. By July 1918 a quarter of a million American troops arrived each month and the German General Ludendorff saw his campaign to win the war come to a close.

References:
The SLEEPWALKERS, How Europe Went to War in 1914, by Christopher Clark, publ Penguin
IN EUROPE, Travels Through the Twentieth Century, by Geert Mak, publ Vintage

Archibald Frederick DAVIES

Born Dawlish July-Sept 1881   Died Flanders, 2 December 1917, aged 36

Rifleman   552746   1/16th (County of London) Battalion Queen's Westminster Rifles

Archibald Frederick DAVIES was the grandson of Frederick Peter Davies (1825-). Frederick Davies was born in Clerkenwell, Middlesex and married Jessie (?) and they had four children, born in St Bride's Middlesex, Jessie (1850-), Clara (1852-), Frederick Alexander (1852-) and Frank (1858-). They moved to Dawlish in the following three years, for the 1861 census shows them living at 12 Portland Place, Dawlish. The father was a widower and his cousin Harriet Johnson was their housekeeper.

> Frederick Peter Davies is shown in census returns as a photographer and occasionally as an artist and secretary to the Gas Company.

Frederick Peter Davies and Harriet Johnson were married in the Parish Church Islington by licence on 9th February 1875, by which date they were both aged 50.

In 1881 they had moved to 21 Brunswick Place, Dawlish.

There is a death registered for Harriet Davies aged 74[104] in 1899. Her husband, a widower for the second time, was 86 at the 1911 census and living with his unmarried daughter Jessie.

> Frederick Alexander Davies was born[105] in Clerkenwell, Islington, London in 1852 and trained as a printer. In 1871 he was working as an apprentice printer at 48 Blackfriar's Road, Southwark.
>
> Frederick Alexander Davies married[106] Mary Jane Knight in Dawlish in the April- June quarter of 1881.

Mary Jane Knight was the daughter of Thomas and Elizabeth Knight. Thomas Knight (1817-1852) was a machine maker and he married Elizabeth Tucker (1817-) and they lived in South Molton. Elizabeth was born in Kings Nympton and she and Thomas had two daughters, Mary Jane (1853-1932)born in [107]South Molton and Louise Elizabeth (1849-1901).

> Louise Elizabeth Knight married John Slee and they had a daughter, Bessie, who appears aged 12 in the 1881 census in Dawlish, and again in 1911 with Frederick and Mary Jane Davies.

After the death of Thomas Knight in 1852, Elizabeth married again, to James Vile. She had been living with him as his servant at Cooks Cross, South Molton in 1861. At that date she was working as a plain needlewoman and Mary Jane Knight was still at school, aged 8.

> In 1871 Mary Jane Knight was a housemaid to Elizabeth Vile (formerly Knight) at 12 Marine Parade.
>
> By early 1881 Mary Jane Knight was still living with her mother, Elizabeth Vile, at 1 Brookdale Terrace, Dawlish where her mother was a lodging-house keeper.

It is possible that Frederick Alexander Davies had moved on from printing to establish a business as a photographer, his father's trade, for that is how he appears in the 1891 census at 9 Marine Parade:

---

104   Death GRO Ref Newton Abbot 1899 Oct-Dec, vol 5b, p 90

105   Birth GRO Oct-Dec 1852, Islington, London, vol 1b, page 250

106   Marriage GRO 1881, Apr- June, N.A., Vol 5b, page 287

107   Birth GRO ref 1853, Jan-Mar, South Molton, vol 5b, p 438

Frederick A Davies,	Head,	37	Photographer		born London
Mary J Davies	wife	37			born South Molton
Archibald	**son**	**9**			**born Dawlish**
Mabel	dau	8			"
Herbert C	son	4			"
Dora E	dau	2			"
Annie Ray	visitor	9			born Chelsea

By 1901 there was one more child, Lilian M Davies, born in Dawlish ca 1892, and Archibald was no longer listed at home. He may have already, at age 19, left to study law in London where we find him in 1911, living at 54 The Crescent, Wimbledon Park, S W London with his wife Lilian, nee Page. They were married at St John's Church, World's End, Chelsea on April 10th, 1909.
Lilian was born in Bellingdon, near Amersham, Bucks, daughter of Edward and Jane Page.

> Edward Page (1836-1906) was a farm labourer married to Jane, nee Pittim (1841-1914). When Jane was widowed she moved to live with a nephew in Tring in 1911. She may have been deprived of a farm labourer's tied cottage on the death of her husband.

Frederick A and Mary Jane Davies had six children but two had died by 1911. Mary Jane Davies died on 24th January 1932 at 51 Withycombe Road, Exmouth at the age of 79 and left her possessions to her daughter Mabel Davies, spinster. Her husband died in March 1953 at the age of 100[108].

Archibald Frederick Davies is mentioned in an article in the *Dawlish Gazette* as 'confidential clerk to a well-known firm of London solicitors, by whom he was held in the highest esteem.' It also appears that Archibald and Lilian Davies had a son ca 1913.

It is not clear when Archibald enlisted with the London Regiment (Queen's Westminster Rifles), 1st/16th Bn. He was with a Trench Mortar Battery when he was killed 'instantaneously' in the final phase of the battle of Cambrai. A regimental war diary shows that the battalion had been in action on the 30th November and were withdrawn from the front line and resting on 1st and 2nd December, but there was one casualty from other ranks (O.R.) on the 1st and two O.R. on the 2nd December. The diary for the 30th November records the lack of anti-aircraft fire against patrolling enemy aircraft and it may be that shrapnel from a bomb may have caught Archibald Davies unawares?

A F Davies is recorded on the Devon Roll of Honour and on the Dawlish Boys' School Roll of Honour.
Dawlish War memorial inscription: DAVIES A.F.   RFN.   LON.Q.W.RFLS

Devon Heritage site info: 552746   Rifleman Archibald Frederick Davies of the 1st/16th Battalion, the London Regiment (Queen's Westminster Rifles). Son of Frederick A and Mary Jane Davies of Marine Parade, Dawlish. Born in the September quarter of 1881. Died 2 December 1917, aged 36.

Commonwealth War Graves entry: DAVIES, ARCHIBALD F. Rifleman   552746

---

108   Death GRO ref Devon Central, March 1953, vol 7a, p 395

02/12/1917   London Regiment (Queen's Westminster Rifles), 1st/16th Bn.
Panel Ref: Panel 12.   Cambrai Memorial, Louverval, France

Last known address: 54 The Crescent, Wimbledon Park, S W London
Next of kin: Lilian Davies, wife

References: Birth marriage death refs   Dawlish Gazette collection in Dawlish Museum
The Battle of Cambrai -   http://www.historylearningsite.co.uk/world-war-one/battles-of-world-war-one/the-battle-of-cambrai/
refs via subscription websites: Census records
Regimental War Diary   Marriage record, Chelsea 1909
UK, Army Registers of Soldiers' Effects   Probate records

Cambrai Memorial, Louverval, France - CWGC

Albert William DAVIS

Born Dawlish, 24th August 1887   Died of wounds 7th December 1917, aged 30
Private   443539   Canadian Infantry, 29th Battalion

Albert William Davis was a Dawlish lad who lost his parents by his early twenties and then emigrated to Canada. Whatever might have been his dreams of a life there, they were rudely shattered by the start of the Great War and he returned to Europe to fight with Canadian forces.

Albert's grandfather, William Cummins Davis (1815-1894) was a Town Porter and married Martha Butler (1819-1890). They had five children by the census of 1861: William (1846-), Joseph (Albert's father) (1850-1899), Mary (1853-), Martha (1857-) and Elizabeth (1860-).

By the 1871 census they were living at 14 Park Street and Joseph was 21 and a carpenter. His younger sisters were dressmakers.
In 1877 Joseph Benjamin Davis married Ann Bessie Lovell in Dawlish in 1877[109] and he took work as a Railway Porter. In 1881 they were living in Manor Row with their first two children, Ida Mary (1879-) and Kathleen B (1880-). They had five children in all but three died and the two survivors (by 1911 census) were Ida Mary and Albert William Davis.
Their father, Joseph, died in 1899[110]. Their widowed mother was living with the two children at 11 Luscombe Terrace in 1901. She died in 1911 in 11 Regent Street, soon after the taking of the census.

> Ida Mary Davis married Hedley Hoar in 1908[111] and she was Albert's closest living relative when he decided to emigrate in 1913.

There is a record that Albert Davis, aged 26, arrived in Quebec City in September 1913 aboard the ship *Royal Edward.*

Following the outbreak of war, **Albert William Davis** enlisted with the 29th Battalion of the Canadian Expeditionary Force on 9th June 1915. *The Western Times of Tuesday 11 December 1917* reported that "after many rejections, on account of weak sight, he was accepted." He was medically examined at Nelson, British Columbia, which lies between Vancouver and Calgary and one imagines that he had set about a new life in Western Canada.

"Earlier contingents, including the 2nd Division which contained the 29th Infantry Battalion of the Canadian Expeditionary Force, had sailed for England and been trained on Salisbury Plain and at Shorncliffe before leaving for the front. Just after New Year's Day, 1916, the Canadian Corps was strengthened by the addition of the Third Division, the formation of which had been authorized the preceding December."

"The fighting of the year 1916 was among the bitterest of the whole war. The first heavy fighting in which the Canadians were engaged was in April around the craters at St. Eloi, at the southern end of the Ypres salient. This sector had been much fought over. Huge underground mines had been detonated; the ground had been churned up by shell-fire; and the rains had made it a veritable quagmire. On April 2nd the Third British Division had established themselves on a line

---

109   Marriage GRO ref Newton Abbot district, 1877 Apr-Jun, vol 5b, page 207
110   Death GRO 1899 Apr Jun, N.A.,vol 5b, p 67
111   Marriage GRO 1908, N.A., July-Sep, vol 5b, p 287

well within the former German defences. The next day they were relieved by the Second Canadian Division. The position which the Canadians took up was not consolidated; and the next day before any consolidation could be carried out, the German counterattack began with the most severe bombardment yet seen in that section of front.

The Canadian advance posts were overwhelmed, and nearly all the gains of the British were surrendered. For over a week the Canadians strove repeatedly to recover the lost ground, but in the end they had to give up the attempt as impossible, and to dig in on the line from which the British had set out.

The arrival in France of the Fourth Canadian Division in August, 1916, brought the Canadian Corps up to what was to become its full strength. At this date the first battle of the Somme had been raging since July 1st. While the Canadians Corps had no part in the early stages of this battle the Newfoundland Regiment which was part of the British Army had been annihilated on July 1st at Beaumont Hamel. It was not however until the beginning of September that the Canadian Corps was moved down to the battle area; and not until the middle of September was the Corps engaged in any serious action.

From the middle of September, however, to the middle of November the Corps bore its full share of the Somme fighting. The first important action in which the Canadians were engaged was the capture of Sugar and Candy trench and the sugar refinery at Courcelette on September 15. This action is notable not only for the fierce fighting involved but by the fact that for the first time tanks were used in cooperation with the Canadian infantry. The following day the Canadians swept on and captured the village of Courcelette itself, in one of the most successful operations of the Somme fighting. For many days the Germans strove stubbornly to retake Courcelette; but their efforts resulted only in further loss of ground and further punishment.

At a later stage of the Somme fighting, known as the battle of Thiepval Ridge, the Canadians suffered heavy losses in the taking of Regina Trench. This was a line of German defences beyond Courcelette which it took the Corps a full month to capture. As the Autumn had advanced, the weather had turned bad, and the heavy Somme mud had made the problem of the attacking troops heartbreakingly difficult. Nevertheless, in the end they succeeded in capturing Desire Trench, which was the German support line, However when the Somme fighting stopped in the later part of November there was little to celebrate. The Canadian Corps had sustained 29,029 casualties for a mere six kilometers of mud.

The end of 1916 found the Canadian Corps finally fashioned into the army which during 1917 and 1918 was to be the spear-head of many attacks. It had now attained the strength of four divisions; and in the fighting about Courcelette, Regina and Desire Trenches the men of these four divisions and their commanding officers had gained valuable experience, experience that would serve them well in their next battle Vimy Ridge. The growth and development of the Canadian Corps was now complete.

It appears that **Albert Davis** may have been seriously injured by shrapnel in an air raid later in 1917 and was brought back to Netley Hospital near Southampton, where he died. The following extract from the *The Western Times of Tuesday 11 December 1917* reported:

> "News reached Dawlish yesterday that Pte. Bert Davis (Canadian) had passed away at the Welsh Hospital, Netley. About three weeks ago his sister, Mrs Hedley Hoar, received official notification that he was gassed and injured in the spine with shrapnel. Up to Thursday last, he was reported to be making excellent progress, and the news of his death

came as a great shock to his relatives. He was in Canada when war broke out, and, after many rejections, on account of weak sight, was accepted. He threw up a good berth, with excellent prospects. Before leaving Dawlish he was one of the most popular lads in the town. As an entertainer his services were greatly in demand for "smokers" and entertainments. His death will be keenly felt by Dawlish people who tender full sympathy to Mrs Hoar in her grief."

Davis A W is recorded on the Devon Roll of Honour and on that of the Dawlish Boys' School.
He is listed in the Book of Remembrance – First World War – in the Memorial Chamber of the Peace Tower in Ottawa.

Dawlish War memorial inscription: DAVIS A.W.   PTE.   29TH CAN.

Commonwealth War Graves entry: DAVIS, ALBERT WILLIAM   Private   443539
07/12/1917   Age: 30   Canadian Infantry, 29th Bn.
Grave Ref: 3013.   Dawlish Cemetery
Son of Joseph and Bessie Davis, of Dawlish, Devon, England.

Last known address: Canada
Next of kin: Ida Mary Hoar, formerly Davis

References:
Free birth, marriage & death refs.   British Newspaper Archive
Soldiers of the First World War, Canadian Government records
Dawlish Gazette 8th December and 15th December 1917
A   Brief   History   of   the   Canadian   Expeditionary   Force   -
www.niagarahistorical.museum/media/03.C.E.F.-ABriefHistorycopy.pdf
Refs via subscription websites: Census extracts
     Marriage refs

Frank Samuel DART

Born Dawlish, 1893   Died Moorlands Hospital, Manchester 19th December 1917, aged 24
Private   268222   Devonshire Regiment, 1st/6th Battalion (Territorials)

Frank Samuel Dart was the youngest child of a well known fishmonger and the grand-son of a Dawlish farm worker, Robert Dart. Robert was born in Dawlish.

Robert Dart (1830-1910) married[112] Anna Windeatt in 1850, and his wife came from a Teignmouth family.

Robert and Anna Dart had eight children and lived for many years in Park Row, Dawlish. Their children were:

John Dart	1851-1909	born Dawlish	father of **Frank Samuel**
Robert Dart	1853-	"	
William Dart	1855-	"	
Ann Maria Dart	1857-	"	a.k.a. Hannah
Ellen Dart	1861- 1863	"	
Henry Dart	1865- 1877	"	
Frederick James Dart	1868-	"	
Emily Louisa Dart	1872-	"	

Birth dates are taken from General Record Office references in www.freebmd.org.uk and a detailed family tree (Ancestry.co.uk - 'Joanne Matten').

John Dart was a well known fishmonger/ fish merchant in Dawlish.

John Dart married[113] Mary Jane Woodrow (1854-1918) in the St Thomas district in 1871.

Mary Jane Woodrow was the daughter of William and Anna Woodrow of Dawlish. William was a naval pensioner and Mary Jane was born in East Stonehouse (now Plymouth).

John and Mary Jane Dart's children are listed in the census entries and Ancestry as:

Henry James Woodrow	1869-	born to Mary Jane Woodrow, father unknown
Ellen Dart	1872- 1873	
William John Dart	1875- 1876	
Ned Dart	ca 1875	born Dawlish
Frederick John Dart	1876-1929	"

> Frederick John Dart married Helena Maude Woollacott in Barnstaple Apr-Jun 1895. He was a ticket collector for the Great Western Railway and she was a fish merchant (1911 census). They had two daughters, Kathie (1902-) and Florence (1906-) that appear on the 1911 census. There had been two other children of which one had died.

Alice (Maud) Dart	1877-	born Dawlish
Emily Anna Maria Dart	1878-	
John Dart	1880-	"

> He married Mary Jane West in April 1904 and he was a Petty Officer, R.N. in 1911 and they had John William Dart (1907-), Frank Samuel Dart (1909-) and Phyliis May Dart (1910-), born in Kingsteignton.

William Dart	1882-	born Dawlish
Percy (Edward?) Dart	1884- 1915	"

---

112   Marriage GRO ref Newton Abbot, 1850 Oct-Dec, Vol 10, p 240
113   Marriage GRO ref St Thomas, Apr-June 1871, vol 5b, p 80

| Elizabeth (Lizzy) Dart | 1886- | " |
| **Frank Samuel Dart** | **1893-1917** | " |

They lived at 2 Shapter's Court in 1881 and at 26 Brunswick Place in 1891.

The census return for 1911 shows that after the death[114] of John Dart on 29 October 1909 his widow, Mary Jane, was living at Brunswick Place, Dawlish with her son Frederick John and his family. It also records that Mary Jane Dart and the late John had eleven children of which five had died before the 1911 census. John Dart is shown in Probate records as a fish dealer and he left £1,133 – 15s – 6d which was a sizeable sum in 1909.

The census of 1911 also shows Frank Samuel Dart, 18, boarding with Martha Smith in Coventry where he was an apprentice engine fitter (motor cars). Other engine fitters were also boarding there.

We know that Frank Samuel Dart enlisted at Plymouth and that may have been soon after the outbreak of war. He appears in this photograph first published in *The Western Times of 9th October, 1914.*

Dawlish Lads in the 5th Devons.

"Dawlish lads who joined the 5th Devons, and who are shortly leaving for India. A noteworthy fact is that the six men are well-known members of the Dawlish Football Club. The names of the members are: -

Back row: Privates **Dart** and Coleman, and Sergt .Loram.
Front row: Privates Blackmore, Yeo, West and Hutchings."

Photo: Boone, Dawlish now in the Museum collection.

(L/Cpl Reginald Charles Blackmore died of wounds in Palestine on 22nd September 1917. q.v.)

---

114   Death GRO ref Newton Abbot, 1909, Oct-Dec, vol 5b, p 66

The 5th Battalion of the Devonshire Regiment 1/5th (Prince of Wales's) Battalion

August 1914: in Millbay, Plymouth. Part of Devon & Cornwall Brigade, Wessex Division.

9 October 1914: sailed for India, landing Karachi 11 November 1914. Came under orders of 3rd (Lahore) Divisional Area at Multan. December 1915 moved to Lahore.

30.12.1915 the Devonshires moved to Basra and joined the 36th Indian Brigade.

12.05.1916 Joined the 14th Indian Division which engaged in various actions as part of The Mesopotamian campaign including;

Advance to the Hai and capture of the Khudaira Bend, Capture of the Hai Salient, Capture of Sannaiyat, Second Battle of Kut, Passage of the Tigris, Fall of Baghdad (1917), Passage of the 'Adhaim, Action of the Shatt al Adhaim, Second action of Jabal Hamrin, Third action of Jabal Hamrin.

4 April 1917: landed at Suez, Egypt. Engaged in Mesopotamia and Palestine.

25 June 1917: transferred to 232nd Brigade, 75th Division.

Sept 1917 Moved to Amara to defend the Lines of Communication of the Tigris Defences.

1 June 1918: landed at Marseilles and proceeded to the Western Front.

The British needed the oil in Mesopotamia for the Royal Navy so that it could replace its coal-fired vessels. When war broke out in 1914 the Germans, who had previously been partners in the enterprise, turned into the enemy, so control of these oil supplies became one of Britain's primary goals. Under the guise of protecting India's borders with Mesopotamia, an expeditionary force arrived in November 1914 with the aim of taking possession of the towns of Basra, Baghdad and Mosul, the capitals of the provinces bearing the same names. At about the same time, Kuwait became a British protectorate after negotiations instigated by Winston Churchill.

Once British interests in the oilfields had been secured, it was decided to consolidate our position by moving along the river banks to Baghdad which ultimately fell in 1917 but not without bloodshed. The Germans tried to foster a Jihad or holy war against the British forces and Turkey itself offered strong resistance to these incursions into its Empire.

The British Force was composed of the Indian Army (which at that time included a number of British Regular and Territorial units) and was totally unprepared for the kind of guerrilla warfare which it ultimately faced in Mesopotamia. It was poorly-equipped and under-trained and caught out by a nightmare logistical scenario. As if that wasn't enough, there were flies, mosquitoes, constant high temperatures and humidity. Sickness and disease spread out of control through the camps and the death rate rose to the point where units simply did not have enough officers and men to continue fighting.

Private Frank Samuel Dart was taken ill and brought back to Britain. The press reports show that he had "a long and painful illness" and had been treated at Moorlands Hospital, Manchester. He died there and was brought home to Dawlish for burial in the cemetery. The following report gives an interesting view of his life before the army, but it does not dwell on the discomfort of a patient travelling by sea from the Middle East to Britain, in contrast to the airlift of casualties in more recent times.

The Dawlish Gazette of 22nd December 1917 gave an early report of his death:

"On Wednesday news was received of the death in hospital in Manchester of Pte. Frank.S.Dart after a long illness. Deceased, who was aged 24, was the youngest son of the late John Dart, and of Mrs Dart, Reed Cottage. He went to India with the Territorials in 1914, and subsequently volunteered for service in Mesopotamia. Whilst there he met with an accident, breaking his leg. Fever and other complications ensued, and he was sent to Egypt and from thence to England. Altogether he was in hospital 18 months. For the past four weeks he had laid in a very critical condition, and his death was not unexpected. The deceased was a fine swimmer and water poloist, besides being a good footballer. Many will remember the remarkably keen and evenly-contested races between Dart and Harry Hartwill for the swimming championship of Dawlish. Both had few equals of their age in the County. The former was better at sprint races, while the latter excelled at the longer distances. In the end "honours were easy" between the two. Many Dawlish lads scattered far and wide in the Empire's service will hear with regret of the death of the former school and playmate in the halcyon pre-war days."

Reference to the funeral report in *the Dawlish Gazette of 29th December 1917* shows the chief mourners as "Mr J F Dart (brother)*(presumably reversed initials for Frederick John Dart),* Mr J Dart, R.N. (brother), Mr R Dart (uncle), Mr F Dart (uncle), Mr R Dart, junr, (nephew) *(possibly Robert Frederick S Dart, son of Frederick John, born Exeter, March Q 1901)";* Also "In affectionate remembrance, from his broken-hearted sweetheart, Eva."

The UK, Army Register of Soldiers' Effects has a slightly unusual distribution of Death Grant to seven beneficiaries, each receiving £7. 3s. 8d. (Mother- Mary, Brothers Fred, John, Sisters, Alice, Elizabeth, Helen June and nephew, Frank Knight. Against the line for Elizabeth it records "At the request of brother William for the benefit of Nephew Harry").

The War Gratuity was also split in seven shares, 5/7 going to Brother Fred and 1/7 each to Chas M Scott and Sis-in-law Helena.
He was awarded the Victory Medal and the British War Medal.

F.S.Dart is recorded on the Devon Roll of Honour and the Dawlish Boys' School Roll of Honour.

Dawlish War memorial inscription: DART F.S.   PTE.   DEVON REGT.

Devon Heritage site info:
268222 Private Frank Samuel Dart of the 1st/6th Battalion, The Devonshire Regiment. Son of John and Mary Dart of Brunswick Place, Dawlish. Born in Dawlish in the December Quarter of 1893. Died 19 December 1917, aged 24.
 http://www.devonheritage.org/Nonplace/DevonReg/TheDevonsinMesopotamia-1917.htm

Commonwealth War Graves entry: DART, FRANK SAMUEL   Private   268222
19/12/1917   Devonshire Regiment, 1st/6th Bn.   Grave Ref: 2128.   Dawlish Cemetery

Last known address: 41 Cope Street, Coventry
Next of kin: Mother, Mary Jane Dart

References:
free birth, marriage, death refs
The Devon regiment in Mesopotamia
refs via subscription website:
UK, Army register of Soldiers' Effects
Probate records

extracts from *the Dawlish Gazette*

census records
UK, Soldiers died in the Great War
Ancestry family tree 'Joanne Matten'

This photograph appears in various publications with differing descriptions, one of which is "the Dodge family, market gardeners at Cockwood" The variety of baskets and piles of marrows suggest that they traded from home as much as providing supplies to local merchants.

Arthur George DODGE

Born Middlewood, Jan-Mar 1893   Died Baghdad, 28 December 1917, aged 24

Gunner   865132   Royal Field Artillery, 1086th Battery, 215th Brigade

Arthur George Dodge was the grand-son of John and Elizabeth Dodge. John (1822-1873) was born in Dawlish and Elizabeth (1821-1895) was born in Hennock.

They were living in Middlewood (Cofton parish) in 1871 and John died two years later at the age of 51. By this time they had three sons:

William Dodge	(1848-)	born	Cockwood
John Dodge	(1851-)		Dawlish
Walter Henry Dodge	(1858-1916)		"

Walter Henry Dodge married Annie Paddon (1865-1942) from Iddesleigh, North Devon. They married in the June quarter of 1890[115]. In 1891 they had their first child, Edith Mary (1891-), and Walter's widowed mother Elizabeth was living with them. She died in 1895, aged 75.

In 1901 Walter and Annie were living at Middlewood Cottages and Walter Henry Dodge was a market gardener. Their children were:

Edith Mary	(1891-)	born	Cofton
Arthur George (1893-1917)		"	
P. A. Elizabeth	(1898-)		"
Walter Percival Valentine	(1899-)		"

A neice, Dorcas Dodge, (1878-) was living with them as "Mother's help", and a brother-in-law, Bertie Paddon (1889-) was also listed in the household.

Dorcas was the daughter of William and Ann Dodge, also living at Middlewood, Cofton, and they had a son, John Dodge (1876-1951) who married the widow of Holroyd Edward Hamlyn (q.v.). John Dodge was a first cousin to Arthur George Dodge.

The family had grown by 1911 when they are shown to have had six children, one of whom had died by the date of the census and that must have been P.A.Elizabeth, because the five survivors are listed in the household of Walter and Anne at Middlewood as:

Edith Mary	(1891-)	single
Arthur George	(1893-1917)	single, working as market gardener
Walter Percival Valentine	(1899-)	scholar
Lionel John	(1902-)	"
Leonard Edward	(1903-)	"

A niece, Mary Dodge (1890 -) is shown as a domestic servant, and Bertie Paddon, brother-in-law is now working in the market garden with Ralph Brooks (1891-) who appears to be from a local (Cofton) family.

Enlistment records do not survive for Arthur George Dodge but it may be assumed that he was conscripted into the Royal Field Artillery. The 1086th Battery was one of the units of the 215th (CCXV) Brigade which was engaged in actions in Mesopotamia, as part of the Indian Army. See also the previous account for Frank Dart.

Various actions of The Mesopotamian campaign include:

---

115   Marriage GRO 1890, Q2, N.A. vol 5b, p221

Advance to the Hai and capture of the Khudaira Bend, Capture of the Hai Salient, Capture of Sannaiyat, Second Battle of Kut, Passage of the Tigris, Fall of Baghdad (11 March 1917), Passage of the 'Adhaim, Action of the Shatt al Adhaim, Second action of Jabal Hamrin, Third action of Jabal Hamrin, Battle of Tikrit (5 November 1917).

Once British interests in the oilfields had been secured, it was decided to consolidate our position by moving along the river banks to Baghdad which ultimately fell in March 1917 but not without bloodshed. The Germans tried to foster a Jihad, or holy war, against the British forces and Turkey itself offered strong resistance to these incursions into its Empire.

In the Mesopotamia campaign more died of sickness than were killed in action. The manner of Dodge's death is not known. The Army Register of Soldiers' Effects often indicates the cause but none is shown here. The register entry shows a distribution of Death Benefit to:

Mother, Anne   Sister, Edith Mary   Brother, Lionel John
Brother, Leonard Edward   Brother, Walter Percival P

The War Gratuity was paid only to his mother Anne, his father having died in 1916.

Cofton church memorial inscription: ROY. FIELD ART.   DECEMBER 28TH 1917

Commonwealth War Graves entry: GEORGE DODGE
Gunner Service No: 865132   Royal Field Artillery   1086th Bty. 215th Bde.
Date of Death: 28/12/1917   Age: 24
Cemetery: <u>BAGHDAD (NORTH GATE) WAR CEMETERY</u> Grave Reference: II. B. 7.
Additional Information: Son of Mr. W. and Mrs. A. Dodge, of Middlewood, Starcross, Devon.
Last known address: Middlewood, Starcross (Cofton)

Memorial to Walter Henry Dodge with inscription to Arthur George Dodge in Cofton, St Mary, churchyard.

Next of kin: Mother, Annie Dodge

His father, Walter Henry Dodge died on 8th August, 1916 and left £3,593 – 9s – 1d. To his widow.

References:

Free Birth, marriage, death refs

Capture of Tikrit - http://www.firstworldwar.com/battles/tikrit.htm

Mesopotamia campaign   - http://www.1914-1918.net/mespot.htm

Refs via subscription website:

      Census data

      Ian Wright family tree (Ancestry)

APPENDIX A Deaths recorded from the First World War – Dawlish Civil Parish

surname	forenames	date death	d.o.b.	unit	Rank
		1914			
Criddle	William John	06/08/1914	02/04/1887	R.N., HMS AMPHION	1st C.P.O.
Mould	Alfred	17/10/1914	01/07/1893	R.N.R., HMS VIVID	Seaman
Wills	John Frank	24/10/1914	01/01/1885	Devonshire Regt, 1st Battn	Private
Bearne	Arthur Henry	01/11/1914	20/06/1881	R.N., HMS GOOD HOPE	Steward 2nd cl
Davis	Frederick Albert	01/11/1914	20/02/1883	R.M.L.I.,H.M.S.MONMOUTH	Sergeant
Pillar	Samuel	08/11/1914	13/01/1894	Coldstream Guards, 2nd Battn	Private
		1915			
Holman	Paul	15/02/1915	07/02/1893	Hon Artillery Coy, 1st Battn	Gunner
Stoyle	Walter	13/03/1915	02/06/1891	Devonshire Regt, 2nd Battn	Private
Crook	Clarence Henry	17/03/1915	01/01/1896	Devonshire Regt, 2nd Battn	Private
Pessell	George John	16/04/1915	3/10/1879	R.N., HMS DUKE OF EDINBURGH	Ch Ship's Cook
Rooth	Richard Alexander	25/04/2015	22/03/1866	Royal Dublin Fusiliers, 1st Battn	Lieut-Col
Jackson	Wilfred George	27/04/1915	03/10/1895	The Buffs(East Kent Regt) 1st Battn	Lieutenant
Mudge	Edward	28/04/1915	22/08/1896	R.F.A. 4th Wessex Brigade	Gunner
Ford	Frederick George	09/05/1915	26/05/1896	R.M.L.I., R.N.Divn Plymouth Battalion	Private
Baron	Alfred Samuel	13/05/1915	09/07/1873	R.N., HMS GOLIATH	Ldg B'tm
Bond	Frederick William	23/05/1915	01/08/1894	RAMC, 1st/24th Wessex Field Ambulance	Private
Jarman	Thomas Frederick	22/06/1915	04/04/1868	HMS VIVID, retired on ill health	Chief P.O.
Crook	Stanley James	24/08/1915	01/03/1895	Devonshire Regt, 1st Battn	L Corpl
Anning	John Gwyne Kerle	25/09/1915	01/09/1893	Devonshire Regt, 8th Service Battn	Private
Cornelius	Sidney	25/09/1915	01/04/1886	Devonshire Regt, 8th battn(Service)	Private
Cotton	Frank Charles	25/09/1915	01/06/1889	Devonshire Regt, 8th battn (Service)	L/Sgt
Crideford	Ernest John	25/09/1915	01/04/1893	Devonshire Regt, 8th battn	Private
Dew	William John	25/09/1915	01/01/1885	Devonshire Regt, 8th battn	Private
Hooper	Albert John	25/09/1915	25/04/1878	Devonshire Regt, 8th battn	Private
Martin	Ernest George	25/09/1915	01/03/1897	Devonshire Regt, 8th Service Battn	Private
Stevens	William Henry	25/09/1915	01/04/1890	Devonshire Regt, 8th Battn	Private
Kerswell	Sidney Harold	14/10/1915	01/01/1894	Royal Fusiliers(London Regt) 3rd Bn	Private
		1916			
Rundell	Gerald Easterbrook	23/03/1916	01/06/1894	Somerset Light Inf, 9th Battn	Private
Davis	Thomas Pounder	19/04/1916	08/04/1876	R.N., HMS VIVID	A.B., RNR.
Browning	Guy Arnott	31/05/1916	15/12/1876	R.N.,HMS INDEFATIGABLE	Chaplain& N.I.
Dew	Alfred Thomas	31/05/1916	03/11/1891	R.N., HMS INDEFATIGABLE	Stoker, 1st Cl
Hutchings	William John	31/05/1916	01/04/1886	R.N.,HMS BROKE	A.B.
Morrish	Frank	31/05/1916	15/09/1873	R.N., HMS DEFENCE	Chief Armourer
Mutters	William Henry	31/05/1916	01/03/1869	R.M.L.I. HMS QUEEN MARY	Private
Jones	Arthur Thomas	31/05/1916	29/05/1887	R.N., HMS DEFENCE	A.B.
Gibbings	George Henry	17/06/1916	01/01/1886	Devonshire Regt, 1st/6th Battn	Cpl
Browning	William W	01/07/1916	01/04/1897	Devonshire Regt, 8th Battn	Private
Bowden	Ernest John	01/07/1916	01/08/1892	Devonshire Regt, 2nd Battn	L Corpl
Doble	Edward	10/07/1916	01/06/1888	Royal Field Artillery	Bombardier

Lake	Charles	22/08/1916	25/04/1884	R.N., HM Submarine E16	P.O.
Lucas	Sidney Charles	30/08/1916	01/01/1892	Devonshire Regt, 1st Battn	L/Corporal
Milward	Etienne Geoffrey	02/09/2016	23/01/1896	Duke of Cornwall's L.I. 7th Battn	Temp Captain
Radford	Carl	03/09/1916	01/06/1896	Gloucs Regiment, 12th Battn	L/Sgt
Bren	Henry Alfred Hogarth	09/09/1916	21/02/1892	Leinster Regiment, 4th Battalion	Lieutenant
Moss	Allan	10/10/1916	1857	Worcestershire Regt	Major
Elliott	William Alfred Victor	03/11/1916	01/04/1897	DCLI, 11th Battn	Private
Honour	Bertram Charles	18/11/1916	01/10/1890	Devonshire Regt, 2/4th Battn	Private
Leaman	Henry	21/12/1916	01/09/1885	S. MID. Royal Engineers,1st/3rd Field Co.	Sapper
Blackburn	Leonard Walter	29/12/1916	01/01/1898	London Rifle Brigade, 5th Battn	Rifleman
		1917			
Chapple	Samuel Alfred	08/01/1917	01/12/1890	Devonshire Regt, 4th Reserve Battn	Private
Smith	Thomas Alfred	13/01/1917	1877	Devonshire Regt, 9th Battn	Private
Burch	Arthur Charles	17/02/2017	05/01/1882	Wiltshire Regt, 1st Battn	Private
Pike	George	19/02/1917	10/06/1890	R.N., HMS THUNDERER	A.B.
Scott	Edward Maurice	24/02/1917	08/11/1893	The Buffs - East Kent Regt, 1st/5th Battn	Private
Larcombe	Francis George	30/03/1917	01/01/1884	Devonshire Regt, 2nd Battn	L/Cpl
Hill	James Henry	10/04/1917	01/04/1891	RAMC Hospital ship SALTA	Private
West	George Carter	15/04/1917	01/06/1877	Australian Field Art'y, 2nd Divn,Trench Mortar	Gunner
Bright	Hubert John	17/04/1917	01/01/1897	Machine Gun Corps	Cpl
Peters	Charles Maurice S	22/04/1917	01/12/1888	Hon Artillery Coy, (Infantry)	Gunner
Knapman	George	24/04/1917	1896	Royal Dublin Fusiliers, 1st Battn	Private
May	Henry	22/05/1917	01/01/1886	Hampshire Regt, 2nd Battn	Private
Scott	Walter Henry	28/05/1917	01/04/1890	King's Royal Rifle Corps,	L/Cprl
Gibson	Harry Norman John	27/05/1917	03/11/1897	R.A.F.(HMS PRESIDENT II, 'F' Squadron)	Aircraftsman 2 cl
Pitts	William	22/06/2017	01/11/1887	Machine Gun Corps, 23rd Coy	L/Sgt
Williams	Wilfred Claude	31/07/1917	01/01/1897	Tank Corps, G Battn	Gunner
Marks	William Joseph	02/08/1917	16/03/1890	RFA	Gunner
Lewis	Thomas Norman	08/08/1917	02/12/1890	Royal Garrison Artillery	A/Cpl
Mayne	Albert	09/08/1917	16/06/1896	Coldtsream Guards. 1St Battn	Private
Blackmore	Charles Henry	29/08/1917	22/07/1890	Canadian Infantry, 47th Battn	*Private*
Hockaday	Percy John	31/08/1917	01/06/1884	Royal Engineers.Telegraph Coy	DIV.Insp. Tel
Hamlyn	Holroyd Edward	16/09/1917	01/01/1895	Somerset Lit Infantry, 7th Battn	L/Cpl
Holloway	William Robert	20/09/1917	02/11/1889	Machine Gun Corps, 69th Coy	2nd Lieut
King	Charles Frederick	20/09/1917	28/10/1882	1st/9th Battn King's Liverpool Regt	2nd Lieut
Blackmore	Reginald Charles	22/09/1917	01/12/1890	Devonshire Regt, 5th Battn(Territorials)	L Corpl
Tapley	William Frank	04/10/1917	01/05/1884	Devonshire Regt, 1st Battn	Private
West	Albert Henry	04/10/1917	01/09/1889	Devonshire Regt, 8th Battn	Private
Garrett	Herbert A	07/10/1917	01/09/1897	M.T., Army Service Corps	Private
Pope	Philip Gladstone	16/10/1917	11/08/1887	Royal Field Artillery, 31st Brigade	Lieut
Stephens	Leonard Reggie	26/10/1917	01/01/1897	Royal Warwickshire Regt.15th Bttn	Private
Blatchford	William	26/10/1917	26/05/1891	R.M.L.I.2nd Royal Marine Battalion	Private

Pook	Thomas	26/10/1917	01/01/1880	Devonshire Regt, 8th Battn	Private
Davies	Archibald Frederick	02/12/1917	01/09/1881	London Q.W.Rfls, (1st/16th battn)	Rifleman
Davis	Albert William	07/12/1917	24/08/1887	Canadian Infantry, 29th Battn	Private
Dart	Frank Samuel	19/12/1917	01/12/1893	Devonshire Regt, 1st/6th Battn	Private
Dodge	Arthur George	28/12/1917	01/02/1893	Royal Field Artillery, 215th Brigade	Gunner
		1918			
Way (M.M.)	William Richard Brown	14/02/1918	28/04/1881	Somerset Light Inf, 7th Battn	Private
Hallett	Thomas	16/02/1918	13/09/1852	R.N., HMS ZARIA, Depot Ship, Longhope	Lt Cdr (Retd)
Bright	Reginald Charles	19/02/1918	01/01/1897	R.N., HMS MONS	A.B.
Horwill	William Henry	21/03/1918	01/05/1877	King's Royal Rifle Corps,12th Battn	Rifleman
Andrews	Walter Lennox	23/03/1918	01/05/1888	20th Hussars	Private
Snell	Peter	28/03/1918	01/04/1896	Royal Field Artillery	Gunner
Selley	Andrew Alexander	04/04/1918	08/03/1896	R.N., HMS VIVID	Officer's Stwd
Abell	Percival Ernest	10/04/1918	01/06/1896	Gloucs T.M.Btt (Regt, 8th Service Battn)	Private
Luscombe	Frederick Samuel	10/04/1918	01/11/1880	R.N., HMS MAGIC	A.B.
Geidt	Charles Uppleby	10/04/1918	06/08/1894	Royal Flying Corps	Lieut
Crook	Edmund Charles	12/04/1918	01/07/1883	South Wales Borderers, 11th Battn	Private
Baldue	Frank	09/06/1918	28/02/1873	Canadian Forestry Corps	Private
Carman	Wilfred	20/06/1918	20/11/1890	Devonshire Regt, 5th Battn	Cy Sgt Major
Fortescue	*Margaret Jane*	*27/06/1918*	*23/07/1878*	*Canadian Nursing Service*	*Nurse*
Gilpin	John Sparkes M	13/07/1918	01/06/1890	Devonshire Regt, Graduation Battn	Private
Church	Arthur Gilbert Walsh	20/07/1918	13/07/1894	Devonshire Regt, 1st/5th Battn	Captain
Cutcliffe	John	26/08/1918	01/01/1887	East Yorks Regt	Lieut
Harris	Henry John	26/08/1918	01/12/1892	Devonshire Regt, 1st Battn	Sergeant
Moore	Arthur John	27/08/1918	01/03/1887	Coldstream Guards, 2nd Battn	Private
Harris	Percival Samuel	28/09/1918	01/10/1893	East Lancs Regt, 11th Battn	Private
Blackmore	George	04/10/1918	01/01/1900	Machine Gun Corps	Private
Leaman	Stephen	06/10/1918	01/01/1887	Royal Welsh Fusiliers,14th Battn	Sniper
Nicholls	John Jeffry	12/10/1918	01/10/1891	5th Canadian Army Medical Corps	Pte/ Ambul Drvr
Honour MM	Reginald Alexander	17/10/1918	01/09/1894	Coldstream Guards, 1st Battn	*L/Cpl*
Kemp	Kenneth Reginald	18/10/1918	01/01/1896	(C de C) R oyal Army Service Corps	2nd Lieut
Cruse	Harry	20/10/1918	01/01/1889	Devonshire Regt, 1st Battn	Corpl
Kerswell	James Edwin	25/10/1918	10/04/1878	Royal Engineers, Yeomanry Divn	Sapper
Cole	George Henry	06/11/1918	01/10/1896	Royal Warwicks Regt, 2nd Battn	Private
Burch	William Henry	09/11/1918	30/08/1897	R.N., HMS BRITANNIA	A.B.
Dallman	Leonard Charles	06/12/1918	01/09/1896	Royl Field Artillery, 113rd Brigade	Sergeant
Scott	Harry Reginald	07/12/1918	01/10/1891	Yorkshire Regt, 5th Battalion	Private
		1919			
Evans	John	17/01/1919	01/09/1874	R.N., HMS ALBEMARLE	Chief Stoker
Bowden	Sidney Charles	19/01/1919	01/01/1897	Coldstream Guards, 5th Resrve Battn	Private
Thornhill	William Edward	21/01/1919	01/01/1873	RAMC, 99 Field Ambulance	Sgt
Abell	Sidney Thomas	01/02/1919	01/09/1890	Devonshire Regt, 3rd Battn	Private
Crews	*William H*	*27/02/1919*	*01/01/1865*	*Devonshire Regt, Depot Battn*	*Private*
Kingdon	Frederick Robert	18/03/1919	01/06/1890	Royal Engineers, "G" Depot Coy	Sapper

Brimicombe	James	04/04/1919	07/02/1890	RFA	Act/Bombardier
Wills	Samuel Gordon	27/04/1919	05/03/1887	S.S.BELGIC / S.S.BELGENLAND	Ldg Smn
Ruddle	Richard	26/07/1919	01/01/1888	RHA	Gunner
King	Percival	23/10/1919	01/01/1887	HMS WINCHESTER	Eng Lt Cdr
Jones	Samuel	23/10/1919	01/01/1890	RAMC	Private
Nichols	Albert	25/10/1919	01/01/1899	Somerset Light Infantry	Sgt
Black	William John	11/11/1919	01/04/1888	Worcestershire Regt, 6th Battn	Corpl
		1920			
Brook	Frank	30/06/1920	26/07/1889	R.N., HMS KILMAINE	A.B.
Hill	Russell	24/11/1920	01/01/1897	Gloucestershire Regt	Lieut
		1921			
Edmonds	Philip Augustus	09/01/1921	01/01/1893	Royal Fusiliers(London Regt) 3rd Bn	Private
Ager	Ernest	05/03/1921	06/05/1880	RAF	Air Mech
Horn	William John	12/04/1921	18/05/1899	H.M.S.VIVID	Ord Smn

APPENDIX B - Names in alphabetical order with dates of death

Part One of this Series covers those who died in 1914-1915, This volume covers 1916-1917 and the final volume 1918-1921

surname	forenames	date death
Abell	Percival Ernest	10/04/1918
Abell	Sidney Thomas	01/02/1919
Ager	Ernest	05/03/1921
Andrews	Walter Lennox	23/03/1918
Anning	John Gwyne Kerle	25/09/1915
Baldue	Frank	09/06/1918
Baron	Alfred Samuel	13/05/1915
Bearne	Arthur Henry	01/11/1914
Black	William John	11/11/1919
Blackburn	Leonard Walter	29/12/1916
Blackmore	Reginald Charles	22/09/1917
Blackmore	Charles Henry	29/08/1917
Blackmore	George	04/10/1918
Blatchford	William	26/10/1917
Bond	Frederick William	23/05/1915
Bowden	Ernest John	01/07/1916
Bowden	Sidney Charles	19/01/1919
Bren	Henry Alfred Hogarth	09/09/1916
Bright	Reginald Charles	19/02/1918
Bright	Hubert John	17/04/1917
Brimicombe	James	04/04/1919
Brook	Frank	30/06/1920
Browning	Guy Arnott	31/05/1916
Browning	William W	01/07/1916
Burch	William Henry	09/11/1918
Burch	Arthur Charles	17/02/2017

Carman	Wilfred	20/06/1918
Chapple	Samuel Alfred	08/01/1917
Church	Arthur Gilbert Walsh	20/07/1918
Cole	George Henry	06/11/1918
Cornelius	Sidney	25/09/1915
Cotton	Frank Charles	25/09/1915
Crews	William H	27/02/1919
Criddle	William John	06/08/1914
Crideford	Ernest John	25/09/1915
Crook	Stanley James	24/08/1915
Crook	Clarence Henry	17/03/1915
Crook	Edmund Charles	12/04/1918
Cruse	Harry	20/10/1918
Cutcliffe	John	26/08/1918
Dallman	Leonard Charles	06/12/1918
Dart	Frank Samuel	19/12/1917
Davies	Archibald Frederick	02/12/1917
Davis	Thomas Pounder	19/04/1916
Davis	Albert William	07/12/1917
Davis	Frederick Albert	01/11/1914
Dew	William John	25/09/1915
Dew	Alfred Thomas	31/05/1916
Doble	Edward	10/07/1916
Dodge	Arthur George	28/12/1917
Edmonds	Philip Augustus	09/01/1921
Elliott	William Alfred Victor	03/11/1916
Evans	John	17/01/1919
Ford	Frederick George	09/05/1915
Fortescue	*Margaret Jane*	*27/06/1918*
Garrett	Herbert A	07/10/1917
Geidt	Charles Uppleby	10/04/1918
Gibbings	George Henry	17/06/1916

Gibson	Harry Norman John	27/05/1917
Gilpin	John Sparkes M	13/07/1918
Hallett	Thomas	16/02/1918
Hamlyn	Holroyd Edward	16/09/1917
Harris	Percival Samuel	28/09/1918
Harris	Henry John	26/08/1918
Hill	Russell	24/11/1920
Hill	James Henry	10/04/1917
Hockaday	Percy John	31/08/1917
Holloway	William Robert	20/09/1917
Holman	Paul	15/02/1915
Honour	Bertram Charles	18/11/1916
Honour MM	Reginald Alexander	17/10/1918
Hooper	Albert John	25/09/1915
Horn	William John	12/04/1921
Horwill	William Henry	21/03/1918
Hutchings	William John	31/05/1916
Jackson	Wilfred George	27/04/1915
Jarman	Thomas Frederick	22/06/1915
Jones	Arthur Thomas	31/05/1916
Jones	Samuel	23/10/1919
Kemp	Kenneth Reginald	18/10/1918
Kerswell	Sidney Harold	14/10/1915
Kerswell	James Edwin	25/10/1918
King	Charles Frederick	20/09/1917
King	Percival	23/10/1919
Kingdon	Frederick Robert	18/03/1919
Knapman	George	24/04/1917
Lake	Charles	22/08/1916
Larcombe	Francis George	30/03/1917
Leaman	Henry	21/12/1916

Leaman	Stephen	06/10/1918
Lewis	Thomas Norman	08/08/1917
Lucas	Sidney Charles	30/08/1916
Luscombe	Frederick Samuel	10/04/1918
Marks	William Joseph	02/08/1917
Martin	Ernest George	25/09/1915
May	Henry	22/05/1917
Mayne	Albert	09/08/1917
Milward	Etienne Geoffrey	02/09/2016
Moore	Arthur John	27/08/1918
Morrish	Frank	31/05/1916
Moss	Allan	10/10/1916
Mould	Alfred	17/10/1914
Mudge	Edward	28/04/1915
Mutters	William Henry	31/05/1916
Nicholls	John Jeffry	12/10/1918
Nichols	Albert	25/10/1919
Pessell	George John	16/04/1915
Peters	Charles Maurice S	22/04/1917
Pike	George	19/02/1917
Pillar	Samuel	08/11/1914
Pitts	William	22/06/2017
Pook	Thomas	26/10/1917
Pope	Philip Gladstone	16/10/1917
Radford	Carl	03/09/1916
Rooth	Richard Alexander	25/04/2015
Ruddle	Richard	26/07/1919
Rundell	Gerald Easterbrook	23/03/1916
Scott	Walter Henry	28/05/1917
Scott	Edward Maurice	24/02/1917
Scott	Harry Reginald	07/12/1918

Selley	Andrew Alexander	04/04/1918
Smith	Thomas Alfred	13/01/1917
Snell	Peter	28/03/1918
Stephens	Leonard Reggie	26/10/1917
Stevens	William Henry	25/09/1915
Stoyle	Walter	13/03/1915
Tapley	William Frank	04/10/1917
Thornhill	William Edward	21/01/1919
Way (M.M.)	William Richard B	14/02/1918
West	George Carter	15/04/1917
West	Albert Henry	04/10/1917
Williams	Wilfred Claude	31/07/1917
Wills	Samuel Gordon	27/04/1919
Wills	John Frank	24/10/1914

APPENDIX C   Reference Sources and working method

1

The starting point was the list of names recorded on the War Memorials of Dawlish, Cofton and Holcombe, within the civil parish of Dawlish. There are in addition individual memorials, and the project researched sources that gave further information about their service careers and of the families at home.

2   Working methods

The project has used as many sources as available to cross-refer for accuracy. The primary sources used were:

http://www.cwgc.org/ Commonwealth War Graves Commission website gives the names of all recorded dead from WW1, and later wars. The least information includes place of burial and where commemorated, but it will often expand this to include forenames, names of next-of-kin, and other data. To search for casualties it helps to know the Regiment and/or service number.

https://www.forces-war-records.co.uk/   Forces War Records (a subscription site) may provide further information about medals awarded or entitlement to medals and regimental histories. It has lately added records of those wounded.

http://www.devonheritage.org/WarMemorials.htm is a site which gives brief information about each person listed on town War Memorials in Devon. Some of the 'facts' are questioned by the Dawlish WW1 project from later searches which have been made easier by the more recent access to online data.

http://www.freebmd.org.uk/   freeBMD is a valuable site to help identify the date of Birth, Marriage or Death where a family history is being developed and is best used in conjunction with a site giving access to Census records, which will generally allow a family tree to be assembled. Dates may only indicate year or quarter but they will give General Record Office (GRO) references to allow access to birth, marriage or death certificates. A number of these were obtained where ambiguity existed and other reference material could not be found online. Copies of Birth, Marriage or Death Certificates are best ordered from the GRO website.

Census records from a subscription service such as Ancestry http://www.ancestry.co.uk/   This will allow a search of all census data from 1841 (partial census) every 10 years to 1911 (the last accessible at this time).
The public library offers access to a census search on its own subscription, but may be time limited to ensure fair use. Very often a casualty 1914-1919 can be found in the 1911 census and then tracked back every 10 years to build a family structure.

http://www.naval-history.net/   is invaluable for placing Naval or Royal Marine casualties by date and location. In many cases the action in which a person was involved is also described in detail.

Army enlistment records from 1914-1919 were mostly destroyed by fire in the Second World War Blitz but Medal Records survive and can be accessed from family history sites, as can the Register of Soldiers' Effects which are pages of original ledgers listing the Death Grant and War Gratuity paid to next-of-kin.

Army Officer records are held at National Archives, Kew.

Royal Navy and Royal Marine personnel records are held at the National Archives, Kew, and can be downloaded for a small charge. These will identify date of joining, physical characteristics, postings and promotions.

Dawlish Gazette archive at Dawlish Museum This source is used to give additional information that is not easily obtainable elsewhere. It is not on open access but a request for assistance should be addressed to Dawlish Museum, The Knowle, BartonTerrace, Dawlish.

The National Newspaper Archive is available online (subscription service) and there is local regional coverage from Exeter and Plymouth based newspapers. Weddings and funerals in Dawlish were often reported.

WARNING   Users of family history websites may gain access to family trees constructed by other people of varying skills. It is not wise to abstract data from another person's tree without checking with other sources that the data is reliable.

Devon Family History Society. This source is valuable for those members who can visit the Tree House in King Street, Exeter (off Fore Street) and obtain assistance in their family history search. **enquiries@devonfhs.org.uk**

The Devon Roll of Honour is a contemporary list of names, similar to those on the Town War memorial, and held by the Devon Archive/Heritage Centre, Great Moor House, Sowton, Exeter.

Dawlish Boys' School Roll of Honour   -   This is located in the Dawlish Community College, Elmgrove Road, in the students' entrance hall and reception. It gives the names of those Dawlish boys who were killed during WW1 who had attended Dawlish Boys' School.

This is a brief outline of the search methods used in building individual biographies for the Services of Commemoration which were held on the centenary of each death, and have been used to build the website.

www.dawlishww1.org.uk   carries the data for all deaths of Dawlish men and one woman in one location, and is free to use.

Acknowledgements

First, an apology to the memory of Mr Fuller, my last history teacher at Charterhouse, when he said in 1954, 'with the death of Queen Victoria we complete the syllabus'. My hand shot up to ask if he could tell us about the cause of the First World War. His reply was 'That is not yet part of history. It is too recent.'

In 2013, the approaching centenary of the First World War brought attention to the town's War Memorial and the lack of general knowledge of those named, or of their families who lost fathers, brothers or sons. An interested group was led to apply to the Heritage Lottery Fund and to Dawlish Town Council for funding to study this topic. The applications were successful and a working group was formed to identify targets and we worked together over the five years.

The individual members shared tasks but there were certain key roles played by: Revd Roger Whitehead and Ann Leigh who co-ordinated approaches to churches for participation in Services of Commemoration over the four year programme, and to provide a temporary altar for use at each venue; Keith Gibson who spent many hours turning the pages of Dawlish Museum's collection of the weekly newspaper *The Dawlish Gazette* to recover contemporary reports of Dawlish casualties; Tom Elliott who liaised with the Dawlish Branch of the Royal British Legion over participation in ceremonial events; Sheila Ralls, Sheila Wain, Michael Clayson, Campbell Brown and Bob Vickery who searched available resources online to construct mini biographies for each casualty; all the clergy and members of the co-ordinating group who have contributed to making each Service a very personal tribute; Teignbridge District Council for the care of Dawlish Cemetery Chapel which has been prepared for our use on many occasions.

We waited to commission a website until we could appreciate the extent of available data, and then were helped by The Weatherheads, Huw and Angie, who took instruction and then constructed a web site that has been used by thousands across the world to discover material about their families. We have received many welcome comments from people in the Commonwealth and other parts about the ease of use and the content found on the site. Keith Gibson and Bob Vickery undertook the task of loading collected data to the site where it resides as;   www.dawlishww1.org.uk

There have been many outside the working group who have provided insights into special areas of interest by undertaking enquiries or contributing from their own extensive researches, and they include John Jackson for the Jackson family; June Snell for access and use of her researches into the Way, Ford and related families; Kedrun Lawrie for correspondence in Flemish regarding past and present Belgian refugee family members; Michael Clapp regarding his ancestor Alice Clapp who first recorded Belgian names; Alastair R W Rooth for contributing personal family material on his grandfather Lt Col Richard Rooth; Arrabella Whitworth Jones and her late mother, Catherine, who offered access to photographs of their ancestor Maude Hildyard, the Quartermaster of Dawlish Red Cross VAD; Roy Gamblin for material related to Frederick Jarman's family; the late Campbell Brown for detail of Holcombe casualties; others too numerous to mention who have opened their family albums and joined the congregations at Services of Commemoration to make known their family relationship to the casualty being remembered.
This is the second in a group of similar format books to cover the 124 war dead. Part One, 1914-1915 was published by Amazon/Kindle in February 2021.

References are to some extent covered in the section on Tracing Family Histories, on page 197. Specific references are given in footnotes while many books have been used as source material or as working models during the project, including:

"The War Illustrated", being a 9 volume bound edition of a weekly illustrated paper "A Pictorial Record of the Conflict of the Nations";

"First World War" by Martin Gilbert, Publ BCA 1994, a compendium history which has informed parts of the linking texts;

"Devon During the First World War", Devon Remembers Heritage Project, publ South West Heritage Trust 2018;

"We will Remember Them", The Men of Tavistock who died in the First World War, by Mettler and Woodcock, publ Tavistock and District Local History Society 2003;

"A Foreign Field" by Ben Macintyre, publ Harper Collins 2001, a detailed and atmospheric account of the early days of the war and of the German devastation of civilian communities;

"In Europe", Travels through the twentieth century, by Geert Mak, publ Vintage 2007;

"Somme", The Heroism and Horror of War, by Martin Gilbert, publ John Murray 2006;

"Somme Battlefield Companion", publ The Commonwealth War Graves Commission 2016;

"The Battle of the Somme", The National Commemorative Event to mark the Centenary of the Battle of the Somme, 2016;

"The Donkeys", by Alan Clark, publ Hutchinson 1961, publ Pimlico 1991, a celebrated account of the problems encountered with battlefield commanders during WW1;

"Goodbye to All That", by Robert Graves, publ Penguin 1960, an account, often critical, of the leadership during WW1;

"Jutland 1916", Death in the Grey Wastes, by Steel and Hart, publ Cassell 2003, a detailed account of the prelude to and execution of the battle and its resultant effects on naval warfare in WW1;

"Storm of Steel", by Ernst Junger, publ Penguin Modern Classics 2004, being the battlefield experience of a German soldier during WW1;

Many online sources have been essential to identifying casualties and their service history, most notably the Commonwealth War Graves Commission (cwgc.org), supported by detail drawn from census returns listed on some subscription websites (in this case ancestry.co.uk) or at public libraries with access.

It is quite likely that some family stories contain misattributions and we will be pleased to make corrections to the texts or illustrations. Comment can be made via the "Contact" panel on our website.   Robert Vickery, convenor of the Dawlish WW1 group

Printed in Great Britain
by Amazon